Calling to the White Tribe

Rebirthing Indigenous,
Earth-Saving Wisdom

Calling
to the
White Tribe

Rebirthing Indigenous,
Earth-Saving Wisdom

Ed Mc Gaa, Eagle Man

MOON
BOOKS

Winchester, UK
Washington, USA

First published by Moon Books, 2013
Moon Books is an imprint of John Hunt Publishing Ltd., Laurel House, Station Approach,
Alresford, Hants, SO24 9JH, UK
office1@jhpbooks.net
www.johnhuntpublishing.com
www.moon-books.net

For distributor details and how to order please visit the 'Ordering' section on our website.

Text copyright: Ed McGaa, Eagle Man 2012

ISBN: 978 1 78279 134 8

A CIP catalogue record for this book is available from the British Library.

Design: Stuart Davies

Printed and bound by CPI Group (UK) Ltd, Croydon, CR0 4YY

We operate a distinctive and ethical publishing philosophy in all
areas of our business, from our global network of authors to
production and worldwide distribution.

CONTENTS

This book is dedicated to the World's greatest Step-Mother and Spouse, Mary Ray McGaa.
Jan 13th 1943 - April 27th 2011.

Foreword

The cycle of life is simple; it travels from death until rebirth and all our living, experiencing and learning is done in between. And with each cycle we would aim to expand upon that which has already been revealed to us ... or that is how it once was. The contents of this book uncover a very hard hitting truth, that we, in modern Europe, have strayed so far from our Natural Path, turning our back on our ancestral ways, that all our lessons are in danger of being lost and we will plunge into ignorance, chaos and despair as we are torn from our past and our authentic Great Spirit and the creative force of All.

As a native Scottish person I was surrounded by the natural world during childhood but struggled to come to terms with what I instinctively knew and felt, and what was being taught and imposed upon me. Had I not found a great teacher and mentor in Swein McDonald, The Highland Seer, I would not have survived, nor would I have learned to hear and act upon my Calling, seeking out Ed McGaa, Eagle Man.

What Ed gifted me over the decades; he also gifts everyone within this book. As a highly respected elder of the Lakota, he is in a wonderful position to assist other people by frankly and honestly spelling out where we have gone wrong and how we may still rectify our errors. As Ed points out in this book the Native Americans have had a much shorter time of being exposed to the controlling and debilitating forces of organised religion, whereas in Europe it has virtually obliterated our ancestral ways; its teachings, experiences, rites and our ability to live in harmony with Nature.

As I was being taught 'the old ways' at home, it was still very much 'underground'. To speak of it was considered dangerous. But now lights are flickering from across the 'pond' shining upon us as this book explains the where, how and why we 'fell' and more importantly how we can still rise again and restore that which is our true inheritance. Taking us through our fall from 'grace' into the arms of a man-made idea of 'God' we can begin to understand and act upon the legacy of our ancestors by looking at the surviving tribal people on our planet who are now standing firm in their traditions and their relationship with the earth upon which we are an integral part.

Getting in touch with our 'Celtic' roots, the tribes that collectively covered much of Western Europe, we are encouraged to draw upon the true majesty of our being; seeing ourselves again as sacred and divine, rather than detached from it or lesser than we are. Regaining our self-respect is key to leading a more passionate life, it is about quality not quantity – there are simply too many of us now in survival mode rather than thriving and adding to the story of rich human tapestry. It is also suggested by setting the records straight in Europe we can redress the balance globally, impacting on all humankind and the way in which all life can thrive.

Barbara Meiklejohn-Free, The Highland Seer, Shaman, musician and author of the best-sellers *The Heart Of All Knowing* (O-Books) and *The Shaman Within* (Balboa, Hay House US).

Introduction

A tyrant must put on the appearance of uncommon devotion to religion. Subjects are less apprehensive of illegal treatment from a ruler whom they consider god-fearing and pious. On the other hand, they do less easily move against him, believing that he has the gods on his side.

Aristotle

Why am I, a Native American addressing the people of the British Isles? Because in my homeland, the Americans, who perhaps need to hear this most, simply won't listen! But humanity's 'spark' and with it the fundamental obligations as Earth's custodians cannot be allowed to simply fade away and so I couldn't imagine a group of people better placed to now carry the torch. More and more of your young people are totally disgruntled embracing neither a religious nor spiritual path. They want to get on with their lives, many choosing atheism, while others are seriously interested in the Natural Way. This book is intended to aid those who have similar views.

It is still hoped that some Americans at least will also learn from this writing and begin introspection. I am pleased to admit that the more intelligent and less gullible among them are attempting to probe our ways but they are few in comparison to the many ignorant who choose to satisfy themselves with superstition, false luxury, fairy tales, celebrity watching and extreme materialism as their life goals and meanwhile continue to gobble up disappearing resources.

We have a statement; 'Live for the generations unborn.' It means we should live our present lives in provisional regard for the approaching generations unborn as well. Nowhere in the White Man's teaching, including his black, religious book - his Bible, is such a selfless statement recorded. This statement will

3

not be found in the Koran either. Both of these man-written, man composed books which are held forth by their adherents as 'God Written' issue absolutely nothing about the impending environmental crisis now fast upon us and the health implications that precede it which we are having to face already. Diet and the type of water one consumes is a highly important factor for healthy living. Evidently our food and water is now polluted to sufficient degree as evidenced by the above diseases affecting mostly all humans as they age: All the more reason why we should go back to Spirituality which can lead us to a healthier attitude regarding our food and water supply. Aside from the soulful and pragmatic fruits of Natural Way Spirituality, this paragraph alone could be the most valuable lesson!

But instead Organized Religion plays a leading role in the 'mortgaging' of future generations; 'Live for today and the hell with the Generations Unborn; mortgage them!' And the environmental dilemma due mainly to exponential over-population is the greatest economic atrocity that needs to be addressed by at least one author who has the pragmatic based courage to stand up and deliver.

Islam and Christianity

My friend Nancy Miller, when asked about the followers of these faiths wrote,

They (Christians and Muslims) fell into the trap of religion, rather than the freedom of spirituality, due to fear and ignorance. Churches are political creations, with no more interest in promoting truth than any other political body. They exist to promote themselves. The worst thing to happen to the followers of Yeshua of Nazareth was Paul. He twisted the words of the seer Yeshua, and formed them into a political entity. Then came Constantine and Justinian (and their Popes), who completed the rape of truth, and forced it down the throats of everyone in their sphere of influence. You either capitulated, or got very dead, very quickly. The Middle Ages, through our times, built on those lies, and now here we are. Yeshua never said he was 'God' or even 'the Lord'. That was another 'Paulist' invention. He did say that 'all' people were manifestations of the Creator, and told his followers that everything he was able to do, they were able to as well. He never created a religion, or opposed any other beliefs.

Why bring up other religions you may wonder? Simple. It was Dominant Religions that subverted, suffocated and in many countries obliterated all traces of Natural Way lifestyle thus leading to a total disregard for the powers of Nature, which is now coming down on the whole planet due mainly to man's sheer ignorance and greed. In my own country, Christian missionaries lobbied our Congress and not unlike General Franco of Spain, manipulated our law makers to ban our religion/spirituality as well.

We have two of the world's largest religions, Christianity and Islam, basically in total ignorance, or at least not admitting the ongoing environmental dilemma before us. No doubt, such omission is because their Black Books, their so-called prophets, say nothing about environmental danger. Only the harshness of advancing Nature will correct them, which it definitely will!

Japan's Fukushima is an excellent example of total disregard for the powers of Nature. The radiation leaks will last and damage for centuries. Values and ways that worked for thousands of years for the original inhabitants - the Indios Rojo (Red Native Americans), and the once powerful Celts too, are capable of working on the Environmental level now. Instead, the White Man's religion thwarts deceptively, needed environmental healing medicine. Reliable and proven example from the past is needed right along with the present disciplines; thankfully, some of the other modern nations not controlled by religious hierarchies are following and implementing toward proven success.

My primary reason for writing this work is to allow a viewing of what a tribe, even in this modern day, has preserved regarding Nature's Spirituality and to pass on to the good people of the United Kingdom that which was related and flourished in their lands several thousand years ago under the Mother Earth influenced Celts. What you may learn here is what also coursed through the blood of your lineage and is still there. Learn it well and eventually carry it on to other nations for I believe it is within the uniqueness of the British Isles that our 'natural way' could blossom back, gaining a strong, needed foothold and then onward to neighboring lands.

The Environment, albeit Nature's deadly teachings brought on by foolish Man himself, will ever be your readily observant and supportive ally. Nature's present day warnings are obviously not supporting its detractors. What I have experienced in your lands enlightened my journey and removed the hopelessness I found in my homeland despite the abrupt spiritual revival of my own people, the enlightened Sioux, who are such a small, unheeded fraction of America's ignoring populace. My discoveries in England, Scotland and Wales were akin to a Knights Templar viewing a distant, whimsical Holy Grail, an Earth saving grail, fleeting away across meadow and glade. Take your time to learn it well although I must warn that Nature's disasters for mankind can become quite expedient. A rebirthing of 'simple truths' await that I have found lacking in the other ways that have been forced upon us.

Historically, at least, I hope that you will find our story, our survival - the story of the North American Native American to be quite interesting and thus will hopefully dispel the many falsehoods heaped upon us by dominant society writers and media as has also been implemented against your people who respected Nature in their attempts to incorporate such into their faith which disregards Nature. Not only will I tell you about our

Indigenous history and ways but I hope to reveal much about modern America as well.

Nineteenth century America's dealings with us, mainly through their U.S. Army as we successfully fought them will be revealing as they broke treaties and we were forced onto Native American Reservations, mostly barren lands that were not much good for farming and making a living on. We are now allowed to come and go freely from our reservations. We were initially confined, forbidden to move from one encampment to another. Our religion/spirituality was branded as pagan and heathen, terms I resent. Adolf Hitler even studied the American confinement system, in implementing similar methods for the Jews. We were not exterminated on our reservations, instead were fed scant rations, but it was the confinement that was placed upon us which bothered us the most. When the First World War came, we were needed for the military. Our warriors were good at it. After brief military training they boarded troop ships to fight the Germans from the trenches of France. Upon their return our reservation confinement was lifted. Later, we were allowed to be citizens. To the Sioux (Lakota) newly won freedom was well worth the journey to go fight in the first of many wars to come. My Uncle on my Mother's side fought overseas in that war.

Mongol and Viking

Where did America's earlier inhabitants come from? We Sioux-Lakota are mostly of Asian descent. Among the Northeastern tribes of North America there exists a trace of Viking blood. This same DNA trace could also be Celtic. These tribes, which the Sioux are descended from are almost a half foot taller than many of the Southwestern tribes and those indigenous inhabitants of Central and South America as were the original Vikings in comparison to the smaller Europeans further south. The Vikings enjoyed a richer protein diet, salmon mainly and free to hunt diet supplementing wild game. The Northern American tribes enjoyed a rich bounty of meat; buffalo, deer, wild turkey, numerous smaller animals and abundant fish which they were also free to hunt unrestricted.

Only the nobility were allowed to hunt in the vast forests of Europe. The common man apprehended for hunting game to supplement his family's diet would have his bow fingers severed. When my tribe fought the U.S. Army we were generally at least a half foot taller than our European descendants; the size of the Union and Confederate civil war uniforms of the mid 1800s are exemplary proof. The Mongols and northern Chinese also were considerably larger than the southern Chinese. The Mongols had a richer protein diet which added to their size. American Army and Marine Veterans who fought against Mongol divisions in the Korean War will readily attest to the size difference between the Mongols and the Koreans. Medieval Europe historically was beset by annual famines which continued until the major foods of the Americas, mainly corn, beans and potatoes came to their farm lands. Ground grain gruel was the common fare of medieval Europe.

In Spain, I noticed how tall the northern Spanish people were. Could this have been from the tall traits of the Celts who once roamed their lands and obviously flourished upon the readily available game that once abounded? The South American tribes are no doubt descendants of Southern Chinese boat migrants landing on the western coast of South America. Again, size contrast is a distinguishing feature between the Mongols of the North and the South China Sea coastal people.

I feel, at times, as a frustrated Jewish writer would have felt, back in the time of Nazi Germany. Let us surmise that this writer was deeply patriotic and had even worn a German uniform in the earlier World War. He somehow had the foresight and the vision of what the rise to power of a man like Hitler would bring down on his country and not just the nearly total destruction of the

Jewish people within. Or possibly an equal example; let us imagine a Japanese writer in the 1930s and the real danger he could envision with the rise up of the ultra-Samurai-ism of a controlling Hideki Tojo. Further, if somehow such a writer would know of the foolish idea of attacking an industrial giant of the world - the United States, it would not be just the suicidal folly of leadership they would warn of but worse, the deaf eared, lemming like, blind following of the citizens of both countries would never listen to such a writer.

So where are the environmental commentators of Native American descent? They do not exist. Admittedly, most Native Americans have not been raised in their culture. We have a host of pretenders, mostly the Native American Academics, but a few are immersed in their culture, historical knowledge and Spirituality. With those credentials you will never get your foot in the door of modern media America. You have to be a clone of culturally backward America to qualify. A traditional respecting and Nature knowledge gathering Native however, stands as much chance as a snowball in hell or a Jewish writer in Nazi Germany.

The White Man in America is swallowed up with his European heritage, quite disinterested in the Native American's past despite the raw fact that he will have to learn our value system to survive the environmental consequences fast approaching. It will be like the automotive mechanic, Mr. Good Wrench, who appears in a car service uniform in television commercials. He states with a wry smile, full of common sense warning, 'See me now, or see me later!' Your vehicle will need service from him sooner or later. Strongly and aptly implying that the longer one waits the greater will one's servicing needs become … and hence, the greater the bill. But most ignore this just as Native Americans are warning America about the Environment, but to no avail.

America unfortunately, is a 'Fairy Tale' land. It is still intoxicated on the resources that once flourished before they were voraciously consumed by the European immigrants. Multiply and produce, always build bigger (and not always better). We were told in school that America was the 'Land of Unlimited Resources!' Now the resources are gone. But humans will change! How so? I have to issue this following phrase with a smirking smile that will even out do Former President George W. Bush. Climate Change!

Mother Nature's Planetary Heating is now making millions of believers. It was almost overnight that millions in the Northeast who were hit disastrously by 'Frankenmonster', Hurricane Sandy coupled with a high tide, a full Moon and an advancing 'Nordeaster' storm to add to the disaster that unquestionably 'educated' the densest populated area of the United States. They were like a man stumbling up groggily from a knockout punch knowing he had been conquered by his opponent. Nature leaves no question about who remains in control of this planet. Re-elected President Obama suspended his presidential campaign bid at a critical time in what was then thought to be a very close race with former Governor Mitt Romney, who ridiculed Climate Change. A Republican Governor, Chris Christie, a harsh critic of the President, 'took off his boxing gloves' so to speak and worked side by side with the President during the aftermath and in the end of their Duty gave positive plaudits to the President such had Nature's wrath changed him. Later he called the President congratulating him on his re-election.

I suppose climate change ridiculers' reasoning is that their Bible says nothing about the world's greatest forthcoming disaster, even though it becomes such an obvious reality with the increasing havoc that plays out across the planet let alone the disappearing Arctic Sea ice and melting glaciers. Simply observe Greenland! They remain 'locked in' but this last election and such a devastating storm will prove to subtract many a Republican adherent from their lists is my future prediction. I firmly believe the Earth Power as created by some mysterious Vast Creator will prove me out. Unfortunately the Planet's scenario will not become a rosy, Hollywood ending scenario. I do hope, for the sake of humanity, that I am dead wrong. Who is the culprit? As these pages turn, the source will be repeated considerably – Over Population!

Despite that 'Everything will be okay,' is the claim of those who have been programmed by the 'Happy Endings' of fairy tale land. The Hollywood movies and television soap continue the charade. No one in America is allowed to break that spell. A few scientists speak out and even our former Vice-President, Al Gore, and the environment receives some lip service but the serious issues of Planetary Heating, Clean Water, Water Shortage, Pollution, Thinning Ozone and Gone Resources are danced around. No one, especially Organized Religion (which controls a number of American politicians) will not touch or mention the obvious approaching, exponentially increasing crisis of over population.

Eventually, the White Man will have to copy what China and your country have already arrived at regarding Over Population. How can China initiate and employ such a stance? Simple: That country is not controlled by Organized Religion! I have not visited Italy yet but I do meet many Italian tourists yearly and am no longer surprised when the majority of them I meet pay only lip service to the Church of Rome. Initially, when I first heard their negative support of 'The Church,' I was surprised but now, after several years hearing the same, I believe that even Italy is following the way of the rest of Europe. Possibly Ireland, at least part of it, may still be holding out although much anger exists in that land concerning the covered up pedophilia scandals.

Missionaries Facing Spiritual Perseverance

The American government began to herd the Natural Way

people off to Reservations over a hundred years ago, mainly by bringing in their Christian missionaries to destroy all visages of Native American Culture (Nature based values). This was a mistake. It is my firm belief that foolish America will become doomed towards a system of less than mediocrity through their thwarting of Nature. Corrupt political leadership and foolish misuse of what Resources are left is steadily destroying my country. 'Discipline' is a word that modern Americans shy away from, unlike the early colonial forefathers of old who utilized effective discipline which then became seriously eroded. In but a few centuries we now see the dire, disastrous results of greedy, selfish stewardship.

When the missionaries came to my reservation they almost obliterated Native Spirituality. They were under the protection of their own created and congressionally lobbied for religious ban placed upon all Native American tribes. They preached zealously of a man-God born of a virgin woman whom will appear in the sky someday, 'saving' all believers and punishing the rest. They invented a super powered Devil or Satan that would do the punishing and even attempt to harm us in this life. (We Sioux have never observed this man concoction.) This falsely fearsome idea was preached in the boarding schools where our youth were confined for nine months of the year away from their parents. The appearance in the sky someday of God's human appearing offspring for ultimate environmental or related disastrous curing calamities is a bit much for my mere brain, more so than the virgin birth idea, even. I hate to see the mass of the world rely on that particular belief and thus give Mother Nature's reprisal more of a head start than it has now.

What makes Native Americans so 'different' from the all-encompassing, merging, assimilating and 'Superior' Dominant Society which came to surround us? It is a proud stubbornness regarding complete assimilation. For the larger tribes in the west, we were blessed by vast geography which allowed a protective 'distance' and because of this semi-isolation we were able to retain our language and our Spirituality despite the government's effort to eradicate our past. Basically, it was just too difficult for the zealous Christian missionaries, who brought their own form of government into our lives, to 'get to' all of us. We also have had a much shorter duration to be 'under the spell' of these meddling missionaries. My tribe, the Sioux, the Lakota, have only been on the limiting Native American reservation territories for just over a century. It takes longer than a mere century to break down the tribal language and cultural values.

In the east, tribes have had 200-300 years of direct subjugation and rule of the White Man. Consequently they have lost their language and Spirituality but those remnants in this present day modern society are now borrowing from the Western Tribes; their ceremonies and Spiritual concepts. Formerly, 'assimilated' American Indians now want to return to being so called 'real' Native Americans, especially reconnecting back into our Nature respecting Spirituality. They are suddenly aware that environmentally, the so-called 'civilized' way is just not working for them and is detrimental. It must be those age old values, 'Values of the Blood' that have come back, risen up within them to catalyze such a driving desire which one can observe when they come out to our traditional reservations to observe or become a part of our ceremonies and celebrations. Maybe it is because they want to, 'Simply respect Nature.' It must be noted; the eastern tribes and many mid-western ones, once, not very long ago, shunned and denied the old Native Ways. I mention this fact not so much in the line of some form of deserved persecution, but on the contrary I want to illustrate a firm example as to just how powerful the materialistic seeking world of the Dominant Society and their Organized Religion can become to a conquered people.

In the far West, the large Navajo Tribe and Hopi have managed to retain their language and Spiritual concepts despite being under 400 years of brutal Spanish conquistador influence and occupation. Their sheer numerical size and vast geography was a major blessing for their stubborn success - my opinion. The southwestern tribes are far more superstitious and more loaded with related taboos however, than the tribes coming out of the northeastern areas of the continent. No doubt the conquerors' superstitions have had a longer period to make their effect. Farther south the Central and South American Native Americans did not fare as well either. The Spanish church was ever present sanctioning such brutality and ready and willing to enslave the Native Americans in the gold and silver mines to take back the metals to Spain and Portugal. The gilded altars in the churches were solid proof.

Spiritual Perspective

Many present day Native Americans, have shed the Spiritual beliefs of their ancestors yet adamantly claim 'true Native identity'; while ridiculing true traditional respecting Native adherents. This man - God belief excuses many American citizens from holding any interest in our ongoing environmental impact. 'Oh well, God/Jesus, will not let us down' they resign. Admittedly, this God-will-take-care-of-everything concept appears to be quite a rewarding theory but too difficult for a true Nature respecter to swallow. It agitates to the extreme the true believers when you dare to critique or disagree with their views but with the environment at stake, they have to be challenged.

These followers of the White Man's religion control a considerable portion of American politics to this day but fortunately for the planet not Europe. Their religion has made exceptional progress into the majority of Native American tribes across America as well. The derogatory terms, heathen and pagan, have been placed upon the followers of the Natural Way. Most tribes have lost their old Spirituality (Religion) due to the powerful government sanctioned Christian Religion of the White Man's way. They will adamantly claim that the government has honored the Separation of Church and State proclamation based in the Constitution but oh how the Organized Religions are particularly favored. I simply have to mention the words 'Tax Free Churches' to squelch their clamor.

My tribe, the Oglala Lakota Sioux, managed to keep our language in order to keep our values which differ considerably from the White Man's values. This historic struggle will be depicted in later chapters. The average American citizen has little interest in our Native Indigenous culture and values however, despite its needed application to the many serious problems, not environmental problems alone, which are now plaguing this America. Strangely, I see what China is doing, a so-called 'God-less Society' as termed by our Right Wing media; China's needed discipline to survive and non-allowance of Organized Religion into its government. America is quite the opposite. Organized Religion, especially the Right Wing 'Tea Party' is making serious inroads into American Politics and the environmental issues are the least of their concerns. A good automobile bumper sticker would read; 'Protect the Rich. Vote Tea Party!' (Republican Party). Another would be: 'Save Social Security - Tax the Churches'.

This book is primarily intended to enlighten the awakened European population regarding Spirituality thought as was once the philosophy and lifestyle across your land. It may appear that I am complaining about my country and praising others as we read onward. I think that by bringing forth some of America's serious problems, the reader can learn or observe the folly of a nation that has ignored the Natural Way. America is no longer 'the Land of the free', it is now becoming severely shackled economically along with 'Homeland Security' and the supposed threat of Terrorism from the Islamic fanatics. The ultra-right Christians would love to start a 'Holy War' to obliterate Islam and in the end convert the Jews to Christianity. This sentiment statement is now uttered in the Catholic Apostle's Creed which is voiced in Sunday services across the nations of the world. Hopefully this readership will learn well the dangers of unlimited allowance of extreme religions and the damage it can bring about on innocent, moral, patriotic and ethical people, whilst finding a true path to peace and prosperity in the heritage of their indigenous pasts.

Chapter I

Religion & Spirituality

When Man speaks of Religion or Spirituality, He should speak only in a suppositional sense or attitude, with the exception, of course; that which he directly observes. For, it is indeed an incomprehensible Mystery.

In our Universe, at least, most believe we have an ethical and moral Designer, Force, Ruler, Originator, Maker, Creator, (God). The speed and exactness of a computer, a mobile phone are brilliant, seemingly magical examples of what this Great Force allows from and through what it has designed. Mere, egotistical human thinks that he has created the invention; never realistically reasoning that all invention has to begin with this Mysterious Force which my people call Wakan Tanka (Wah khan tan kah) - Great Spirit.

There is little visibly left of the Celtic Way from what I have directly observed in recent travels to Europe. It has been thoroughly obliterated by Organized Religion. You are foolish to go to the churches to try and find it. If you truly seek what the ancient Celts practiced, utilize plain common sense and go to an Indigenous tribe that has managed to keep their Spiritual connection to the Natural Way ... and little different than what the Celts basically practiced. This writing will bring the indigenous to you although many non-natives, especially Europeans, are now journeying to some of our Western Native American tribes and observing ... and learning.

What is Spirituality? What is Religion?

Organized Religion has a history of deprecating Nature as a spiritual base. Religion often disagrees with the findings of modern science whereas Spirituality is more often supportive of scientific discovery and findings. After all, the scientist is simply probing, investigating, and studying a specific area or field of Creator's nature. First let us begin with Indigenous Man, who was immune to the detours, the detractions of modern living. Furthermore, he had direct access to the teachings of ever-present, all-surrounding Nature. Wild game could be in view with every step. There was no not covering pavement, view blocking sky scrapers, no brick and mortar, let alone planetary, life threatening, and life ending pollution which Man creates. Indigenous Man's lifestyle was dependent upon Nature's provision, whether it was soil tilling or hunting or both. If one was to learn Spirituality - his was the perfect classroom.

My tribe managed to preserve their Natural connection, the Natural Way or 'Nature's Way'. Yes, and even yet to this day. Our forebears lived this belief system prior to the coming of the White Man – the Wah shi chu. Despite the Academics and the Wah shi chu missionaries who did the immediate damage to spiritual preservation, my tribe preserved and are now returning (Ahtaa hehnucehnu - hastily) to the old Natural Way (our Native Spirituality). Our ceremonies of thanksgiving are returning and being presented once more to Creator and its Spirit World by the Lakota people, who for the most part are now part Wah shi chu due to the increasing inter-marriage, or should we say 'outer-marriage'. It obviously makes no difference to the participating Spirits that enter our ceremonies and refresh us spiritually.

The Celtic tribes who once roamed freely throughout most of Europe for several thousand years were quite parallel – spiritually to the Sioux, the Iroquois, the Chippewa and most of the Northeastern North American Indigenous tribes: this holding is my strong suspicion. Nature is Nature and on both sides of the Atlantic she reveals the same. Man's basic interpretations, if they remain devoid of superstition, (man's creation), the parallel beliefs should remain similar - is another of my beliefs, suppositions. Eventually, the blocking out of Nature due to 'civilized advancement' along with modern Man's input of religious superstitions (all concoctions of this strand of Mankind) brought on a myriad of religious beliefs and onward to an outright avoidance of Nature's teachings and further onward to even a vilification of that which could be spiritually fruitful within what ironically is created by the very Creator itself ... and there we have Organized Religion to this day.

Obliteration

Man could not control Nature nor alter or dilute what it can and will display, therefore it had to be religiously obliterated and those who chose to remain steadfast to the Natural Way were condemned, persecuted, and eventually exterminated to the extent that their Spirituality eventually vanished. And such is what basically happened to the ancient teachings and recordings of the collective Celtic Wisdoms. Europe had a much longer exposure to Organized Religion and therefore suffered complete obliteration of its indigenous wisdoms and belief systems. My tribe has been only exposed to Organized Religion but a century - not long enough to extinguish the Natural Way from the ongoing generations.

The same course of obliteration happened to the belief system of tribal peoples of the western hemisphere but it has not happened to all of the tribes in North America. My tribe was besieged by Wah shi chu Christian missionaries who were quite successful with their federal government lobbying despite supposed democratic constitutional secular protections to ban indigenous tribal religion (Spirituality to the tribes). Some of the western United States' tribes went 'underground' however, to keep their belief system alive. Following the aftermath of Dr. Martin Luther King's Civil Rights Movement in the 1960s, the American Congress finally woke up and passed the Freedom of Religion law a decade later after MLK; hence removing the unconstitutional, unlawful religious ban.

A strong resurgence; a return to Native Spirituality has now occurred and the old spiritual ways, still preserved, are now flourishing vigorously on the Lakota reservations - mostly in the state of South Dakota. Surrounding tribes are also returning to their ways including those tribes in Canada especially the Cree. They come down to America and attend our summer Sun Dances. Some Sioux go up to Canadian Native American Reservations (Reserves) and attend their ceremonies which beseech to the Great Spirit (Creator). ,The Lakota can give you a window to your ancestor's valuable beliefs if you garner the Wisdom (common sense) to look through it.

Native American ceremonies, songs and prayers will be explained in this writing so you can enter the 'mind-think' of a people, the North Native American, who was very much akin to the spiritual outlook of the ancient Celts of Europe. Like I said, 'Nature is alike on both sides of the oceans.' Their teachings which are based on unchanging Nature were strongly alike. Both attempted to find the intricacy of the Higher Power (God; to some) mainly through 'What' and 'How' this vast Creator Entity reveals its Nature for moral and ethical guidance rather than seeking universal knowledge from the foolish blathering of Man.

Modern Man has traversed widely in his attempts to 'know' what is actually impossible to truly perceive. Yet he's been quite successful in branding his formulated concepts onto society. Man has established a religious hierarchy which controls through fear along with false, unsupportable promises. And the 'bleating sheep' followers choose eagerly to adhere to this rather than to seek realistic learning and true knowledge, free from superstition and false claims, which now are becoming quite dangerous for planetary survival. They (the sheep) are programmed, medicated, embalmed to deny that which only a much Higher Power than mere Man can adequately provide.

Evangelicals shun hierarchy and build their own vast

mansions from their Sunday Service monetary collections and televised to draw the sheep; preaching how God will reward them financially. Their faces are notably tight, voices forceful and fearful while quoting biblical verse. Most religions are quite homophobic, denying vehemently that Creator makes all things, entities, breathing and non-breathing, moving and non-moving - the way they are. My tribe simply states that a Winkteay (one born as a non-heterosexual) is made that way by Creator and no chastisement or negative treatment of such individuals should be allowed or is condoned because one does not injure or hurt what Creator creates. The Spirit World awaits all and justice will be served on violators.

Jehovah's Witnesses held to a certain number who will only get to enter 'Heaven' but altered that Biblically deciphered amount once this particular sect grew in membership. Mormons wear special 'God pleasing' underwear. Muslim women must always keep their heads partially covered when in public, some sects demanding a burka. Catholic nuns only recently came out of a special hooded covering that was quite restrictive. Priests and nuns all take a vow of celibacy and yet pedophilia scandals have run rampant throughout the church hierarchy leading toward numerous lawsuits thanks to this new age of exposing communication.

Environmentally, many Christians ignore planetary heating, dismissed by their 'Rapture/Resurrection' belief that their God concept will appear and solve any and all environmental problems besides rewarding the adherents and of course punishing the non-believers. I hope that they are right! Such is just a few of the startling beliefs Man has come up with from his many organized religious sects. But a few centuries back, one could or would be put to death, and most often after torture, if one would disagree with such religious precepts. The penultimate chapter will indeed expose such atrocities that Organized Religion has inflicted on innocent people.

All mainstream Christian and Muslim establishments believe emphatically that a 'Devil' or 'Satan' exists, and prey upon humankind to detour their journey away from a rewarding heaven and on into a fiery, quite unpleasant 'Hell' where one can expect eternal torture. Traditionalists of my tribe believe a Spirit World exists where all humans will eventually enter and there one is judged by those whom one has offended untruthfully and by those whom one has honored truthfully according to positive morals, ethics and what the animal world certainly exhibits for us – Truthful Duty to offspring, pack or Tribe during one's Earth Journey. It is difficult for most culture respecting Sioux to think Ultimate Creator has any need for a White Man's Satan; let alone allow such a thing in a Creation which provides for us all. Therefore, our culture is much less superstitious, or afraid of the dark. Certainly such an attitude is a needed armor against the religious charlatans of the world.

We also have 'Honest Observation' in our armory, which is defined as looking clearly at what Nature reveals to us along with an awareness of the Past. Honest observation also holds a cautious respect for Nature's power. To regain the Natural Way, one can expect false, denigrating accusations to be hurled back upon those, including the probing, investigators of Science, who simply are seeking real Truth.

Great protectors of Mother Earth were the old generations of Indigenous people; quite unlike the fruitless negativity we have experienced from observing and hearing Dominant Society's Organized Religious practice down through centuries and now inwardly supporting life threatening pollution mainly from unchecked commerce while ignoring Earth's dire warnings. Yes! Organized Religion is completely devoid of Environmental care and concern. Where is such supporting evidence in their highly touted bible? Heating of the Planet, Water Shortage, Gone Resources and Over Population are the four major causes of the future calamities besetting our planet's survivability. I should correct that statement: rather it should be – human's surviv-ability upon the planet. Mother Nature will survive; humans may not!

Such oncoming disaster is so visible in this modern day that Organized Religion is now forced into desperate retreat but yet they still hold fast to their downplaying and minimization of such serious threats to our planet. Their 'black books' of human prophecies speak nothing of the above subjects, rather one major proverb or command dictates: 'Multiply and subdue the Earth.' In my opinion, over population is the most serious threat to our existence and the wildlife upon the planet also. One country alone is taking serious steps toward minimizing over population – China. This country also places a check on Organized Religion as well for they are well aware of Organized Religion's ability to control. If Organized Religion would have controlled China in the past century, their population would no doubt have doubled by now! India, adherents of Organized Religion, will eventually surpass China in sheer number.

Western Europe does not yet set political based restrictions on population limitation (in England they are looking into limiting populous through changes in their social welfare system) but the citizens themselves are practicing commendable curtailment of the sizes of their families. Eastern Europe is also awakening toward a similar sustainable practice. The planet's western hemisphere in comparison, does not practice population control especially Mexico and those South American countries still held in the grip of Organized Religion, predominantly the Catholic Church.

Mexico would become desolate, but their check valve is illegal immigration into the United States which it will eventually control due to the lack of awareness of the materialistic numbed Americans. Math is math but America remains too distracted with their existing comforts to realize the approaching end of successful secularization due to the eventual loss of control of their own country. They are akin to alcoholics whom remain steadfast to their addiction oblivious to all that is falling away around them.

Leadership

What dedicated, self-less leadership has Organized Religion spawned? We can simply look at the corruption, greed and self-promoting non-leadership that the American Congress (all Organized Religion proponents) has spawned for itself to answer that question. Not only have the politicians enriched themselves but the tax free Churches have also, especially the hierarchal ones and the televangelists.

Indigenous peoples were equally Matriarchal and Patriarchal. They saw that Nature (God's Creation) was balanced and therefore their Spirituality would be as it should be and remain accordingly as all things made, (created) displayed were far more exemplary, more dependable than what mere man would utter. Many of the Celtic women rose to Bardship; the keeper of the records, the Keepers of the proven, workable wisdom. Like the Celts of old regarding Woman, she has a high place also in Lakota Sioux society. The Animal World, the female often leads the hunt. The herding Wamaskaskan (animals), the old matriarch elephant leads to water and grasslands. The Bulls follow. Often the Alpha wolf pack leader is female; the female lion leads and engineers most of the hunt. That is the way God made it. Among the Sioux and the Iroquois, the woman is powerful as it was among the ancient Celts.

The Pilgrims who arrived in America in the 1600s knew nothing about 'Democracy'; they would later adopt it through two observant envoys to the Iroquois Confederation of five tribes - Thomas Paine and Benjamin Franklin. Paine remained with the Iroquois, learned their language and took the wonderful political and social valued gift to Europe where it blossomed so well that it brought down the decadent, selfish and corrupted monarchies.

By directly observing what Creator has put before us - Nature, we can easily learn how our own countries should be organized and operated fairly. To practice the Natural Way, however, requires keen, thoughtful observation of Creator's workings; more than just a few songs and some ceremonies, however.

The Natural Way is a matter of living your beliefs and to know, understand, feel and be all that surrounds you which is Nature made and not man-made. It is a lifetime of moral and ethical application. The more astute you develop your mind to perceive and look for clues and meaning set before you by this Ultimate Creator, the more you prepare that miraculous mind for your own lifestyle while here. One's goal should be a deep, serious ongoing consideration for a preparing of the mind for that much longer duration in that other world beyond – the Spirit World. The more advanced you develop yourself from direct observation, the more advanced your mind, your spirit, your soul will become to be more advanced for the Spirit World, which most Native North Americans sincerely believe awaits beyond. This supposition also means one must de-clutter and remove clogging superstition, harmful appetites, greed, ego and ignorance from the mind. Watching soap operas, shopping sprees, celebrity watch and such related empty fascination is not rewarding preparation for the Beyond.

Nature respecting two-legged (human) believes that Creator is All Truth, All-Knowledge. The more truthful you are, the more knowledge you seek, especially Nature reflecting knowledge, the more God-like you become. Quite simple is it not? Conversely, the more you stray away from truthful morals and a harmonious lifestyle, the farther away you become from the fruitful goal that awaits in the Beyond. I further believe that this Beyond is a place of All Truth and All Knowledge as well. Would not an All Truthful Creator make it so? But its offered advancement will not be attained by an unprepared, selfish, unfocussed and disinterested mind. I also believe, unlike some of those in Organized

Religion, that only the mind (Soul, Spirit) goes on! Yes, some believe the entire body and its worldly desires elevate also, usually for the satisfaction of the male members in the form always of extra wives or mates for his pleasure. These beliefs are purely marketing devices, highly successful for recruiting Church or Mosque membership. The more Truthful, the more real Knowledge you seek, the closer you become like Creator. Yes, fairly simple isn't it?

Nature's Discipline

It would be very foolish to attempt one's life journey with an absolute disregard for Nature's discipline. Americans especially, are programmed through media to believe 'Hollywood' endings. But Creator has designed Nature to teach discipline. The Native American out on the Great Plains knew that he had to hunt hard during the summer to put away adequate dried meat for Nature's long, approaching winter. Failure to do so meant death. This was called, 'wintering over'. Nature does not offer forgiveness either. Does a tornado, a hurricane or typhoon return and put all the pieces back together again? Does a drought, or a man caused dust bowl as in the 1930s in the Mid-western states of America return and replant the farmers' burnt out crops? Likewise a tsunami, an earthquake or mudslide (usually man-induced), offers no forgiveness. Even in modern countries blessed by abundant resources, record floods often bring destructive damage to their croplands and cities.

Ignoring what created Nature repeatedly warns us, can become quite dangerous. How Japanese engineers could so foolishly, stupidly, disregard, ignore God's evidence of repeated earthquakes and go ahead and build a nuclear reactor next to God's ultra-powerful sea water is beyond me! (In a historically proven Earthquake area!) Obviously they became so immersed in their engineering studies and consequently divorced themselves from a healthy respect for Nature and Nature's ultimate powers that they totally ignored Nature. I was asked what relationship did I believe Creator, if any or possible, is sending Man a message regarding such a calamitous disaster. I guess I would have to answer, 'Creator, or It's Spirit World that possibly looks after our Tierra Madre; maybe they (Observing Spirits) are teaching Human to begin a much deeper respect for Nature's forces'. The Ocean is obviously a major, powerful force as well as is Man's discovery – Atomic Energy. The two of them should be learned, respected and realized to distance both as far apart as possible.

Forgive Me!

Organized Religion has one believing that one can be quite ignorant of world surroundings, non-observant, self-centered, a greedy person without positive humanitarian goals or practice, oh yes ... and super paternalistic, woman baiting, woman hating too ... and you may live 'happily ever after'. All you have to do is utter just before you die, 'Forgive me Dear Lord. Forgive me!' Bingo! The doors of heaven will open wide for you. I don't think so! Such a successful marketing ploy, however, that obviously appeals to the greedy and ignorant of all classes. At least half of the woman gendered Spirits in the Spirit World will no doubt vehemently agree with me on this particular point. Therefore I have endeavored; with the help of many other like-minded acquaintances to project to you a fuller menu (Earth centered) to gradually digest and go onward to what I believe will be a far more productive life. You will, no doubt, become a careful protector of a living Entity - the Earth Mother whom we are all part of since when we were first conceived in our lineage mother's womb. It is all very simple yet human has managed to complicate and make difficult what is so easily observed from Nature - Creator's (God's) Created Creation.

The past centuries Man had the luxury to make his multiplication of erroneous living but now, in this age of Exponential

Population Multiplication, such overly consumptive lifestyle breeds extensive pollution which is racing our Planet toward human's doom. The Planet will go on spinning but it is Man who will become doomed. Detractors, nay-sayers and of course the alibi chorus for Organized Religion are most welcome to quote me on Exponential Population Multiplication. Someday we can have a hotly contested discussion - in the Spirit World where the aces will be mine!

What Are Spirits?

Quite simply, they are former humans who prepared themselves while they traveled here at one time and went on into the Spirit World in a higher state than the non-observant and were 'better equipped' so to speak to now progress more fully into the World of Knowledge - the awaiting Spirit World. Those who loaded themselves down with the worldly vices created by man; extreme materialism, blinding ego, numbing consumption of narcotics and/or alcohol, selfishness, abandonment of offspring, power seeking, control seeking, falsehood in its many aspects, disloyalty to family, tribe, Nature etc.; all plus more of such blinding conduct to honest observation of our surroundings and fellow beings imparts such a strong negativity upon one's own Spirit (Soul to some) that, in my opinion, will make it very difficult for such individuals to progress in Creator's realm of knowledge that awaits us all. Creator is All Truth and All Knowledge, is it not? Providing that One believes in a Higher Power.

And the Devil?

Organized Religion quickly employs its usual 'Work of Satan' accusation to any book that disagrees with its stand. I once had a priest shake his fist at me and foolishly threaten, 'Ed McGaa, you are possessed by Satan.' I pushed his puny arm away and laughed, 'Priest, we don't have any man-made devils. That's your creation. You can keep it!' He was trying to stop the resurgence of our annual tribal Sun Dance of Thanksgiving to Benevolent Creator and of course futilely losing control of their once powerful grip on our Native American reservation which was speedily happening; thanks mainly to the catalytic Martin Luther King Civil Rights movement freeing up the Negroes from decadent 'Jim Crow' prejudicial treatment. If anyone should be canonized, sainted, beatified it should be MLK! Throw in the white one (Martin Luther) as well. Talk about bravery. There was a very courageous man who took on the Catholic realm at a very dangerous time. Martin Luther broke the spell, the complete control of the violent, murderous, torturing, monopolistic medieval church of his time: Such a brave, courageous person to revolt against such decrepit inhumanity. A later chapter gathered from preserved evidence suffered by later dissenting church adherents will prove how despotic one controlling organized religious institution can become.

Creator is All Truth and All Knowledge. Would such an entity allow quite the opposite in its realm? You can learn from observation of Nature. What exists, even a tiny dragon fly can be a worthy teaching. The Christian and Islamic 'Devil' does not exist. Have you ever seen one? Don't expect to unless you have been on some hallucinating drug possibly and which your deranged mind has possibly made up. It is a perfect man designed tool to keep you under control.

A Lesson in Observation

Let us take four wires; A gold one, a copper one, an iron one and an aluminum one. Let us also utilize a wooden dowel or a rubber strip about the same size and length of the metal wires. Now let us hook up an electric connection that will pass the mysterious electrons that are hooked up to the vast grid systems crossing the planet and even run the computers and laptops that reach out mysteriously to other countries across the oceans. In less than an eye wink we can transgress with others due to the working mystery of these electrons such is their capability allowed by the Great Inventor.

Now let us explore the speed and ease which the electrons will travel through each metal wire, remembering, acknowledging that such capabilities of allowance or hindrance is a characteristic from Ultimate - the Great Inventor. (Yes, we have many names for IT! We also will not describe IT as a He or She!). It is a bit too vast for such foolish non-observant based nomenclature despite what the masses of the World utilize. Great discoverers were often vilified for their successful probing and accurate realizations. The gold wire will allow the least hindrance toward the electrons followed by the copper and then the iron wire. The aluminum wire offers the most resistance. Gold is rather expensive and scarce so hence copper is utilized most by our electrical and related electronic providers. The wooden dowel allows no passage and the rubber strip provides complete blockage.

The parable of this brief study is a direct example of nature observation. No you do not need to be on a mountain top, upon the high seas or observing a herd of buffalo to study the wisdom of Nature and what it can teach you. Our minds are an accumulation of a mass of electronic interchange that converts what we observe to memory and related conduct of ourselves according to what we experience and what we *choose* to experience. The Memory goes on and in most of us who believe Spirit-wise; goes with us into the Spirit World. Yet the totally definitive explanation of what truly IS an electron cannot be fully explained by the most gifted scientist. Such is the Mystery of the Ultimate, the Great Maker. Human is so foolish to quarrel and argue over what is totally inexplicable. The Northern Native American realized this fact and did not waste their time on such a subject. I was blessed to attend several meetings of various holy men of differing tribes with my mentors - *Chief Fools Crow and Eagle Feather. Such a commonality of respect for the Great Mystery was a common virtue.

I hope to advance toward the gold wire state for my journey into that Beyond as well as for personal progress while here. Endeavoring to have succeeded in accomplishing the least impedance of God's Truth (Creator's Truth) while they were here upon their Earth journey was the success of those Spirits that now return to observe and sometimes aid us in our journey. This is a strong supposition that I harbor. Those who seek the clutter illustrated in degrees by the other wires and the abrupt non allowance, complete blockage of the two non-metals shows to me a revealing example and what natural wisdom seeking can impart. Creator is All Truth and All Knowledge. One can take it from there!

Chief Fools Crow, Oglala, (1890? 1891? - 1989), the most famous North American holy man of the latter 20th century. He lived modestly at Kyle on the Pine Ridge Reservation. Along with Chief Eagle Feather, Sichangu Holy Man, (1914-1979) he was responsible for the return of the Sioux Sun Dance in modern times. Spirituality and Historic author, Thomas Mails wrote an interesting and revealing biography on the venerable and spiritually powerful leader, Fools Crow.

Mind Fulfillment

To just learn how a particular tribe (in this case the Lakota) performs its ceremonies, speaks or sings its particular songs and prayers will be but a shallow representation of Earth respecting spirituality, if that is all that one seeks. Granted, songs are wonderful tools to call out to the Spirit World, birds utilize it all the time to communicate. Human's prayers and beseechment (the seeking of positive spiritual communication) are all good to speak forth; be one alone, in solitary or voiced as a group in ceremony, but life goes on to offer each of us much deeper mind fulfillment, if one projects the desire to learn more of Creator's demonstrated knowledge in order to prepare for advancement onward to another beginning that lies beyond.

Direct Observation and relating to all can lead one to those powerful Sioux words, the phrase, Mitakuye Oyasin (Mee dtak ooh yeh Oh yah siin) - We are All Related, We are All Relatives or For All my Relatives. The initial chapters of this book will present indigenous ceremony, however, mainly to demonstrate just how powerful communicating ceremony can be for those tribes who through their own steadfast resourcefulness, have maintained their cultural connection to such an awesome and amazing power. My own personal experience from being a pledger for six annual sun dances in six successive August summers on my reservation conducted by two Sioux holy men of deeply spiritual, communicative wisdom was indeed a mind filling experience which has lasted well into my later time.

No Need for a Leader

For those who embrace the Natural Way, the last thing we should ever do is go out and find some sort of 'Leader' for this Earth and Environment respecting spiritual path we have chosen: Teachers whose knowledge is based on true experience; Yes. But a singular, hierarchal leader above a linear, elevated bracket of sub-leaders; No! It is far too encompassing for some mere human to attempt to be directing, controlling, manipulating, attempting to expand through false promises and as most common; siding in with a future dictator who promises repayment for opiating the masses he wants to control. This last methodology has been perpetuated down through time as a highly effective cooperative ploy for would be dictators. The Church and The Dictator would be a challenging book for some future author. It may take a bit longer for the Natural Way to right itself from the past ravages of Organized Religion, but as it evolves back - which it will: it will be stronger, far more meaningful and reaching than what we have witnessed regarding the pitiful, insufficient, often corrupted Way of Organized Religion with its many self-serving, unfocussed 'Leaders'...

Nature will always be the real leader of Spirituality, not Man. Nature is now responding strongly and at the same time she is doing some serious teaching. Man's greed and desire to control has now provoked the wrath of Nature. It is just a matter of time, no doubt a steady series of increased suffering for human to finally, hopefully come to an awakening. It is here now, the first strong warnings which the world around us still ignorantly ignores especially the religious leaders of today. We do not need some head Guru, Pope, Patriarch or Ayatollah! Humanity now has a powerful ally, which allows me to be optimistic, despite the oncoming environmental dilemma. Humanity can now communicate and is doing so more efficiently each advancing day. World changes never considered before are steadily happening. It is happening. The people of Europe are at the forefront. This is not a writing of fairy tales, 'hocus pocus' or superstition. You will find far more superstitious beliefs, practices and proclamations emanating from the two largest religions upon the planet than you will in the spirituality of the traditional Lakota Sioux or of the ancient Celts. Could Creator (God) finally be tired of Superstition which has caused death and destruction through the centuries even presently? With the forthcoming environmental edicts about to emanate from reacting Nature herself in these suddenly aware times; quite possibly Creator is beginning to show us how disastrous our superstition based (along with ignorance and wasteful, materialistic appetites) folly and disrespect for Its Creation can become. The 'New Age' brought forth the impressive Harmonic Convergence; but not unlike Organized Religion, New Age could not or would not shed Superstition. The Natural Way has no superstition. Nature cannot have it unless devised, implemented and inserted by mythology-phobic Man.

It is time that Indigenous people speak up and it is time that Dominant Society keeps quiet and listens for once. The ongoing environmental catastrophe tells you to 'introspect' and listen to a people who have lived safely, harmoniously with Nature down through many more centuries than Dominant Society has. From my observation, the White Man is bent on the appearance of obtaining personal salvation. The Native American is more concerned with planetary salvation. He is not worried about reaching 'Beyond', as long as he follows and respects the true rules of Nature over the attempts of Man. It did not take Dominant Society long to undo the successful environmental pattern the Indigenous Peoples employed.

We do not believe that we need to be 'saved' from our Benevolent and All-Providing Creator who made us. Such super-stitions the White Man has placed upon us, even banning our religion and language to force us to comply. Religious extremists hatched a federal built and staffed all-Native American 'patients' (mostly Sioux and Chippewa) insane asylum built at Canton, S.D. to primarily contain our religious leaders. Thanks to the Martin Luther King civil rights movement the Federal (Government) ban was finally lifted in 1978 through the Congressional Freedom of Religion Act. In the meantime, we faithfully served our country beginning in WWI and on into Vietnam, Iraq and now Afghanistan and who knows what others will come. There are plenty of wars for U.S. Citizens to enter into wherein the sons of the rich most often avoid the actual battle scenes. The following scenario actually happened. Without further preaching, this is what happens for those that seek the Spiritual ... at least for the Lakota Sioux.

Chapter 2

Encounters with the Spiritual

On the final day of a Sun Dance in the late 1960s, a lone cloud appeared far to the south as eight dancers waited to be pierced*. Chief Eagle Feather and I were the first. I had returned safely from the hell of Vietnam, as predicted in an earlier ceremony conducted for me by Chief Fools Crow. In that ceremony which took place before I left for Vietnam, I took the Sun Dance pledge, 'If I can come back, I will dance the Sun Dance.' All that was predicted for me regarding battle, came true. There are various reasons why sun dancers take their pledge and now we were at the height of that fulfillment.

The large Sichangu Sioux holy man stood next to me urging me to watch what was happening far away to the south. A distant growing puff of white cloud was the only image in the hot August sky. I was too tired to offer it much attention. I was also thirsty and hungry from four long days of fasting and fulfilling my sun dance pledge. I have to be honest, at that particular moment in my life; I was simply counting off the final hour of the grueling sun dance. I imagined the relief I would soon be feeling when the ceremony and my four day vow would be over.

Details of Sioux ceremony will be explained in a later chapter. Piercing is performed by the medicine person to each pledger (sun dancer) who has promised Creator his 'pain so that the people, the Earth, will live'. A sharp awl is pushed under and through the chest skin (not the muscle) and back out again to allow a polished wooden skewer into and partially out of the 'tunnel' that the awl created. This small, strong band of skin now holds the skewer. The end of a rope from the sun dance tree is brought forward and with a leather thong, the rope is bound to the two projecting ends of the skewer, connecting sun dancers to Mother Earth. It is all voluntary; no one is forced to endure it. Woman never has to be pierced in the Sun Dance. She gives her pain 'so that the people may live' in childbirth, which could kill her thus facing far more danger. Therefore she is honored, respected by never being pierced.

The cloud seemed to be approaching. It was a vast western sky with no other clouds visible. The dry Badlands' air was still, yet the cloud seemed to be moving towards us. I could feel a dull throb where I had been pierced in my chest. I held my rope's weight in one hand to ease off the pain. After a few minutes the pain changed my chest to numbness. I eased my grip on the rope and let it hang freely while shuffling a slow dance step to the drum beat coming from the drummers at the edge of the sun dance arena. We watched each dancer lie on the bed of sage face upward at the base of the sun dance tree and be pierced by the sun dance Intercessor, the Sun Dance Chief. Chief Fools Crow would push his sharp awl in and through the chest skin and back out again, then insert a smooth wooden peg into the first cut and tunneling under the skin he would push the tip back out. Onto this hardwood skewer he would tie the pledger's rope to the peg with a leather thong. The other end of the rope was attached high up on the tree implanted at the center of the sun dance arena.

Surrounding the arena was a pitiful crowd numbering only several hundred traditionalist Sioux. This was not a large number coming from the Oglala tribe that numbered at least 25,000 people back then, the neighboring Sichangu tribe, representing some of the pledgers, including Chief Eagle Feather, were also sparsely represented. Hiawatha Federal Insane Asylum (Canton, South Dakota) no longer existed but the fear of 'The Ban' by the government and instigated by the Christian missionaries lingered.The numbers of the traditional faithful was pitiful in those days. The reservation missionaries with the unconstitutional help of the federal government had done their job well -

from their viewpoint. Little did we know or realize that the return of Native Spirituality would build like a tremendous storm. Thousands would return to the way of their ancestors and our lone Sun Dance would become numerous in but a few decades. Thousands of new pledgers would arrive. One Sun Dance would not be able to fulfill its four day vows. 'It's coming closer,' I remember Eagle Feather's awed tone. The cloud about the size of a football field approached slowly. I should have been in awe but I was so weak and tired, I simply wanted the ceremony to be over.

Fools Crow came toward me after the last dancer was pierced. 'Hau, Nephew.' Bill Eagle Feather exclaimed, 'That cloud is coming right at us!' The cloud was approaching the edge of the camp-ground which was full of teepees, tents, and trailers; all surrounding the circular Sun Dance arena with its lone cottonwood tree at its center, decorated with colored prayer cloths. The drums were throbbing seeming to speed their hypnotic crescendo; that pulsating, haunting tone which one hears only at a Sun Dance. As a Sun Dancer you will hear it for an eternity. It is so powerful; the pain in your chest seems to be carried away with its soothing, magical tone. Fools Crow took me by my sage gauntlet tied around my wrist and walked me inward toward the tree. All the dancers came inward, dancing a slow shuffling gait to the heavy rhythm of the drums, blowing their eagle bone whistles. We touched the tree and blew our shrill whistles. The tree shrilled back!

We danced backward to the end of our ropes. The ropes tightened and our thongs held firm. Fools Crow signaled with a nod and we all danced back toward the tree, our eagle bones shrilly tweeting. Again the tree sang back! Four times in all we would dance inward. The cloud was directly above as we touched the tree for the final time. It sent down soothing, light rain on the dancers and the praying crowd. We went back to the end of our ropes. The drums throbbed as if we were standing before a gigantic, singing waterfall. Some sun dancers would have visions as they leaned back against their bond with Mother Earth. The silent on-looking crowd would send up their prayers to Wakan Tanka, the Great Spirit whom we assumed was watching from somewhere. Eventually all would break free and the ceremony would be over.

Was Creator watching over that particular ceremony? Who controlled that cloud or rather, what controlled that moving billowing object of Nature which purposely made such a timely appearance on a windless day? There was no fearsome, rolling thunder or terrifying lightning, no punishing hail stones; just pleasant, soothing, cooling, light rain. Is that a sign that whatever controlled that cloud, might be somewhat pleased? What would be your reaction had you seen such a miraculous sight? Indeed, this was a very powerful experience. Would you deny what your eyes had shown you? Would you be such a coward and never reveal what you had observed? The world is full of such cowards on their life journeys, oblivious to why they are here. Some folks would find it impossible to believe. How can some people be so indoctrinated by other humans that they would refuse to believe what their own God-gifted eyes reveal to them? They will actually be lying before God, by denying, will they not? Such is the power of the indoctrination other humans hold over them! Sheep are easily led.

We were beseeching, formally calling, formally acknowledging. Creator acknowledged back. But modern materialists of today are simply ignoring what they see with their own eyes. They actually do not want God or any power to interfere with their disastrous taking and could not care less about the generations unborn. I hardly think a Creator will rush to our rescue unless we change our attitude. This ceremony was direct observation. It happened! We will next explore a few more startling spiritual quests. Eventually the history and leadership of these planetary and Creator respecting people will be presented as well. It is the type of real, truthful, selfless leadership along with Nature forms of beseechment that needs to return or else we are all doomed. I believe knowledge mainly comes from experience. But knowledge can also come from truthful associates who impart it. Like the Lone Cloud Sun Dance; the following actually happened, although before a smaller audience. I have often wondered, 'For what reason would the Sioux, up and leave what appeared to be a lush paradise (Carolinas) and finally arrive at the harsh Great Plains?' My answer would be the very same Spirit Ceremony that you are about to witness. And all that I can offer for verification is that many such ceremonies have been and are held by members of my tribe and other tribes. Or feel free to read the works of Dr. Wm. K. Powers, a noted anthropologist who has written several books on the subject (*Yuwipi- The Native American's Spirit Calling,* University of Nebraska Press, 1982).

I am not into convincing anyone, but I do not shy away from actual observation and real life experience. Skeptics are free to look me up in the Spirit World. By now, I think that most readers will be convinced that I actually think one exists. Again, I do not insist that you necessarily have to believe as I do. Like the 'Lone Cloud' this was another of my mystery projecting experiences and was observed by others. The participants were all University related, some sporting rather high degrees academically along with accomplished track records from an academic point of view. Unfortunately, Dr. Bryde whom I have depended a lot upon for much of my Sioux historical material has recently passed away. He was present at this happening. The years have gone by; Lula Red Cloud, who was but 20 years at the time, is the great, great granddaughter of Chief Red Cloud and was also present. Lula can verify what took place back in 1970. Without further distraction let us continue ...

University of South Dakota

At the request of the University Administration, Chief Eagle

Feather came to the University of South Dakota to conduct a revealing Yuwipi (Spirit Calling) ceremony. At this ceremony, in the late '60s, many so-called 'credible' people attended. These were university professors with graduate degrees. (Therefore, I guess, a detractor would almost have to assume that they were maybe more 'credible' than most ordinary people.) This ceremony was for the benefit of non-Native Americans and was held at the University of South Dakota to find five students and their pilot/professor who crashed a light, single engine airplane somewhere in the cold, remote, snow-covered region called the Nebraska Sand Hills whose terrain is akin to parts of Mongolia and Northern China.

They were returning from Denver, Colorado to Sioux Falls, South Dakota, and encountered a blizzard. The pilot developed vertigo and it was presumed the plane had crashed on the windswept Nebraska Sand Hills and was covered by snow. An all-out search began, even the Nebraska National Guard was used, but after a while it was too expensive and futile to continue. The search was called off. At that point the University of South Dakota Native American Studies program, where I worked part time since my major occupation was a law student, Native American Studies had connections with Sioux holy men and none other than the President of the school called upon them for help. At the ceremony, I sat next to his beautiful blonde wife, Connie Bowen.

Bill Eagle Feather asked for a map. He specified that he wanted 'the airplane kind of map (WAC chart) and not the ordinary road map.' A line was drawn from Denver to Sioux Falls, the light passenger plane's intended destination and Eagle Feather proceeded to study it before the scheduled evening's ceremony in the basement of the school's museum. The aircraft held a maximum capacity of five passengers plus the pilot. The ceremony began with Eagle Feather's ceremonial peace pipe being offered to the Ultimate Powers under one Benevolent and

All Providing Creator. Lula Red Cloud, a student, held the pipe after the opening. Chief Eagle Feather was bound, and lightly wrapped in a blanket. We then lowered the huge man face-down, a rug provided some comfort for him on the hard floor. After the tobacco offerings were spread out and the lights turned off, the ceremony began in total darkness.

The singer boomed out the calling song, an eerie loud, high pitched, staccato wail that sounded so ancient that one's genes knew that it was ancient and told you so. After a few minutes of this calling and drumming the Spirit People (or Spirit Forces) entered, flourishing in the form of blue-green lights. Around and before us, above us and in close to us; at times they flourished seeming in tune to the mesmerizing drum beat. The calling song to the spirits finally finished as all who sat there were placed into a spiritual void totally separating them from all that was earthly. Such a power was before us that had one asked another what was their own name, they would not have been able to answer or care to.

A brief discussion seemed to occur between Eagle Feather's muffled voice and some other entity. This entity which was the called upon was simply Spirit (Wahnahgi). The conversation did not last long. A moment of silence then a song was called for and once it began, the lights reappeared and seemed to exit through the wall. Eagle Feather called for the song of Chief Gall of the Hunkpapas. Whatever it was that had communicated to Eagle Feather, it had now left the room. The singer sang out, and at the conclusion of a special song, Grey Weasel, the entity, Eagle Feather's spirit helper, came back again.

A purring sound filled the room. The patter of small feet was accompanied by the excited chattering of a weasel. A weasel in America is very much like a ferret or an ermine or mink. Ferrets are kept as pets by a few people and allowed to roam freely in their dwellings. Eagle Feather began to talk in Sioux to the animal, and the visitor chattered (spoke) back and purred as the holy man spoke. They continued to converse for a period until finally the animal no longer chattered but purred slowly. Then Eagle Feather called for the same song. A woman sang. When her song finished, a loud crack came from the center of the floor and something slid toward the keeper of the pipe. I felt it impact into my feet with a sharp jab. I actually leaped sideways and into the lap of Connie Bowen. Sheepishly, I remarked to her that something had hit me. You must remember that all of this was taking place in the darkened room within the bottom of the university museum building.

Predictions

Once the song ended, Eagle Feather called out, 'Ho, Grey Weasel has made seven predictions:

1. The airplane crashed in a storm not far from a town that has two creeks with almost the same name. We should send an airplane out to look for it. A man and woman will fly that airplane.
2. The animals will point to where we should go.
3. If we fly where the animals point and head past the town with two creeks, we will fly over the plane, but it is pretty well covered with snow.
4. The plane sent out will have to land but everyone will walk away from it. Do not worry; the pilots will be smiling as they look back.
5. In the next day or two some people who are not looking for the plane will be led to it by an animal.
6. Only five will be found. One will be missing within the airplane. She landed away from the others, but she will not be too far away.
7. Her face will be upon an ice colored rock. She has a Chinese (pageboy) hairdo and wore big glasses.

Those are the seven predictions. Now also, a rock that looks like ice has entered the room. It will have these signs I spoke of. Ho, Nephew (meaning me). 'Reach out in front of you and pick up the rock. Hold it until the final song. You are of the rock clan, and you should welcome your rock brother, not be afraid of it.' Somewhat skeptical, or still in a degree of fear from the encounter, I readily handed the rock to Connie Bowen, who asked for it. Before the final song and the lights turned on, Eagle Feather said, 'The two who fly like the winged ones,' meaning my companion and I (both pilots) would hopefully find the crashed plane by flying and using the stone as a map.

The next morning, we flew a Cessna 180, single engine plane from the University town's airport which was close to the Missouri River. As we lifted, I looked down and saw that the deer in the meadows were grazing, and they all were pointing downstream. We banked the airplane downstream. It must be noted that deer usually graze towards evening and seldom are seen in the morning hours. In a short while we came to another stream, a creek which emptied into the river. Deer were standing close to its mouth and all were pointing upstream. We followed the deer's indications which seemed to be foretold on the stone because deer images were inscribed on it.

We came to the two creeks with the same name and flew on to see a town in the distance. One creek was named South Wolf Creek and the other was Middle Loup Creek. Loup means Wolf in French. We passed over the small town of Arnold, Nebraska, a very isolated and remote cattle town. The surrounding land and landscape was very vast with few or no fences and no planted agriculture, only vast grassland for cattle feeding and some stunted trees and tall cottonwoods at springs and dry creek collection points. We figured out that the cloudy, unclear sign on the opaque, ice gray crystal stone represented fog, as we were starting to notice the clouds getting lower to the ground. Across and away from the town we passed over a ranch where cattle were all standing on one side of a soybean/cracked corn cake feeding trough and pointing us toward some deer pulling hay from a haystack and who also pointed us onward in the same direction that the feeding cattle were indicating. Cattle, when feeding, always stand on each side of a trough when they gather no different than when they are taking on water from an elongated container but not these particular cattle at that given moment. We circled for a while over a spot as the fog was pushing us downward, visibility wise we were beginning to get into flying trouble and soon we were homeward bound to avoid the descending fog.

An eerie feeling came over both of us before we banked the airplane back to Vermillion, South Dakota and the University airfield as though those deceased down below us were telling us that we had arrived at their final destination. Eventually, we landed back where we started, just in time because the fog was settling on the runway as we put the airplane in its hangar. It could have been fatal for us had we not returned in time to find the runway because of the oncoming descending fog. Carol who held a commercial flying license was a very pretty, blonde and a good ten years younger than I. My flying skills had been honed by the military especially my combat missions in Vietnam. She had flown many hours in civilian planes despite her youth, now in her twenties but she was a natural, gifted pilot and a welcome addition in the cockpit when adverse weather came in.

In those days many pilots flying small aircraft eventually met their doom fatally due to weather conditions which could isolate you from direct visibility. We both were well aware of what we had escaped from. It was now dark and we promptly drove our cars into town and had several relaxing drinks as most typical pilots would have been prone to do. The modern instruments of today were not invented then. Even when I was flying the million dollar machine, the Phantom F4, navigational instrumentation was relatively crude when compared to the lifesaving (and aircraft saving) instruments now available to pilots. The next day after we had had our narrow escape, close to where we had reversed the plane's course, two coyote hunters followed the tracks of a coyote. The animal's tracks led them to the wreckage of the Cherokee Six airplane. The tail of the doomed plane was exposed due to the rising temperature from the fog. They reported the position and soon rescue vehicles converged on the scene. All of Eagle Feather's (actually Grey Weasel's) predictions proved true.

Well, there you have a ceremony that the preachers, popes, cardinals, and mullahs can never do. Nature's Path is truly the world's most powerful religion/spirituality if prediction and spiritual communication is the standard. It is also the result of the sheer truth and dedication of the intercessor (the conducting medicine person) and, of course, the sincerity of the audience that allows or makes a pleasing atmosphere for the spirits to come in or whatever it is that you wish to call these information giving, knowledge probing forces who come in or want to come in.

I imagine the preparation and sincerity of the old Celtic Seers produced similar ceremony. It is all an allowance of the Ultimate Power. It is not possible unless the Intercessor - the Holy Man or Holy Woman conductor or beseecher - has extreme focus, yes an Ultimate Focus to cultivate an appearance; a bringing in of those Spirit Forces to come into the ceremony. These men or women have cultivated themselves to arrive at what I term; Pure, Pure God-Truth! Organized Religion does not have this ability and never will. They have too much of a distracting outer focus to put it bluntly.

Without harmony and undiluted truth, however, nothing will happen. It is encouraging to believe that the Spirit World will truly be a truthful and sincere place where earthly lies and manipulation will not in the slightest be allowed or condoned. Nothing but pure truth will be the total mental (or thought-wise) atmosphere, possibly. Again, our observation of God's Nature readily displays, God's (Creator's) Nature is always truthful. Should not Creator's Spirit World be likewise? Makes one wonder why we long to stay here!

'Life is but a mere shadow on the wall compared to the complete reality that lies beyond.' I reflect upon Plato's meaning in his 'Allegory of the Cave.' What we experience here, observe here, can and no doubt will be reflected to a related degree in the Beyond. It is obvious that the spirit is able to go back in time and discern what took place. The girl's seatbelt, who was thrown out of the plane, had become unsnapped no doubt by flying debris from a high G force, or possibly by her extreme increased weight due to the spinning airplane's centrifugal force thus breaking the seat belt or buckle. Extreme centrifugal force ejected her through the plane casting her out away from the others. This prediction would be impossible to conjure. The spirit guide obviously has the ability to revisit this happening back in time to be able to report specifically as to the findings. 'One of the six will be missing. She landed out away from the others.' I find that statement impossible to conjure and only able to come from an entity that had 'non-earthly' help.

This Spirit Calling ceremony, could have influenced the Carolina Dakota to advise them what danger was about to cross the Atlantic or the magnitude of the deadly danger (contagious disease) the Europeans had already brought. They up and left a lush existence rather suddenly. This would be highly unusual for an established society comfortably settled in to their surrounding environment. The main subjects or characters (Red Cloud, Crazy Horse, Sitting Bull and Black Elk) in this writing undoubtedly knew of this ceremony and may possibly have depended upon it to some degree when they so successfully fought the White Man's soldiers; who knows? I find that the Yuwipi ceremony has certainly influenced my journey.

Pure, Pure God Truth

Pure Truth extends much deeper than simply 'not telling a lie'. When a human being can develop themself to shed all forms of 'un-truthful' habits, beliefs, false superstitions, exaggeration, irresponsibility, non-appreciation, disregard for thanksgiving, non-observance – especially of Nature's teachings immediately before you and all forms of disrespectful negativism; then that person is beginning to extend oneself into a communicative mode to communicate to those Spirits that surround us. When one does arrive at such a positive state in regard to Pure Truth there is no Consecration, Anointment or related 'Recognition ceremony' conducted by mere man who seems to love to insert various forms of hierarchy into his Organized Religions.

Yes, mere Man, loves to elevate himself. Maybe he wants to be a 'Mini God' so to speak. This attitude doesn't work if one seeks to be able to call in the Spirits! Repeatedly, I will make the statement: Creator is All Truth and All Knowledge. It is all very simple. Many virtues must be practiced, developed and put into action however, for one's lifetime. Sharing, Generosity, Bravery Courage, Observation, Perception, Recognition and more: all will lead one toward a higher state and a definite preparation for a Spirit World which lies beyond, whether or not one will ever care to communicate directly as the Indigenous Medicine persons so do.

While one conducts oneself on such a positive Spiritual journey, one's body will harmonize with the surroundings of Nature and become a very helpful tool as well. Like a dancer at a pow wow whose heart beat synchronizes with the drumbeat and can dance effortlessly for hours; such is the body of a human which can harmonize spiritually with Nature. The animal brothers and sisters exhibit this trait, this connection, every day.

Devil rides again...

What about the alleged power or manipulation of the white

man's 'Devil' or 'Satan?' Well, first, the Traditional Sioux do not believe in such things. They (Man conceived Devils, Satans, Spooky Goblins, Incubi, Werewolves etc.) do seem fairly preposterous. Pope John Paul II sanctioned classes on the clergy to perfect their means to exorcise this white man's devil. It was all on the internet news showing many young priests attending classes on the subject. For them, Satan abounds and must be dealt with. Traditional respecting Sioux reasoning is that a Benevolent Creator has no need to allow such things nor would they be in the 'so-called mind' of such a powerful Force. Where in God-given Nature is there such evidence?

We Sioux have never seen or observed such things and do not expect to. If you have such an entity, why is it we can never observe it? Odd, that so many non-Native American readers (and some turn-coat Native Americans as well) will sincerely believe that the above innocent beseechment, the Yuwipi, intended to bring closure for the bereaved families of the crash victims, which was a direct observation, and even generously intended to help their own kind, will be considered preposterous and thus they will have to invoke some sort of 'Evil' conjuration to it! Not long ago, a few centuries, we would have all been drawn and quartered or burned at a stake for simply wanting to find the six victims. Thankfully, Americans at least, now have the protection of the clause: Separation of Church and State and so far no police have showed up to punish me.

The preceding account will be unbelievable for some, maybe many. Immediately the unconvinced detractors, will cry 'Conjurer! It is the work of their Satan!' Sorry folks. We do not have your Satan. Our Creator has no need for such a Man invention. Now let us go back to the Spirit Calling and to the part where Grey Weasel talks about the girl who was ejected out of the airplane on its fatal spin. Absolutely no way could a so-called 'Conjuror' make such a prediction. The Spirit World remains a mystery but obviously there is enough valuable 'Mystery' to help humans probe into its revelation if properly and respectfully focused. Historically, according to the following similar Spirit communication, written over several centuries ago, proves to me at least, that spiritual communication outside the realms of Organized Religion was alive and well and not of recent vintage.

Capt. Jonathan Carver, Eighteenth Century Spirit Ceremony

Capt. Carver's memoirs, *Travels Through the Interior Parts of North America in the Years 1766, 1767 and 1768*, London, C. Dilly, 1781, is the earliest mention of tribal foretelling ceremony that I have discovered. The explorer was two canoe days' journey from the Grand Portage area which would later become Minnesota territory. Grand Portage is near the northeast tip of Minnesota, and north east of the Lake Superior port of Duluth, Minnesota. This episode is described following the explorer's comments regarding earlier meetings with the Sioux, so this could place him west of Grand Portage. Capt. Carver mentions the Sioux, the Winnebago, and the Assinpoils. The latter could mean the Assiniboine who headed further west. He referred to the Sioux as Nadowessies, Nadewesous or Naddewessiou, an early term for the Dakotas, from these terms came the name that stuck for several centuries - the Sioux. Academics, including Native academics attempting to be politically correct, are presently doing their utmost to send that term the way of the dinosaurs but are having a difficult time with the reservation Lakota, mostly who don't seem to mind being called Sioux. These three tribes mentioned above eventually migrated westward considerable distances except for the Winnebago who remained in the Wisconsin area. Eventually some were sent southwest to Nebraska after reservations were established by the federal government.

Another tribe Carver mentions, was the Killistinoes. The Killistinoes' tribe was more distinctly linked in language with those of the Chippewa and Ottawa tribes. A ceremony was held by a medicine person (referred to as a priest) of this tribe and to such ceremony Capt. Carver found himself invited. The mechanics, so to speak, of the ceremony, bear somewhat of a resemblance to the Yuwipi spirit calling ceremonies I have observed within my tribe.

Let us begin where Capt. Carver was impatiently awaiting a re-supply from Grand Portage for his exploring party. He writes,

> The traders we expected being later this season than usual, and our numbers very considerable, ... we waited with impatience for their arrival. One day, ... the chief priest belonging to the band of Killistinoes told us, that he would endeavor to have a conference with the Great Spirit, and know from him when the traders would arrive ... .
>
> The following evening was fixed upon for this spiritual conference. When everything had been properly prepared, the King came to me and led me to a capricious tent, ... In the centre I observed that there was a place of an oblong shape, ... so as to form a kind of chest or coffin, large enough to contain the body of a man. ...
>
> In a few minutes the priest entered; ... Being now prostrate on his back, he first laid hold of one side of the skin, and folded it over him, and then the other; leaving only his head uncovered. ... two of the young men who stood by took about forty yards of strong cord, ... and rolled it tight round his body, ... one took him by the heels and the other by the head, and lifted him over the pales into the enclosure. ...
>
> The priest had not lain in this situation more than a few seconds, when he began to mutter. ... what he uttered was in such a mixed jargon of the Chipeway, Ottowaw, and Killistinoe languages, that I could understand but very little of it. ... After having remained near three quarters of an hour in the place and continued his vociferation ... he seemed to be quite exhausted, and remained speechless.

But in an instant he sprung upon his feet, ... 'My Brothers,'
said he, 'the Great Spirit has deigned to hold a Talk with his servant
at my earnest request. He has not, indeed, told me when the persons
we expect will be here, but tomorrow, soon after the sun has reached
his highest point in the heavens, a canoe will arrive, and the people
in that will inform us when the traders will come. ...'

The next day the chief took Carver to view the lake. A canoe
came into view as the sun was above, 'sun had reached his
highest point in the heavens,' a canoe came round a point of land
... The Native Americans no sooner beheld it, than they sent up
a universal shout, and by their looks seemed to triumph in the
interest their priest thus evidently had with the Great Spirit.
When the men came ashore they stated that the trader party had
been parted with but a few days before and were to be expected
in two more days and in accord with the medicine person's
prediction.

They accordingly arrived at that time greatly to our satisfaction, ...
Captain J. Carver, Explorer.

First Encounter

My first encounter with the 'supernatural' came when I was a
young Marine warrior about to go to war. After this first
experience, it should be obvious why I never returned to the
White Man's religious indoctrination despite years of catechistic
upbringing including a bachelor's degree from a Benedictine
college, St. Johns University, (MN). There I was quite content
with the surroundings of the good Benedictine monks, who
taught alongside lay teachers. It was a perfect school for my
background, isolated way out in the North Woods of Minnesota
with a pleasant lake, streams and oft visiting, surrounding wild
life. It was a disciplined, no nonsense study environment, yet
encircling Nature offered so much pleasant contentment for my

bloodline. I dearly loved my time at St. Johns along with several teachers, especially the head of the Biology Department, Father Adelard Thuente who was like a second Father to me.

Except for one Chippewa several grades lower, I was the only Native American on campus. Father Adelard was also from the Dakotas and had been raised among my people. Maybe that was why he seemed to show me a special attention, mainly by allowing me to do wildlife studies for extra credit since there was so much wildlife around. Probably, I was a connection to his past, his boyhood. Those were wondrous, rewarding years mainly because I had such a comforting mentor. Yes, I have been blessed with many good and guiding mentors. Like Father John Bryde, S.J., later Dr. Bryde. I never would have been a writer were it not for the historical information I gleaned from Dr. Bryde. See *Crazy Horse and Chief Red Cloud – Warrior Chiefs,* which is based primarily on Fr. Bryde's numerous interviews in Lakota with the old time warriors who were yet alive when he was a Sioux reservation missionary. Instead of writing the historical book himself he generously gave me his notes to complete the endeavor. It is my main seller in my home state - South Dakota.

I appear 'hard' regarding the Church but the experiences my people have suffered from missionaries and their overzealous boarding schools are adequate evidence. I must add one other priest however that has strongly influenced me. Father Bill Stoltzman, now a Diocesan priest in Shakopee, Minnesota was also a former Jesuit. His writings appear in several of my other books. One chapter is almost totally his work. Father Bill tells of his positive experiences in the Sweat Lodge, Vision Questing and Spirit Communication. I asked him if he was going to get in trouble with his Church for writing so vividly and honestly of his positive experiences. He told me not to worry. What he had seen and experienced with his own eyes (from Creator) he could not and would not alter just to please possible Church Doctrine. Truth is Truth and cannot be altered. Father Bill's courage is certainly a shining example of 'God's Pure Truth'.

Like Jonathan Carver, I too was a Captain, a Marine pilot home on leave. My mother said to me. 'Fools Crow is looking for you. He wants you to come down to his cabin. He wants to hold a ceremony for you ... for that Vietnam you are going to.' My mother had five of my brothers go off to war earlier, mostly WWII. She simply accepted it as a regular fact that all of her sons would be involved in combat, one way or another.

She was a staunch Catholic and spent much of her time helping at the off-reservation Jesuit mission in Rapid City, my hometown. I saw more of my mother during my high school years at the mission structure after it was built than at home. It was a gymnasium/church besides a large facility for donated rummage sale, hand me down clothes where my mother spent most of her time sorting and arranging for distribution to the Native American locale and some poor Whites. I spent many evening hours there and on weekends playing basketball. To this day I have a healthy set of legs for my age. My father did most of the cooking. His wife was happy at the mission and he never complained about her absence. He was a basically happy and contented parent, albeit in his advancing years as a parent yet of a high school youth, his last – me.

My only connection to Chief Fools Crow was that I was a pow wow dancer and would dance as a social dancer in the evening time, while the Sioux Sun Dance would be held at the same dance grounds in the early mornings when most of the social dancers were fast asleep in their tents. Chief Fools Crow enjoyed the pow wow social dancing and was always a present figure looking on. My old step-grandmother was there at those early sun dances. You are not supposed to say step-grandmother in my language. A so called step-grandmother is your grandmother. Your step-mom - if you have one - is your Mom. That is just the way it is. Your 'so called' half-brother is your brother. *Mitakuye Oyasin* - we are all related. In those days there was little interest in the return of the Sun Dance, our primary symbol for the return of our Way. There would be no return if the governmental authorities and the colluding, meddling, proselytizing missionaries had their way. By now they had converted the majority of the reservation - so they thought. They were confident they had destroyed the primary spiritual fires; too confident, they would later discover.

Pow Wow Dancing

Pow wow dancing is simply social dancing for relaxation and enjoyment both for the dancers and the on looking crowd as well. We pow wow dancers would dance long into the night, after a lengthy supper break, twirling and turning to the drum beats. It is a magical relaxation. The drums and the singers keep a melodic enchantment. In a way you are a form of fast moving ballerina. Our Sioux women also dance. In those days we did not have the contest and prize money dances which are a major part of the reservation social dancing nowadays. We danced for the sheer enjoyment of just dancing.

It is utterly hypnotic to wear the plains' regalia and whirl and twirl. Tied tightly to your head is a half-foot tall porcupine hair headdress called a pay shah with its two, tall eagle feathers swiveling in bone sockets atop while keeping your bobbing head movements to the drumbeat. Many dancers were bare chested in those days, sporting maybe a necklace of bear, eagle or hawk claws. I wore a bone breast plate which covered my entire front from my neck to my waist. You wear a breechcloth or apron, front and back, fairly elaborate and decorated with sequins, beads; or in my case, a cross stitch of an old Sioux design. At the sides of your breech cloth or apron which is often fringed, you have a pair of fringed buckskin edged, bright, cloth trailers reaching lower, often to your knees. These are weighted toward their bottoms so that they will fly outward as you twirl. Just describing what I used to do offers me a pleasant feeling. At your waist and in the back is centered a beautiful eagle feather tail bustle, with high reaching feathers covering your backside and usually centered with a bright matching design or colors of your breech cloth.

In my social dancing time, eagle feathers were not difficult to come by. There were quite a few eagles on the large reservations which bore adequate food for the large golden eagles which are a bit broader and taller than the white headed bald eagles. 'Goldens' feed primarily on the abundant prairie dogs, jack rabbits and cotton tails. Ranchers in western Dakota were allowed to curtail coyotes using cyanide poisoned jackrabbits as bait back then and unfortunately this procedure would kill many eagles. One could ride horse back into remote areas and most often come across a dead eagle or two. This cyanide practice is now outlawed and harvesting eagle feathers is strictly monitored by federal law.

Underneath one's eagle feather tail bustle and apron or breech cloth, a swimming suit with a pocket for keeping your money would be worn. You needed some change to buy bottles of cold pop for thirst quenching. Tourists keep you in plenty of money when they come up to you, usually at the refreshment stand to ask you to pose for pictures, and usually with their children. Mind you, you are all dressed up and with a slight bit of red 'war paint' upon your face and a braided wig if your hair is short; one does look rather fiercely exotic. Remember that I was in the Marine Corps, where long hair, especially for an officer or a pilot, is forbidden. Usually the little kids often quivered with either awed excitement or maybe from some degree of childish fear of this larger than life human standing behind them. The tourist would often place a fifty cent piece in your hand, or a couple of quarters or even a dollar. It sufficed for your next round of cool beverage when you would soon get thirsty again.

The Tourist

One memorable incident happened when a tourist placed a pair of quarters into my hand after a picture was taken with his two children who I remember as standing quite nervously close to me as we faced the camera. He asked if I was from the reservation. I replied politely that I was born on the reservation but no longer lived there. The previous day I had flown a Marine F-9 Grumman Cougar, cross-country training flight into Ellsworth Air Force Base just a few miles outside of Rapid City.

I landed my Cougar jet at Ellsworth, and rented a civilian plane from a friend named Merrill Belleau at the local flying service and flew on down to the reservation. I would always have to leave my ejection harness, oxygen mask and helmet in his office when I would rent a plane from him during my hometown forays which he would proudly display on a coat rack while I was gone for a few days. Sometimes I would 'buzz' his office with a jet fighter or even shoot a touch and go at the municipal field where the flying service was located. He always got a kick out of that and would have a plane waiting for me. Those were the days!

At the reservation graveled air field my sister Mildred and brother-in-law Ralph would usually show up after buzzing the pow wow grounds a few times. They always kept my dance regalia in their shiny Airstream trailer camper. A retired couple, they were avid followers of the pow wow circuit that was just starting to grow in those days. Native American people were just beginning to recapture their identity. At earlier pow wows, when I was quite young and an onlooker, it seemed that only the old danced and very few of the young adults danced or were in attendance. The Wah shi chu had all the answers then and was bolstered by the many new inventions constantly coming anew. Even we Native Americans marveled at the sleeker, fancier models of cars he produced each year. In awe of aviation, I was spellbound by the new military models he produced and the speed and altitude records that were constantly broken. Everyone, it seemed, wanted to be like the white man. My dream was to become a pilot but deep down inside, I realized that it had to be an impossibility. Such was the self-doubt or skepticism held by a young, less confident, growing Native American in the white man's world.

My sister danced as well and claimed that the dancing and the drumming had healed what was once a painful back condition. My brother-in-law, a big strong white man and a former star football player staunchly supported her new-found interest and could always be seen bustling around the trailer making things comfortable for everyone. If his wife was healthy, he was happy, was his attitude. He dearly loved my sister. She never had children, was considerably older than me and treated me like a son. My Native American dancing had led her to the pow wows where she would hobble to a chair and sit and watch, claiming the drumming soothed her ailing back problem. Once, she simply rose out of her chair and started dancing in the circle. I was startled to see her dancing close by, wearing a shawl. She danced back to her chair after a few circles. Soon she was at it again. In time she was completely healed and even became fairly agile. Her husband credited me for beginning her dance interest and always treated me quite well after her recovery. He did appreciate fully that he had 'gotten his wife back' so to speak. He said to me sincerely on more than one occasion, 'It's pretty tough to see your wife in pain. Looks like those days might be gone.' As I said earlier, the drum beat, which is in tune with your heart beat, can be very powerful …

Well, that was quite a diversion from the tourist who had just placed a quarter or two in my hand. As a Native American writer, you reflect upon what you consider as a worthy story and you just take off on it. This is a habit of the 'storytellers' of old. We generally circle back and get on with the beginning however. So let us circle back to the innocent tourist and his family which he brought to the Black Hills and all their natural splendor which his children no doubt cherish to this day. He asked cordially if I lived in Rapid City and what did I do for a living. Behind my beaded headband over hanging braids, a sweaty face, streaked with a pair of generously daubed, Chinese red lipstick stripes across each cheek bone and wearing a heavy bone breast plate and an eagle bone whistle hanging from my neck, while holding a buffalo horned, black and white horse hair braided, long handled dance tomahawk (was utterly gorgeous), matching beaded arm and wrist bands, buckskin-fringed at that, not to mention the broad eagle feather tail bustle on my back side and matching breech cloth apron or breech cloth covering my front, I guess I did look rather 'Native American', so to speak. I should also mention that small bells like those on sleighs are tied tightly over furred padding at one's ankles and of course, beaded moccasins. All in all, it does give one, especially when you are young and trim; a definite warrior's look. No wonder the two children stared at me in awe as we talked. I guess I 'brought the house down' so to speak, when I answered calmly. 'I'm a Marine Captain, a Marine Corps pilot. I just landed a jet fighter at the air base nearby and came down to dance.' I thanked him for coming to the reservation and wished him an enjoyable safe journey, shook hands with his two mesmerized children and went back to dancing.

I mentioned that I wore a hair pipe bead, breast plate. These so-called beads are 3 to 4 inches long and lie horizontal upon your chest. The many rows are separated by several pairs of stiff leather strips from the top of the chest trailing down to your waist. Bright, large, French brass beads often decorate the edges of the hair pipe as well as an inner row of shorter hair pipe which is ivory-toned. Many or most dancers in my day were bare compared to dancers nowadays. Back then, mostly full bloods or breeds with considerable Native American blood were the vast majority of dancers, so, very few of us wore heavy face paint as they do nowadays since we looked fairly Native American. We considered face paint as a gimmick to hide one's features and as full bloods or half-breeds we felt we had nothing to hide (or gain). I have seen some extremely handsome Sioux men in dance regalia as well as the women who were beautiful. Nothing enhances a person as much as a plains' dance outfit or 'costume' as we used to call it. Regalia is the term now used. When a handsome or beautiful dancer starts to move, you cannot take your eyes off them.

I have to add a note on the now-a-day modern Native American Academics in the Wah shi chu Universities and colleges who cringe when you use the terms 'breed', 'half-breed', 'quarter-breed,' and so on, at least when older Native Americans or real 'Rez' Native Americans not going on to college speak. I had one Academic Native American in college severely chastise me in an e-mail list for using the term 'half-breed.' A 'Rez' Native American came to my rescue by explaining the usage of such terms and told her to 'wake-up' if she is going to attempt understanding reservation Native Americans.

At the dance grounds, a sweat lodge for the small numbers of sun dancers participating would be held in the early morning. When I first saw one, my grandmother had to explain to me what it was and what took place inside such was the typical ignorance of the younger Native Americans of my time due to the very effective 'cultural blotting out' enforced by the reservation missionaries. In those days the advocates for the Sun Dance were attempting to bring it back to the tribe and were facing strong resistance from many tribal members who had been converted to the white man's religion. The strongest resistance came from the missionaries themselves, primarily, on my reservation. Certain Jesuit priests from that order came to convert us in the latter part of the nineteenth century. Their successors were most adamant in their opposition to the Sioux who simply wanted to keep the old way of belief. Such pomposity is the White Man. Not only does he want to take your land; he even has to take your very workable religion/spirituality away from you. To draw a crowd, Chief Fools Crow combined the two events, pow wow dancing and the Sun Dance. With the heavy resurgence nowadays of the ceremony's return, this procedure would be unheard of but those were different times and Chief Fools Crow knew what he was doing.

Fools Crow's Cabin

I picture Fools Crow waiting at the horse gate when we arrived for the *yuwipi* ('they tie him up' or, 'to be bound') spirit calling which the holy man would conduct. The tall, trim holy man held us for a few moments with that mysterious look, the penetrating stare of a hawk or an eagle. Fools Crow was like a Badlands hawk or an eagle - regal, keen, and observant - alone and aloof within his own vast spaciousness, oblivious to the encroaching Wah shi chu world. The straight-postured man spoke from the gate as they got out of the car, 'What took you so long? You should have been here earlier.'

On the way down to the reservation, my sister drove and stopped in at a super market to purchase a considerable amount of groceries for Chief Fools Crow as is the custom of our people when you go to visit a medicine person. You do not take them pretty rocks with ribbons attached as some think they have to nowadays. As I recall, we did not take them a can of pipe tobacco. My mother may have purchased a carton of Camel's cigarettes as that is what she smoked and gave them to Fools Crow as he occasionally lit up a cigarette but the intention of 'giving tobacco' as is the custom nowadays was not the intention of my mother or sister. The large amount of groceries was much more of a custom back then. To this day I wish people would dispel with giving me tobacco when they first come to visit as I am no medicine man and do not intend to be one. I am a writer and a Veteran. Besides, I dislike the taste of tobacco left in my mouth when I rarely smoke a pipe and have seen too many close friends die from it, mostly emphysema; a slow, tortuous death.

'We're sorry, Grandpa,' my sister Mildred answered. 'We

stopped to get groceries.' Grandpa is a common and respectful form of address for Sioux holy men. Chief Fools Crow had no telephone, so how did he know we were coming to see him and even knew we had been delayed to purchase food? This would be my first taste of the Lakota supernatural, as the holy man led us into his mud-chinked cabin. Kate Fools Crow stood by the wood-burning stove and welcomed us with her warm smile. Speaking in the rich Sioux language, we visited and laughed together as the blue enameled coffee pot was filled, meat was cut and put into boiling water, dried *woshapi* (berry cakes), were set in a pan of water and fry bread preparations were made. The laughter flowed. My sister, Mildred, my mother, Sonny Larive and his grandparents, and Fools Crow's son-in-law, Amos Lone Hill, exchanged conversation in Lakota Sioux. Blacktop, a bashful eight-year-old, sat fiddling with the damper on the pot-bellied stove near the west wall.

Spirit Calling

When Fools Crow went to the closet for his medicine bundle, it was a signal for the women to push back the furniture and draw the curtains. Sonny helped prepare for the tying ritual that preceded the *yuwipi*, while Mildred unrolled a long string of tiny cloth tobacco offerings. The four directions were represented by red, yellow, black and white flags, which were placed in earth-filled bowls to form a square before an earthen altar in the middle of the cabin. Mildred wrapped a string of tobacco offerings around the bowls, marking the limits of the spirit area. Sage was passed to all participants, who placed some in their hair and over one ear.

The holy man entered the square made by the string of tobacco offerings to place two leather rattles on the floor before raising his peace pipe to offer an opening prayer. Afterwards, he stood ready to be bound. Sonny tied his arms and hands behind his back with bailing twine before draping a blanket over the

Oglala's head. An eagle feather hung from the top of the blanket that covered the holy man down to his moccasin tops. Next, Sonny wrapped Fools Crow with a rawhide rope, beginning with a noose around his neck and then six more times around his body, down to his ankles. Each wrap represented the seven sacred ceremonies or possibly the Six Powers and of course, the Ultimate Power. While the holy man was lowered, face down to the floor, Mildred sat at the place of honor with the peace pipe, behind the dirt altar with her back against the stove. The kerosene lamp was extinguished.

Amos tapped a drum and sang a centuries-old call to the ancestors of the Sioux, the spirit beings. They came quickly from the west, rattling the stovepipe and swishing the rattles through the room, as if they had been close by, waiting for the call. My Mother commanded me to start praying. Would I return from the war? Would I be a prisoner? We knew the spirits would tell if we prayed humbly. If I promised to live for the people, they would try to protect me, is what I learned later but at the time I was so suppressed by the white man's false stereotypes. Startling, tiny blue lights entered through the stove door behind Mildred while I prayed. They flickered and danced with the heartbeat of the drum, then rose to the ceiling, circled the participants and, then, as the song ended, disappeared back through the stove door behind the pipe holder. I sat down in awe. The buckskin rattles that had accompanied Amos Lone Hill's song, now fell to the floor, silent.

The Wotai (woe tye) Stone

A stranger's gruff voice came in and began to speak to Fools Crow. 'Changu Taunk ahtah.' I heard my sister whisper to my mother. I knew enough Sioux from my parents who constantly spoke it, 'Big Road'. The area where Fools Crow was bound emitted a dim haze. The spirit of Big Road, Fools Crow's Spirit Helper, carried on in conversation with the medicine man. I was experiencing what I termed then - my first ghost. Fools Crow's muffled voice spoke out in the darkness, telling us how a stone had fallen to strike the sacred tree at the summer Sun Dance, while an airplane flew high overhead. The stone bore the image of an eagle within its grain. Later he had a vision. 'I saw the airplane land in a far-off place, and a warrior walked away from it without looking back. He walked toward the sacred tree and stood there with a boy. The stone was brought to the Sun Dance lodge. I took the stone from Eagle Feather and put it in my medicine bundle. It remained in the bundle only a short while and then it was gone.' The group waited while the holy man took several breaths.

'The stone has returned and is now among us here. Eagle Boy, you must pray hard so it will remain.' (My Native American name then, would later be changed.) I answered quickly, blurting out, 'Grandfather, ask the stone to stay with us. Tell the spirit people I offer myself for the Sun Dance. I will live for the people and the power of the hoop.' A shrill tremolo pierced the darkness, followed by a chorus of 'Hau'. The cry came from the women to honor a warrior who would go off to battle. It would be repeated when the warrior returned, or at his grave. Later on, I would alter that pledge, 'I would live for the Way!'

Prediction

Then Fools Crow spoke with uncharacteristic volume and excitement. 'The eagle on the stone is for a warrior who will fly with the winged. Eagle Boy, you shall wear this stone as your wotai. When you are across the ocean, you shall carry it. As long as you wear it faithfully, the bullets shall bounce from your airplane. You shall see the enemy many times. You shall not fear battle and shall laugh at danger.' After a long pause, he spoke more cautiously. 'There is no guarantee, however, that you shall return and become a new warrior to stand beneath the Sun Dance tree with Blacktop, my grandson.'

Fools Crow paused with a cough, weighing what he would reveal. The rattles buzzed. Later I would learn that the old man had envisioned that I would see the enemy 100 times and would vision quest before my Sun Dance ... if I returned. The small blue lights flourished one last time. Big Road made his exit. The rattles clashed, each shaking a different rhythm, their discord breaking the stillness. A concluding song, the untying song was sung. When the lamp was lit, Fools Crow was sitting up untied. His blanket was neatly draped over the stove. The tying rope was wrapped in a tight ball. No one, including Fools Crow had moved during the untying song. The wotai stone, oval and not much larger than a fifty cent piece and twice as thick, waited on the cabin floor and was bound in a buckskin pouch. After the pouch was opened it revealed the small stone; an eagle was clearly discernible in its grain. If you ever come to the Black Hills of South Dakota, dear Reader, go down to a stream and find your own wotai stone. The Black Hills' streams have polished these small stones for eons and they often bear images of animals or earthly scenes.

Spiritual Connection. Spiritual Communication

Where, how does Chief Fools Crow have such unusual, inordinate, awesome connection (power) to draw in 'Spirits' - former ethical, selfless, moral entities of obvious predictive and healing 'Power'? Quite simple, as I mentioned earlier! Unlike Organized Religion's leaders, Chief Fools Crow is far more focused and much less distracted. Greed, Control and debili-tating Ego are void within his constitution and proven, track recorded lifestyle. The guiding Spirits would not work with him otherwise. It is difficult and disheartening for me to believe that there are many readers who just will not understand and even attempt to alibi against the merit of this paragraph. You must always remember that I am the one on the other end of this ceremony. Those SAM missiles fired in Vietnam, miraculously did not – 'get me'! I lived! I cannot dilute this happening and the ceremony leading up to it just to please Organized Religion with all of its thin skinned followers and short comings. Oh well! We shall all meet in the Spirit World – in time. We can sort it all out then.

Combat

I wrote this memory not long after I had finished law school which began immediately after I left Vietnam. Actually, I was only eight days out of a combat cockpit and I was sitting in law school. I had missed freshman week. The following is written in the second person but is an accurate presentation of what happened after I had attended Fools Crow's Yuwipi.

It was nearly noon when he left the debriefing room at the operations Quonset. A helicopter gun ship buzzed low across the distant row of tin-roofed huts sitting on a sand dune. There was little to do at Chu Lai but wait for the outdoor movie, wash clothes and clean the hut. The endless boredom of shifting sand and dreary shacks made him yearn to go home. He had resigned from the Marines to attend law school, but had first requested a combat assignment. His orders home were due. Any intention of remaining in the service had ended with this war. The Marines had allowed him to rise from enlisted rank, but a warrior's role in a war like this one had proved too frustrating.

His grandmother's advice echoed in his memory, 'There will always be a war, Grandson. If they can make a business out of their religion, war can be a collection plate, too.' But the war, despite the frustrations, had provided the way to reach for what he must. Even Fools Crow, a pacifist, never objected to his involvement and had helped his warrior's role with the coming of the wotai.

Later, he would learn to contend that the war was mostly political and economic, no different than most, where the poor were rallied for cannon fodder through a sense of patriotism and, especially in this war, the higher realm, those in control, the elected and economic leaders, strove to keep their warrior-age sons out of combat units, taking no share of the direct and deadliest exposure. In but a short time, he would set his course upon another path and would leave the warring to politicians. Alone with his thoughts for the moment, he rested his head against the ejection seat. Before leaving Vietnam he would fly over one hundred missions. All that had been foretold in the ceremony held at Fools Crow's cabin had come true. Spirit people had entered, predicting that he would see the enemy many times. 'Bullets would bounce from his airplane,' they said.

Spiritual Predictions

The high-finned Phantoms circled like a pair of tiger sharks above the South China Sea. Two electronic-laden Grumman A-6 Intruders orbiting off the coast of North Vietnam were contacted by the F-4s. The Grummans took their positions, holding a separated, lengthy, racetrack orbit, their missile surveillance scanners sweeping inland. The mission's target was located in SAM territory. He was getting close to his last mission. He was due for discharge and new pilots were checking into the squadron. The cruising fighter-bombers turned inbound. The thin beachhead giving way to beige landscape, looked little different than South Vietnam, except for monsoon-flooded rice paddies casting mirrored reflections of false tranquility. The late summer storms were saturating North Vietnam, Laos and Cambodia further inland. Meteorology predicted that Chu Lai would receive heavy rains by noon.

He glanced at his watch. His main gyroscope for instrument landing had turned faulty and he didn't want to make an instrument landing at Chu Lai in heavy rain. The pilots had noted the cloud buildups west of Chu Lai. All Laos and Cambodia missions had been cancelled. He hoped to leave Vietnam before the monsoons; emergency missions were launched regardless of weather and more than one crew and their aircraft had disappeared in the torrential downpours. He unzipped the top of his flight suit, adjusted his pistol shoulder harness and pulled the braided cord at his neck. He tugged to bring the small lump of buckskin from underneath his survival vest. He fondled the buckskin. His orders were due. 'Where are my orders?' he asked as he clutched the wotai pouch. His orders home were overdue.

Square coastal rice fields thinned away to rising piedmont, the rice paddies climbing with the terrain, narrowing to stepped radial bands ending at mountainous, dark green, almost impenetrable jungle. Yet, fifty miles further, somewhere under the thick foliage, a North Vietnamese truck company was hidden and protected by surface to air missiles. The first warning tone issued by the patrol planes crackled like scrambled eggs across his helmet's receivers. His muscles flexed like a prizefighter circling an opponent. The voiceless tones meant North Vietnamese, or more than likely their Russian advisors, had activated radar sets and were no doubt tracking the Phantoms. Both pilots tensed on their flight controls, their feet poised to jam down the rudder pedals in coordination with a sideways slam of the control stick to full aileron.

Any further warning beginning with the spoken code word for the sector, in which they were flying, he would do an abrupt split 'S' maneuver to his right, at the same time igniting both afterburners. Fritz, the section leader, would roll in the opposite direction. The split 'S' maneuver was the most expedient means of losing altitude and changing direction. The plane would roll over on its back like an upside-down turtle before it dropped its nose straight down in a dive. In theory, the launched missiles would be radar locked to a computed destruction point out ahead where target and missile were calculated to converge if evasive action had not been taken. Below, the enemy controller would attempt to alter the missiles' course into the targets.

Fortunately, for the fighter pilots, the missiles' smaller steering surfaces made the projectiles awkward and clumsy in comparison to the fighters. Too much correction and the SAMs would tumble and cartwheel futilely. If the early warning surveillance aircraft detected the upward-bound missiles in time, the fighters usually had a high survival rate, if the fired missiles were detected in time.

Pilot error jeopardized the pair of fighter-bombers from Marine Fighter/Attack Squadron 115. The lead A-6 surveillance aircraft, having flown north longer than the uneasy pilot had wanted, suddenly banked seaward before signaling their counterpart. At this point, the surveillance radar was blind and it was now the mission of the second A-6 patrol plane, trailing further south, to scan the enemy areas inland. Precisely at this moment, the experienced Russian missile technicians fired a salvo of three missiles. Fortunately, an alert radar operator in the second A-6 had anticipated the lead aircraft's turn and was already sweeping his scope inland to locate the Phantoms, while three ascending blips were off the bottom of his screen for a few long seconds. When the three ascending dots appeared, the operator's eyes went wide. He punched the emergency warning indicator without a moment's hesitation.

'Q-B Seven, Q-B Seven!' The code word for fired missiles was shouted out across both pilots' helmets. Q-B was their sector by latitude, Seven by longitude. Both pilots reacted to the code word as instinctively as if their own names had been yelled in alarm. The lead plane rolled left, his wingman rolled right. The inverted pair hung suspended for a long, precarious moment before the black noses dropped, hurtling down, down to the green jungle, miles below. A flash of gray, like a gigantic telephone pole, roared ahead and past the wingman's window. It was the second missile. The first missile had been directed at the section leader's plane and was now tumbling wildly out of control. Preoccupation with the lead missile caused the enemy controller to err, detonating the second missile too late. The shock waves reached out with a solid thump, but no damage was inflicted to his plane.

His inverted machine was just beginning to scream downward under full afterburner power when the last missile flashed from below like a giant spear, detonating much closer. The vacuum shock from this blast snuffed out his left engine, sending the machine spinning. Around and around the F-4 spiraled down, the dark jungle revealing a glistening silver streak bisecting the whirling circle, the peaks and valleys growing deathly sharper. The 'G' forces paralyzed his leg upon the rudder. He strained to release the pressure upon the rudder and pushed back on the control stick toward a neutral position. Down he whirled and he began to panic. Something told him he could not panic. It was the time to concentrate and believe in the Way. Believe in the prediction in Fools Crow's cabin.

The streak of silver transcended to a discernible river before the pilot managed to neutralize his controls, pushing the stick forward against the centrifugal force with all of his strength and pushing his foot with equal difficulty against the rudder pedal opposite from the spin. The stabilator, rudder and aileron surfaces responded, the spin ceased, the dive shallowed and, finally, the plane came under control. Smoke trailed from hot kerosene in the dead engine. He pressed the aileron and rudder controls to point the machine out to the safety of the South China Sea. His adrenaline began to subside. He had been too excited to notice the loss of the engine. The power of just one afterburner, coupled with the supersonic speed accumulated from the dive over ten thousand feet, concealed the loss of the engine. Now, as he brought the throttles out of afterburner, the sudden deceleration warned him of his situation. He checked the dead engine's RPM gage, relieved to find a wind-milling turbine indicating that the port engine wasn't frozen, decreasing the chance of battle damage.

At that moment, Fritz called across the radios, 'Chief, where are you? Are you okay?' 'Feet wet,' He replied. 'C'mon back, Chief,' Fritz ordered, disregarding radio formality as he glared down through his canopy at the telltale smoke trails. 'I got the bastards spotted.' The vindication in his voice flooded through his transmission. He scanned the left engine instruments, satisfied with their readings. He double-checked the fuel flow, pressing the quantity indicators, calculating his reserve fuel. The Phantom was a flying kerosene tank: fuselage cells, wing cells and two external tanks fed the thirsty machine. Abnormal fuel loss would indicate battle damage. It was against battle regulations to re-light an engine that had been taken out of action if one had adequate power to return to base. He had adequate power to return to Chu Lai or Da Nang on one engine and could disregard the section leader's order. Another order, considerably higher, from Air Force Command, decreed that the destruction of SAM missile sites within the DMZ area, including the QB sector, required U.S. Air Force clearance. Even if missiles had been fired, a half-hour waiting period was required before attack. Fighter-bomber pilots were at a loss to understand this directive. Was it to allow the Russian crews time to escape? The telltale smoke trail left by the SAM missile did not last a half-hour.

The regulation made his decision for him. He recalled, with disgust, proclamations made by dove senators on college campuses. It was his last mission, unless emergency missions demanded his duties. What would they do? Ground him and send him back to the States? He laughed aloud. 'Let's get the bastards,' he remarked and banked the Phantom hard; skyward and inland. The silent engine lit without incident. Satisfied, he pointed the big machine back toward Finger Lakes. Fritz called out his altitude and position, boldly oblivious to enemy radio surveillance. He lit both afterburners to scream back to the section leader, homing on a black orbiting speck.

'Fritz. Are you in a left hand turn?' He called. Without answer the lead F-4 darted downward. He slowed his afterburner speed to take careful distance from the F-4's bombing run. Fritz carried seven napalm bombs. Slowly, it seemed, the Phantom F-4 descended, flattening out its dive to approach at under 450 knots. Napalm fuses were 'touchy' and often proved to become duds if flown at higher speeds. Fritz came in low, around 500 feet off the jungle and lesser foliaged slopes. A flash of fire erupted from below the machine while the pilot bent his plane hard to the left to get a look at his drop. He immediately began swearing over the intercom. 'God Damn it, Chief! I'm two hundred long.' (Which meant for the trailing pilot to drop his bombs two football fields (200 yards) shorter of the napalm fire). The dog bone bomb selection switch was clicked to six 500 pounders and armed (half the load of the fighter bomber.).

The right thumb rose over the 'bombs away' button while the fingers held the control stick. A slight tap or two adjusted the rudders at his feet while his left hand on the throttles controlled his now flat approach at close to 500 feet, his speed over 450 knots as the bombs did not have the napalm's detonation problems. When the estimated 200 feet approached the bomb drop button was pressed while the pair of throttles were pushed forward to full afterburner; the control stick leaned to his left and the port rudder pedal pressed firmly by his foot. Almost immediately the ground seemed to erupt behind him as he turned the plane hard to get a view. A flaming secondary explosion erupted from the jungle when the first load of six bombs detonated. 'Right on, Chief,' Fritz yelled with exuberance across the radios. The section leader expended his remaining napalms close to the fiery jungle, sending a ricocheting fire streaking a half-mile, obviously igniting a missile, like an errant fourth of July rocket or a Roman candle flaming through the jungle tops. The last of his bombs scattered the diminishing fireball below with resultant lesser explosions.

After several victory rolls, the section joined back in formation, departing south across the mountains north of Da

Nang. Out ahead of the monsoon, scud clouds were lowering below the mountains to the coastline, moving toward Chu Lai and Da Nang. Within an hour, the rains would be drenching both bases. At a thousand feet, both Phantoms streaked above the landing end of Chu Lai runway, the lead plane peeling away, breaking sharply to arc smoothly back to the touchdown point. The wingman held his course for several seconds more above the runway then rolled ninety degrees to the horizon, following in a wider arc to increase the landing separation from the leader. The drag chutes deployed as each aircraft landed.

The pilots offered little at the debriefing. They reported possible secondary explosions, presumably a minor truck depot. Possible ground fire was alleged; anti-aircraft fire was reported to be negative. The aviators were thankful they were not career men and that they'd both be rotating back to the States soon. He walked across the sand dunes with his RIO and Fritz, their conversation oblivious to the mission. Instead they laughed, reminiscing about two attractive schoolteachers the pilots had met in Okinawa. They stopped at his hut for a rum and coke, despite the time of day.

After Fritz and the RIO left, He sat on his locker beside his bunk and mixed one more rum and coke. It had been a good mission. He languished confidently, assured that there were fewer Russians to fire missiles at the fighter-bombers. He never finished the liquid in his canteen cup. The ever-present heat and the rum made him drowsy. He fell back on his air mattress and was soon asleep. Before he fell backwards, he managed to stand and hang his shoulder holster and pistol on a nail above his mosquito netting and then placed his wotai pouch across the pistol butt jutting from the holster. While he slept, the mainte-nance crews checked his aircraft to correct the gyroscope. Despite the engine squelching blast, not a mark was to be found on the huge Phantom. 'You will see the enemy over one hundred times, and the bullets will bounce from your machine.' Fools Crow had told him. Now dear reader, you should well understand why I have returned to the Natural Way!

Chapter 3

Origins

The Mongol or Northern Chinese migrants swept down from the North in scattered groups. A lesser group came from Scandinavia much later. The Eastern North American tribes bear strong Nordic facial features mixed in with the parent Mongol blood; wherein Asian facial characteristics are flatter, especially the nose. Scandinavian features have quite prominent noses as do the Eastern North American tribes. The Lakota/Dakota came to the Great Plains from the East and also bear prominent noses as pictures of the old time warriors depict. To detractors and dissenters, I simple offer a welcome to come to our Sioux Native American reservations and see for yourself.

Across Asia into Alaska

We have introduced the North American's spectacular ceremonial communication; now let us probe where these people came from. Humankind had lived in eastern Asia at least half a million years at the onset of the Ice Age, slowly moving farther east and north. By perhaps seventy thousand years ago, expanding ice sheets had lowered ocean levels enough to expose a land bridge linking Siberia and Alaska. Animals had used such a bridge before, and man, too, would drift across in search of game, unknowingly occupying the Americas. Later studies hold humans to be here 250,000 years ago.

This highway to the east was open during several periods, as the world's ice cover and sea level varied over millennia to expose or drown the land that today lies under the Bering Strait. But scholars disagree as to when man first traversed it. Some say there is no conclusive evidence for humans in the New World earlier than about 12,000 years before the present BCE (Before the

Common Era) would be better – can you adapt your figures to this convention? (BP Before Present). Other scholars argue it's about 30,000 BP; still others speculate that dates far more remote will eventually be proved. Recent finds in the Yukon's Area Old Crow Basin ice frees during even the most severe glacial periods - supporting an occupation date of at least 27,000 BP.

From where in Asia did the migrants come? A number of Old World sites have yielded tools and other artefacts which suggest a people who may have been ancestral Americans. Only fifty-six miles of water separate the continents of Asia and North America at their closest point. Even this stretch of water is divided by the Diomedes Islands, two tiny hillocks of rock that lie almost in the middle of Bering Strait. With the islands as stepping stones it seems logical to suppose that people may have entered the New World by this route. Through time, glacial ice caps covered vast areas of the planet during various Ice Ages resulting in a considerable moisture tie up worldwide and hence depriving and lowering the oceans, hence the shallow Bering Strait Sea disappeared and a land bridge existed. Even when the ocean existed there is little doubt that crossing over by man or animals was feasible but a few thousand years ago. In this day and age, the ice becomes thick beginning in October and eventually freezing over enough for animals and man to cross over. Before U.S.S.R. prevention, Eskimos from Siberia and Alaska traded freely with each other by crossing over. If ancient man did not walk over or back and forth over the Strait on dry land, he could easily do so on the ice.

Academics and Wind Cave Myth

Some scientists including a known Native American author, Vine Deloria, have debunked the idea of a Bering Strait originated land crossing, holding out the massive, restrictive, glacial ice barrier moving slowly southward would prevent any further human passage. Numerous Native American academics have jumped on board with Deloria; as his is a rather 'chic' and popular stance among academic circles who would rather accept superstitious or mythological theories as to a tribe's beginnings. Many North American tribes hold to a; 'We came out of the ground; or from the ocean; or from a particular mountain' story.

Many members of my tribe, the Sioux, claim that we emerged out of a cave now called Wind Cave in the Black Hills of Western South Dakota; named thus from its small opening when it was discovered by a White Man on horseback in the latter 1800s. This then was our earliest beginning concept. The small fist sized aperture increased the velocity of the wind mysteriously coming from it and he claimed it blew his hat off; upon investigation the small opening was discovered. In time, excavation followed and it is now a state tourist attraction where seasonal tourists can explore several underground miles of its expanse.

I guess, in their estimation, we milled around in that cave for quite some time. In this academic created mythology, humans do not have to fulfil their biological needs when they have to wait in caves for a century or so or more. As long as it is 'Chic,' they can question and condemn what we common sense approaching types conceive. Few, if any, learned scientists uphold such anti-biological theories.

No provisions or water is needed to be consumed. No heating or cooling system is needed in their cave origin theory. I think all caves are fairly dark, actually totally dark; must have been a bit difficult for the tribe to hold council meetings. One's excretory system would have had to shut down totally otherwise the cave would become a rather unpleasant place to live in while waiting, especially over a period of a century or two; maybe much more. This alone would have to diminish the 'chicness' of such a situation. I personally refrain from visiting some countries where I discovered a degree of foul smells emanating from their sewage system regardless of how so called 'modern,' was the hotel I would be staying in. Waiting in that cave would have proven fairly difficult for me.

It is indeed puzzling how my ancestors theoretically emerged through that small aperture before its excavation and began our reign complete with, somehow, magically, suddenly supplied horses and weapons beginning in the Black Hills of South Dakota. Later, in this writing, we will discover that the major source of our horses came from the Arikara. The Bering Strait migration is vehemently denied by these folks. As of yet, however, I do not believe or at least hope that the majority of tribal membership does not ascribe to their theory. One has to wonder how all of these people waiting in such a dark cave could exist for eons. Such is mythology however for it conveniently ignores the common sense essentials of every day life's demands and obviously which Nature demands. I just cannot place, what mythology would like for me to believe, no matter how far-fetched, over, obvious and observable Nature. I do not believe in taboos either but almost feel it is a tad sacrilegious to ignore or worse, deny Nature's demands. I do not consider mythology, when I write about the Sioux, as anything more than passing fantasy. Such information is not offered as a historical happening.

Mythology followed the horse man's discovery as mythology often gets created by humans upon events and discoveries. Would I consider the 'Original Parents' - Adam and Eve as mythology. Certainly! Some readers will not want to hear that but ... when their offspring simply goes over a hill so to speak to meet and beget their wives then the story, myth, fable becomes no less illusory than the Wind Cave myth. In my opinion, mythology is mere superstition. It is quaint and can be made into richly fictitious story telling but nevertheless to honest men of reason I might add, common sense; it is simply entertaining superstition. It often becomes dangerous superstition because down through time huge wars have been fought, won or lost over purely mythological superstitions which were instigated by narrow minded, power crazed religious zealots who came to believe their own mythical creation. To this day we see the violent schism between the Sunni sects and the Shiites of Islam. It has been ongoing for centuries. Not long ago the Catholics and Protestants of the Christian faith, likewise, were physically at each other's throats. For centuries, thousands (hundreds of thousands) of Europeans were tortured to death over superstition of the victims (mostly innocent women) being 'possessed' by this Devil or Satan that Organized Religion still vehemently proclaims.

The National Geographic Magazine's extensive article on the Bering Strait migration (1979) was based on scientific study which seems to reasonably portray what did occur several thousands of years ago. If one has to choose between the two theories, I think that those who have nurtured a bit more of the term 'common sense;' will be the folks that I side with. Modern photography of we American 'Native Americans' is firm evidence that we earlier Northern migrants definitely descended from Asiatic blood - namely the Mongolian people and Northern Chinese who crossed over when, during that period of time, the ocean receded significantly to allow a bare strip of crossable land to connect both continents.

Glacial ice barriers were confined to the edges of the Alaskan Peninsula and the mountainous areas to the north and south, however, the central section, including the Yukon Valley, was almost entirely open and ice-free. The whole arctic slope was also free of glacial ice. Men and animals lived in close proximity to these ice masses, flourishing from the increase in vegetation at their edges which in turn flourished from the moist seasons. During the last glacial periods, early American entered from the Bering Strait opening, crossed over into the Yukon Valley and then onward into Canada and points East and South. How long ago is debatable. Estimates now generally vary from a few thousand years up to 50,000 years and with some exceptional estimates claiming several hundred thousand years.

Scientific fact and evidence, however, points to the front door for ancient America being the Bering Strait. Man crossed over and first lived in what is now called Alaska. His footprints would eventually lead down or southward into Saskatchewan, Alberta and on into the Great Plains. From the Great Plains he would discover more abundant lands and easier living, warmer and more comfortable. In time, many would become sedentary and plant crops. Others would never give up the hunt. Most would combine the two occupations; food planting and hunting. Some would become ardent fishing people and/or coastal food gatherers supplemented by hunting forays inland.

Kentucky, for example, the 'dark and bloody grounds' would abound with arrow heads, spear points, pottery and a host of implements as this hunter man would turn to agriculture and become sedentary yet always supplement his food supply with the hunt and or fishing. His new invention which would come much later - the bow and arrow - which he could also use while stalking ponds and streams, was his major game provider except when he had to tackle big game. Then, the spear performed the task. More artefacts would be found in those areas obviously where the climate was less hostile and more comfortable which meant that the southern states of America would someday have the most numerous indigenous populations along with the most abundant, easier accessible game but this would be a long time coming, if we study the migration trail out of Asia. It would be a very slow process.

Eastward Chino/Mongol bands would migrate; breaking off from parent bands or tribes and travel eastward, thence south and southeast into what is now Canada. It was not mere centuries that they would wander, steadily following the migratory game but for millennia they would travel. Into what is now America, some would head south but if size is any indication, the larger Mongol descendants (when compared to who would cross an ocean and land in Peru and Ecuador) would find their way east and southeastward. Finally the long journey for these bands, from a Bering Sea shore, the descendants would end their long journey at the Atlantic. All along the Atlantic coast many would settle as well as inland throughout the South and mid-North America, mostly, generally where the winters were not too harsh and relatively free of the dangerous blizzards and heavy snowfall of the more northern areas. It was a big land with plenty of room.

At this point I want to state that this was the most probable migration for which would be the Northern Tribes who are larger in stature than the South-western Native Americans and on down to South America, who are smaller still. Regardless of size, the Asiatic features would still remain. Sioux were often well over six feet tall when they fought so successfully against the U.S. Army in the 1800s; incidentally, the early European was not much over five and a half feet when he first came here. Look at the Civil War uniforms. The White Man's movies have severely distorted the image of the more modern Native American of but a century or so ago. In time, after the White Man would consume a steady supply of higher protein not available in Europe during the Dakota/Lakota westward migration times, he too would become larger and taller. In these modern times this same feature is happening in Japan where more protein is available. In America, the situation has evolved out of proportion wherein such a high ratio of obesity is now occurring.

There were many, many tribes settled across North America when the White Man first came ashore so much later but in the east we will focus upon one particular tribe because that tribe (or Native American Nation), the Lakota/Dakota (and later termed Sioux) offers the most information for us to delve into and explore. Most importantly is the hard fact that this tribe was still 'Traditional' and resisted the White Man's 'Assimilation Policy' which means they still lived and practiced their tribal ways complete with retaining their own religion and language and not being confined to a Federal 'reservation' until but barely over a century ago.

Ancient Values

Come to our Native American reservations among the larger tribes, Chippewa, Sioux, Canadian Cree and Cheyenne where the full lineage still runs strong and observe for yourself. Search our early photographs, the black and white footage of early cameras. Go to Canada as well and observe. The strong Asian resemblance relationship is clearly evident. It will be difficult to question that most of the Northern Tribes came from the plains of Mongolia and/or Northern China. Our south-western tribes of America, smaller in size, may not be from Mongolia or Northern China but instead could have migrated from Southern China up through South America as many scholars contend.

These southern tribes are much smaller in stature than the North-eastern Native Americans of North America as are the southern people of China, Vietnam and Thailand etc. in comparison to the Mongolian people and Northern Chinese who are larger, taller people. The Sioux, Cheyenne and Iroquois are taller than the South-western Navajo and Pueblo and the Aztec and Mayan of Central America. Was it our heavy protein meat diet that was also the primary ingredient of the Mongols' diet? Could the southern tribes have come by boat across the broad Pacific and landed on the western shores of South America? A theory exists that this was a possible migration, landing boats or rafts in Ecuador or Peru, as was the Bering Strait for the Mongols' theory. Regardless of detractive theories, size and resemblance of facial characteristics along with simple common sense is direct observation.

The Indios of South America do bear a resemblance to the Southern Chinese. For one, both are smaller people and facially there are strong Asian features among the Native South

Americans. Either way, the migrating people entering South and North America clearly bear a far closer resemblance to the Asian people than they do the European people or the Africans or the Australian Aboriginals. The west coast Native American tribes and the Eskimos of the far north have the strongest Asian features of all. Besides our physical traits, we are of those undying traits (or should we say values?) that are proven unaffected through changing time and long duration and which seem to remain immune to complete evolvement regarding complete assimilation despite being surrounded by 'Dominant Society' and its constant attempts to suppress our cultural values and even our true history. Many tribes in America and Canada however, have been forced to abandon their true heritage.

My writing friend, Jack Weatherford won the blessings of the Mongolian government and wrote a very interesting book on the Mongolian leader, Genghis Khan. Its main research material came from the Mongolian archives untainted by the Western world. Even the cooperating Prime Minister of Mongolia has read his book. It is what I would call a 'Wake up' book. Some Americans have read it and found their opinions of the famous leader to be extremely altered toward a far more positive view. I will quote the history and actions of Genghis Khan at times throughout the book where I see a relationship to what the American Chino/Mongolian descendants, the Native Americans have accomplished.

Understand that much of what Americans know about China and Mongolia becomes severely distorted by our government and our so-called free and democratic media. Basically most American news regarding China and its surrounding countries in league with China becomes slanted toward the age old European characteristic, we call Euro-centrism. This premise holds that all things European based, and now American based, are superior to whatever the other side can do or has done. Asian inventions somehow wind up as their inventions. Rare credit is ever recognized from great leaders such as Genghis Khan who changed the world in so many positive implementations and ways. I have now received a different view of China regarding the great struggle between Chiang Kai-shek and Mao Tse Tung.

As a young teenage student, I recall that my high school history class held out that it was somehow China's fault which led to the occupation of China by several European countries including Japan. This was in the era just prior to WWII. The Boxer Rebellion was blamed on the Chinese even though it was held in their own country. Later, in high school, I was ridiculed for standing up for the Chinese and sincerely asking why the foreign countries were meddling there in the first place.

Hmmm, was that my ancient Asiatic based blood that caused me to speak up? Later yet, in college, I asked more related questions regarding Eurocentric historical presentations and received similar ridicule.

It was in the latter '50s and five 'Greatest Issues' affecting America were given to selected scholars by my University to write upon. None of these concerned the brutal segregation of the American Negroes practiced primarily in the southern states of America. Wouldn't have, shouldn't have that been the key issue? Why were not our Native American Boarding Schools at that time an issue? There were not many American Native American students who sided with me as I went on through seven years of advanced education culminating in a law degree.Of those Native American students who 'laid low,' on the subjects of the Native American boarding schools, religious freedom and the corruption of the Federal Bureau of Native American Affairs staffed mostly by paternalistic Wah shi chu; many would go on and become Masters Degree holders and take up academic employment in the Universities or federal government Native American service related positions. None of them would speak out on the Euro-centrism so rife within the Academic world and our related governmental supported bureaucracies.

I termed them 'Indian Academics' and these cowards will receive their due in later chapters. To this day I have not seen one book by them mentioning the banning of our Spirituality or an expose of the federally operated Canton Native American Asylum erected primarily to eradicate our Spiritual Leadership wherein not one White Man was ever incarcerated. I have actual pictures of this Gulag for Native Americans, mostly incarcerated Native American medicine and spiritual leaders in several of my books. When my tribe struggled during the Dr. Martin Luther King civil rights awakening era in the '60s these tribal based Academics were not there in the 'Trenches of Change' with the traditional bent tribal Native Americans who were openly challenging the unconstitutional restrictions placed upon our Spirituality. The white non-reservation youth had yellow school buses that picked them up for school and later in the day brought them home to their families. We simply wanted the same for our youth.

America is a free country and I have no objection to what people choose to believe, as long as they do not get over zealous and attempt to cast harm on those who will not join in their views. Superstition has killed millions down through time along with unimaginable mental and social suffering fostered against the non-superstitious. If I enter a Spirit World beyond, if there is one, I want to proudly look back and reflect that I allowed few superstitions to guide my trail. What I can directly observe from my surroundings and/or become influenced from plausible scientific theories is the basis of my beliefs and that includes origin as well.

I have worked closely with the Chinese and Mongolians regarding a certain agricultural partnership implementing large dairies even larger than those we have in America. They will provide more needed milk especially for their youth which is a positive goal. This interest has allowed me an inside look at these two countries' government and economic modus operandi. Much of our old Indigenous leadership traits and governmental values I see reflected within their working philosophy which is successfully unfolding in those countries in these modern times. They would not be where they are at as a world leader had Generalissimo Chiang Kai-shek won the Great Chinese Revolution. The change his regime brought to Taiwan (primarily with enormous American aid) is highly touted by Western media, scholars, pundits and our politicians. They use Taiwan as a showcase to claim Western style democracies' superiority over China. Their false ego and Euro-centrism erroneously ignores the size difference and magnitude of mainland China's situation following the Great Civil War, in comparison to a much smaller Formosa (Taiwan) with constant infusion of American foreign aid. Where is China at now? Economically, China is a giant among nations. Patience, Discipline, Sacrifice and Time is beginning to reverse the field of play. In America, our future generations of children are 'mortgaged' so to speak, due to the national debt' and that economical yoke is due mainly to financing America's constant wars. China does not 'mortgage' their future generations.

Tibet and China

The following is taken from the article *Friendly Feudalism: The Tibet Myth by Michael Parenti*. The article appeared on AOL Internet, December 26, 2011 and under Huffington Post and Kansas City Star; In my view organised religion has a negative impact on Nature communities, so how does one without prejudice understand the dynamics behind an occurrence as controversial as the Chinese invasion of Tibet? The following extract challenges us to consider the view that perhaps the Tibetan religious authorites were using organised religion as a tool of oppression too?

I. For Lords and Lama

... not all the many and widely varying forms of Buddhism have been free of doctrinal fanaticism, nor free of the violent and exploitative pursuits so characteristic of other religions. ... During the twentieth century, Buddhists clashed violently with each other and with non-Buddhists in Thailand, Burma, Korea, Japan, India, ...

As with any religion, squabbles between or within Buddhist sects are often fuelled by the material corruption and personal deficiencies of the leadership. ...

But what of Tibetan Buddhism? Is it not an exception to this sort of strife? ...

In the thirteenth century, Emperor Kublai Khan created the first Grand Lama, ... This ... Dalai Lama seized monasteries that did not belong to his sect, and is believed to have destroyed Buddhist writings that conflicted with his claim to divinity. ...

... Tibetan Buddhist sects engaged in bitterly violent clashes and summary executions. ... In 1792, many Kagyu monasteries were confiscated and their monks were forcibly converted to the Gelug sect (the Dalai Lama's denomination). ...

... Religions have had a close relationship not only with violence but with economic exploitation. Indeed, it is often the economic exploitation that necessitates the violence. Such was the case with the Tibetan theocracy. ...

Old Tibet has been misrepresented by some Western admirers as 'a nation that required no police force because its people voluntarily observed the laws of karma.' ... In fact it had a professional army, ... that served mainly as a gendarmerie for the landlords to keep order, protect their property, and hunt down runaway serfs. ...

... The poor and afflicted were taught that they had brought their troubles upon themselves because of their wicked ways in previous lives. ...

... feudal theocratic Tibet was a far cry from the romanticized Shangri La ...

II. Secularization vs. Spirituality What happened to Tibet after ... 1951? ... .

... the Chinese after 1959, ... did abolish slavery and the Tibetan serfdom system of unpaid labour. ...

III. Exit Feudal Theocracy
... The Shangri-La image of Tibet bears no more resemblance to historic actuality than does the pastoral image of medieval Europe. ...

... In theocratic feudal Tibet, ruling interests manipulated the traditional culture to fortify their own wealth and power. ...

In Conclusion, Parenti states: ... The question is what kind of country was old Tibet ... Tibetan feudalism was cloaked in Buddhism, ... It was a retrograde repressive theocracy of extreme privilege and poverty, ...

My conclusion? For humanity 'myth' is very difficult to give up. For an intelligent human; what should be the truthful, unbiased, non-distorted observation of history? What you have just read exposes yet another example of deliberate, dangerously groomed, false promises. Organized Religion, imbedded with superstition, relying on and encouraging ignorance leads to power and control. It starts with superstitious myth, then perpetuated ignorance. Those who do the manipulating wreak their new found power over the unquestioning ignorant. Lo and behold - we have complete control. However, I would like to clarify that my view is purely in support of my thesis against organised religion and does not deign to be indicative of the views held by outside agencies and organisations involved with the publication of this book.

Chapter 4

Exodus

The Mongols called the place the 'City of the Khan'. His Chinese subjects called it Dadu, the Great Capital, and it grew into the modern capital of Beijing. The city was host to merchants from as far away as Italy, India and North Africa. Where so many men lingered, as Marco Polo pointed out in great detail, scholars and doctors came from the Middle East to practice their trades. Roman Catholic, Nestorian and Buddhist priests joined their Taoist and Confucian counterparts already practicing in China. Muslim clerics, Native American mystics, and, in some parts of Mongol China, Jewish rabbis added to the mixture of people and ideas that thronged the empire. The city was a true world capital. Genghis Khan was more 'spiritual' than akin to any religion. He would fast and pray alone on a sacred mountain range in Mongolia.

The Mongol legal code of 1291 specified that officials must 'first use reason to analyse and surmise, and shall not impose abruptly any torture.' By comparison, at the same time that the Mongols were moving to limit the use of torture, both church and state in Europe passed laws to expand its usage to an even ever greater variety of crimes for which there need be no evidence. Unlike the variety of bloody forms of torture, such as stretching on the rack, being crushed by a great wheel, being impaled on spikes, or various forms of burning, in other countries, Mongols limited it to beating with a cane. In modern America, which Organized Religion proclaims as a 'Christian Country,' Dick Cheney, former Vice President, championed 'torture' and manipulated its usage on foreign suspects.

The Sioux

Before the Dakota/Lakota migrated westward out of the Carolinas, they were not termed 'Sioux' then. Later they would pick up that name. Siouan speaking tribes of the Carolinas that did not migrate were the Wacama, the Catawba and the Biloxi. The Biloxi moved as far south as South Carolina, yet never left the East with the main body of migrating Dakota/Lakota (Sioux). The Wacama remained in North Carolina and have a creation or origin myth that a comet, or some space entity, crashed in nearby Lake Wacama. This is where the Sioux came from, in their own mythological viewpoint. Some Eastern Sioux think we come from the star group Pleiades, often visible in late summer. Sure seems like a long journey in my personal opinion. I visited the Wacama tribe several decades ago just prior to the publication of my first major published work, *Mother Earth Spirituality in the latter 1890s*. I made a trip: a sort of a 'Roots' trip, if one reflects back to Alex Haley's cinematic work on the African slaves coming to America and named 'Roots'. I did not have to cross an ocean however; instead, I had a talk with the tribal chairwoman of the Wacamas. She said that the last Siouan speaker, an old Grandmother, had died some thirty years before. 'We are all Christians,' she admitted, 'we know little of the past or our culture as your tribe does.' This would have been our story as well, had we never made our Exodus. Actually, we would not have much of a story to tell and our culture and Spirituality would have been lost.

Since The 1500s

The history of the Sioux during the past five hundred years can be traced from their origins in the Piedmont area of the Carolinas. To their North were the Iroquois, the most powerful of the North American tribes. The Iroquois were a united confederacy, made up of five organized tribes. The next most powerful tribe in North America was the Cherokee. Their domain lay south and south-westerly of the Piedmont where they enjoyed lush agricultural lands. European ships were passing up and down the Atlantic coast by this time. For it was a century since Columbus and the first newcomers brought their fatal diseases, wiping out or severely decimating many coastal tribes. The Shawnee were most likely already west of the soon-to-be-migrating Sioux. The Sioux were called Lakota or Dakota in those times. They regarded themselves as the Friendly People of the Seven Council Fires. Later, they would pick up their 'Sioux' name from the French explorers on their journey westward. At the time that Columbus landed on a few islands south of Florida, I believe someone entering into the Piedmont, of what would later become the Carolinas, would have heard the term, 'Hau Koda or, possibly - Hau Kola', which means 'Hello friend' in Sioux.

We can imagine the Sioux living comfortably in the Piedmont area that provided adequate soil for tilling and planting. Meat supplemented their diet: primarily deer and wild turkeys, which foraged all the way to the Mississippi River. Their houses were not the conical buffalo-hide covered dwellings that came later, they were square or rectangular frame structures made of sturdy saplings and covered with bark and thatch from lesser branches, often with leaves for insulation. Winters were milder than the climates of the northern United States. Overall, they were quite peaceful, as were many of the agricultural tribes who had little need or desire for pursuing another tribe's possessions. Their diet consisted of corn, squash, beans, potatoes, tomatoes and the rich array of wild game the land offered. Fish also supplemented their diet. Journeys to the nearby Atlantic coast brought them succulent seafood as well. Such a rich diet occasioned them to be much larger than the early European. If you happen to explore a British museum, the knight's armour on display will not fit a man much over 5 foot four inches. The eastern North American was within the six foot range at those times. Truly, they lived in a virtual paradise. It remains a mystery why they would up and vacate such choice living conditions and head westward. No one has yet to come up with an adequate explanation for that mystery but some theories are well worth studying.

The Westward Move

Some scholars believe it was the constant raids by the powerful Iroquois to the North. If this was the case, then why did they continue to move so far away from their adversaries — two thousand miles in all? The Cherokees to their South were considerably more peaceful than the Iroquois. No doubt, the Cherokees appreciated having the Sioux as a buffer between them and the powerful Iroquois. The westward move soon became a mass migration, and very few stayed behind; only the Catawbas, Biloxis and Wacamas primarily. They would soon be swallowed up by the European tide of immigrants fleeing their own homelands. Europe was not a particularly choice land to live in at the time the Sioux were leaving their productive lands in the Carolinas. Europeans were barely removed from serfdom, brutalized by a harsh church that was still in the throes of the Inquisitions. The Europeans had two immediate masters: the church hierarchy and the land owning nobility of barons and earls, little different than what you learned from the Tibet article written by Michel Parenti. Of course, the King and his court were ever in the background and would draft the serfs and landless people as cannon fodder for their many wars. They knew nothing of the Democracy the American Native Americans were enjoying at the time Columbus was making his journey and even later, when the Pilgrims landed.

Pilgrims

On Sept. 6, 1620, the Pilgrims set sail for the New World on a ship called the Mayflower. They sailed from Plymouth, England with 110 people aboard. The long trip was cold and damp and took 65 days. Since there was the danger of fire on the wooden ship, the food had to be eaten cold. Many passengers became sick and one person died by the time land was sighted on November 10th. Plymouth, USA, which was named by Captain John Smith six years earlier, offered an excellent harbor, with a large fresh water brook. The bay itself, provided a resource for fish and shellfish. The Pilgrims biggest concern was attack by the local natives. But the Plymouth Bay natives proved to be a peaceful group, as were most of the coastal Native Americans in comparison to the far more warlike Europeans, and did not prove to be a threat. The Europeans had a history of constant wars up to this time. Instead, even the peaceful Native Americans who would teach them to survive would be branded in time, as warlike savages and hostiles. They were seen as pagans because of their religion: a creator based spirituality, which taught them to be kind to strangers regardless of their color and differing beliefs.

Over half of the Pilgrims died during the long first winter. In the spring of 1621 an Native American walked into the Pilgrims' camp bearing the words 'Welcome'. His name was Samoset. He had learned English from the captains of fishing boats that had sailed off the coast. He returned with another Native American named Squanto, a Patuxet Native American who spoke even better English. Squanto told the Pilgrims of his voyages across the ocean and of his visits to England and Spain. It was in England where he had learned to speak so well. But when he returned to his homeland, he discovered that his tribe had been wiped out by the white-man's diseases. He was the last of the Patuxets. Squanto's importance to the Pilgrims was enormous, and it can be said that they would not have survived without his help. It was Squanto who taught the Pilgrims how to tap the maple trees for sap. He taught them which plants were poisonous and which had medicinal powers. He taught them how to plant the Native American corn by heaping the earth into low mounds with several seeds and fish in each mound. The decaying fish fertilized the corn. He also taught them to plant other crops with the corn. Beans and squash for example, mutually benefited each other, as well as the corn plant.

The harvest in the following October was very successful. The Pilgrims found themselves with enough food to put away for the winter. There were fruits and vegetables, fish to be packed in salt, and meat to be cured over smoky fires. The Native Americans annually held tribal Thanksgivings to their Higher Power. Obviously, the Pilgrims were influenced by this acknowledging conduct and held a Thanksgiving for their survival and appreciation, which has grown into a national holiday. Chief Massahoit of the Wamponoag tribe arrived with over 50 braves and helped the Pilgrims to celebrate the event. Sadly, the Native originators receive little credit for this event.

The Move Westward

By the 1600s, the Dakota/Lakota were already on their great move westward. The Iroquois were mentioned as a possible reason for the Sioux's sudden migration from their comfortable surroundings. One would wonder as to what significant event would drive out an entire tribe - other than another, more powerful, invading tribe. If that was the case, the Sioux would have been severely mauled, and the victor would have picked up an enormous line of captives. But this was not the case. It was no doubt the deadly diseases that the early ships had brought to the coastal tribes, as in the case of the Patuxets. This scenario is indeed a more plausible theory than attacks by another tribe. Again, I offer the nagging question, why wouldn't they migrate two thousand miles to distance themselves from such fatal diseases? I have a third theory, which I can now bring forth since the Reader is more acclimatized to Native culture. Was it the Yuwipi – the Spirit Calling connection that warned the tribe to make their wise Exodus?

Exodus

Down the Ohio River Valley, the Sioux moved on. Not in one mass but gradually, band by band and in varied sized groups. Possibly, bands joined for security to minimize resistance of the other tribes along the way. They crossed the large expanse of Shawnee territory with little or no opposition. Maybe the Shawnees didn't want to take a stand against a tribe appearing to be on a continuous move except for winter camp-overs. Food was plentiful then, there was even a species of 'Forest Buffalo,' a bit smaller than the heavier plains' bison but enough of them to adequately feed wintering-over humans. Eventually, they congregated in the Midwest, first which was then called Ouisconsin, now termed Wisconsin. Here they would encounter the Chippewa and later the Cree farther north as early as the 1600s. The Shawnee were the largest tribe to be confronted along the way. They seemed to have smoked the peace pipe with the Sioux bands, granting them unrestricted passage. As stated earlier, it was not one mass movement. It may have taken the Sioux a century to reach the Mississippi, sometimes settling on their journey, but gradually heading westward and the majority of the migrants turning upstream when they reached the Mississippi.

When the main body of Sioux reached the Mississippi some bands broke off and crossed the great river. The Mandan eventually crossed to settle far upstream. The Arkansa, and more likely the Kansa, may have crossed the great river near the Missouri confluence. Joe Medicine Crow, tribal historian of the Crow Native Americans in Montana, states that the Crow broke off from the main body of Sioux on their upstream journey at the mouth of the Wisconsin River. The Crow then wandered for a century toward the shores of Lake Superior and eventually crossed westward over the Great Plains, finally settling in Montana where they remain today. They would scout for the U.S. Army, and in time, against their former relatives the Sioux.

After the main body of Sioux congregated near the headwaters of the Mississippi, fierce opposition from the Chippewa sprang forth. Then, as the Sioux moved even further north, the allies of the Chippewa, the Cree, waged battles with the newcomers. Fighting was quite primitive by modern standards. Flint knives, stone axes, bows and arrows were the warriors' tools. At first the Sioux got the best of their foes as they traveled northward against both opponents. It was during this time that the name 'Sioux' was first placed upon the invading Lakota/Dakota, meaning allies or friends, which they preferred to call themselves.

Nadowessi

The adventurous Captain Jonathan Carver brings us to an early contact with the Sioux in the eighteenth century. Carver was instrumental in the transmittal of the naming of the Dakota/Lakota as 'Sioux'. Neighbouring tribes primarily to the north - Objibway, Chippewa and Cree - referred to the Dakota/Lakota as Nadowessi, which meant lesser enemies as compared to the bigger enemies to the east; the Iroquois, the powerful confederacy who pushed them westward. Faced with an endless stream of European immigrants, the Iroquois moved west and northwest up the Hudson valley and consequently drove the Chippewa (Ojibwas) out of their ancestral lands surrounding the St. Lawrence Seaway. The newcomers moving up the Mississippi south and west of the three northern tribes initially proved themselves as deadly and aggressive enemies on the move. The French, as was there custom, came along and added x or ioux to the Chippewa/Cree term and we have Nadowessioux. That term was soon shortened to the word Sioux, a combination of French and Chippewa.

Although the term 'Sioux' is a practical name — which combines the Lakota/Dakota designation – some college educated Native Americans and many academics (Native

American and non-Native American) in particular disapprove of the term 'Sioux'. However, a sign on a tribal building wall, back on my home reservation, simply reads 'Oglala Sioux Tribal Council.' The Tribal Council stationery also reads 'Oglala Sioux Tribal Council.' On the adjoining reservation less than a hundred miles east, their signs reveal 'Rosebud Sioux Tribal Council.' If it bothers an academic that we are 'incorrect', they should first complain to the Tribal Councils instead of employing academic circles to change our name, which we have grown quite used to.

Any name can be a source of pride and respect when we have dignity and a proven track record of fighting successfully in many battles. I suppose I can qualify as an academic if degrees are a prime qualification, which I disagree with of course. I have a Doctorate of Jurisprudence but it was my experience and initial fortitude - common sense actually - to be with the real old-time holy men and other great teachers, like Ben Black Elk and Hilda Neihardt (daughter of John Neihardt, author of Black Elk Speaks). This is where I received a considerable amount of my knowledge, along with Doctor John Bryde's influence, where it pertains to tribal history. Dr. Bryde spoke fluent Lakota. As I have mentioned, he spent many years among the Oglalas as a Jesuit missionary. Add to this mix another mentor, Dr. James Howard.

I flew both men throughout the state of South Dakota as a commercial pilot, while working my way through three years of law school. Both were teachers at the University. Dr. Howard also raised two adopted Native American children. Long hours in the cockpit sitting close to two knowledgeable scholars revealed much of my tribe's history as the Dakota landscape passed beneath us. Participation in the ceremonies, especially at the time when they were being revived by the old-time medicine people, was a godsend. I must credit fate or the Forces for giving me the opportunity to acquire such valuable information. A truly traditional Native American would credit the Spirit Forces, who to us still abound upon the land. They placed me in those times, according to my belief system, the moment, and the place; which was more than coincidental.

Bear in mind, this was a time when a majority of Native Americans - even Sioux - were brainwashed in the Christian missionary and federal government ran boarding schools to deny their heritage when it came down to the spiritual or religious side. I recall, as a law student about to speak at an event at one of the South Dakota colleges. My theme was 'Go back to your culture.' Russell Means, the renowned Native American Activist, was also a speaker. The then reigning Mrs. South Dakota, an attractive part Yankton Sioux wife of a successful basketball coach - both of Sioux extraction - publicly stated to the news media she would turn down her speaking request because of the presence of myself and of course Russ Means. We were 'persona non grata' because we advocated our spirituality as worthy of going back to.

Very few Native Americans back in the 1960s rallied to support us: we who were bound and determined to bring back the old way. I was not at the forefront but I did join them. The old traditionalists led then, mainly the holy men. The Native American academics were notably absent. That is why so few of the academics can honestly quote the old time medicine people as their close advisors. Look at their books! I look at these few academic authors who write about our spirituality and especially our Sun Dance; none of them have ever been in the demanding and gruelling (deeply moving event) Sun Dance! Only one academic do I know, Dr. Chuck Ross, a Mdewakanton Sioux, has been in more sun dances than I have and now conducts the ceremony in the Black Hills. Chuck is an author as well. I will take experience over academia any day when writing of a people's deepest beliefs and their resultant culture. Enough said! Once again, I proudly quote those historical newspaper headlines, 'Sioux Wipe Out Custer!' We will not be undermined by the labels of Dominant Society, or anyone else who wants to label us without our express permission.

While we are on the subject of names; what about the term American Indian or Red Indians; which is constantly brought before us? Dr. Beatrice Medicine, a Sihasapa, Teton Sioux and a noted anthropologist passes the following on to us:

> The term American Indians, the most recent gloss for North American aborigines, is now in disfavour with many tribal groups and individuals. The National Congress of Indians, a powerful self-interest group, has passed a resolution (1978) opposing its use at their last convention. Throughout the historic Native American-white interface, such names as 'North American Indians,' 'Indian Native Americans,' 'AmerNative American,' 'Indian American' and 'First Americans' have been in vogue at various times. In this essay I use Native American and American Indians inter-changeably. As for the focus of the essay, the Lakota who are often labelled 'Sioux,' 'Teton Sioux,' 'Western Lakota,' and 'Dakota' in the anthropological literature, I use the term 'Lakota,' for I am referring to the Western Sioux who speak the Lakota dialect of the Siouan language. I also use designations such as 'Rosebud Sioux' to indicate the reservation as a social system to which one assigns oneself. This is accepted procedure by most Lakota Sioux.

Dr. Bea, is my 'Native American Aunt,' another of my teachers and was always a strong supporter and now deceased.

In the summer time on various Sioux reservations, there will usually be some old-timers sitting around discussing yesterday. If you get the chance, ask them what tribe they are from. They will reply that they are Sioux. If you ask them what particular band they are from, one will point to himself and say, 'I am an Oglala Sioux.' He may point to another and state, 'He is a Sichangu Sioux from over there on the Rosebud.' Then, ask them if they are Lakotas or Dakotas. They will respond that they are Lakotas. Perhaps one will remark, 'We are Lakotas, the Dakotas are far to the east; but, we are all Sioux.'

Sioux Held Their Culture – Others Did Not

Indeed, the Dakota/Lakota were considered enemies by those who came across their path, and offered resistance to the many groups on their westward journey out of the East. I have often made the statement that the Sioux are the last of the large tribes to be reined in from their natural, Creator given freedom; and hence, this is the major reason why they have kept so much of their culture compared to the other tribes who have spent much longer with the dominating white man and his 'melt-all' culture and concepts. The Sioux have only been 'in' for a mere hundred years. This was a blessing for us and is the major reason why we still speak and retain our language, and why we have kept our religion intact. It is simple math; less time with the dominant culture and you retain more of your own culture.

The majority of America's once prolific tribes have lost their language and know nothing of their religion. It is not their fault however. Time, along with geography, has had a lot to do with their loss. A tribe spending two hundred years with Dominant Society can easily lose their roots. Four hundred years with the white man's destructive methods for rooting out native culture and it is a miracle that some cultural roots manage to survive. The Navajo and Pueblo suffered under the brutal Spanish occupation and, their equally destructive, Spanish church: which made slaves of the people, digging for silver and gold in the many mines dotting the southwest.

Geography protected the tribes to some degree (especially the vast spaces of the West); yet, the Pueblo, Zunni and Navajo religious concepts differ considerably from the Northern tribes. A major example is their belief in Evil Spirits and various forms of what I call 'Fear Superstition' much like the Christians and Muslims believe. In my own opinion, the Spanish church influenced their religion over the 400 long years they suffered under brutal rule, until Congress finally passed the freedom of religion act in 1978. To this day, missionary churches still hold the most prominent sites within the Pueblos.

The Wacama Sioux tribe of the Carolinas, has lost their old language and culture. Now, however, we have recording machines, video cameras and compact disks that they can use to regain and preserve the old ways. They are able to regain their language, customs and culture (possibly at least, the old spiritual ways) as many tribes, however, are now attempting to preserve their language and regain their ceremonies. Native American language courses are very popular, and the sweat lodge itself is becoming a prominent ceremony far and wide across America. Those who respect and utilize the sweat lodge, typically learn many Sioux songs.

The same situation that happened to the Wacama, the loss of language and customs, would probably have developed for the main body of Sioux had they not exited to the west. As a large tribe they would have undergone their own Trail of Tears — as did the Cherokee tribe,had they not left on their own. The 'Trail of Tears' was another example of the government breaking another Native American Treaty. They gathered up the peaceful Cherokee and had them march across the Mid-West from the East all the way to Oklahoma Territory which was in the center of the new Nation - America. Many died from that long march. More than likely, they would have been exterminated had they not complied with this journey. The less exposure to Dominant Society, the more cultural retention a tribe will maintain. This is not a difficult formula to understand. This explains why the Sioux are probably a more reliable North American tribe to study in relationship to understanding what Nature based people believed in. Choosing, like wolves, to migrate away from overwhelming threat; they were the last of the large tribes to come in from their freedom on the Great Plains.

Physical Comparisons

I have observed that the Sioux and Iroquoians are not similar in looks compared to most of the other tribes. The once-bordering Cherokees may be grouped in with the Sioux, since they are certainly the lightest complexioned, Caucasian featured people of any North American tribe I have ever seen. The Mandans (whose main reservation is far north along the Missouri in North Dakota) are almost as light as many Cherokees, but they have more Native American features than the Cherokees. I am speaking about Mandan individuals whose blood is over half Mandan. Contrary to many Europeans: they do not have the features of a receding hair line just above the brow, no monks'-spots (premature balding at the top of the skull), and in general, are not 'hairy'. Instead, as with most Plains Native Americans, they are almost without hair on the chest, back and extremities. The Mandans are tall and heavy boned people like the Northern Europeans, but have a 'commonality' in their facial appearance; whereas just about every Cherokee I have met (who was not enrolled from the Oklahoma reservation based in Tahlequah, Oklahoma) seemed to have differing, unrelated, Caucasian dominant features.

The Hunkpapa Sioux in areas of central North and South Dakota are large people in general. The Hunkpapa are slightly darker than the Mandans, but similar in appearance and relatively hairless — with little or no facial hair. Most Siouan people have a heavy head of hair where it counts - on top of the head - and do not go bald, even in senior age. Their hair may thin, but I have yet to see a full blooded Sioux that went bald (unless some sickness caused it). The hair also stays black much longer it seems. I can personally attest to that claim. Over two decades ago at my high school class reunion, white hair and/or baldness was already making its appearance among my non-Native American classmates, and was almost totally encompassing among the majority at our recent last gathering except for me and a few other Native American blooded classmates.

Mississippi Headwaters and Further West

In the early seventeenth century, driven by the Iroquois, the Chippewa were being confronted on a new front by the Sioux. According to Dr. John Bryde, (Modern Native American Psychology) the Sioux won the initial battles; as they had grown accustomed to doing on their migration trail westward from the Carolinas. They had previously swept through the Shawnees, the related tribes west of the Carolinas and those settled in the fertile Ohio River Valley. They quickly gathered a reputation for being fierce fighters. When they came into the Minne-ahtah (Land of much water) region, the Sioux were made up of three groups or divisions: the Tetons; the Yanktons, including the Yanktonai; and the Santees, who were made up of four tribes. The Santees encompassed the Mdewakanton, Wahpeton, Wahpekute and the Sisseton. All Santees spoke the 'D' dialect of the tribe's language and referred to themselves as the Dakota. The Santee tribes may have been the earliest portion of the great Sioux migration; for they ranged far into Wisconsin.

Westward

As mentioned earlier, the main body of Sioux explored the headwaters of the Mississippi. Despite some earlier battles, the Yanktonai tribe made peace with the Cree who lived to the north of the Sioux while the Cree allies, the Chippewa, were further east. With the peace, came intermarriage between the Yanktonais and the Cree; even when the rest of the Sioux were vigorously attacking the Cree. Before 1660 the Sioux were winning most of the battles; in 1658 the Sioux won a bloody fight according to Radisson an early French explorer. In 1670, however, the Cree and their Algonquin-speaking allies traded in their furs for French guns from the Hudson Bay Company. They angrily retaliated against the Sioux for the earlier battles. In 1674 the Cree attacked and killed Sioux envoys at Sault Ste. Marie. The flash of gunpowder and smoke from many yards away — with its accompanying loud 'Bang' — would soon send shivers through even the most stalwart of the Sioux warriors, who were still inexperienced with gun fire. The loud sound accompanying each firing, and resultant death or wound, was a terrible experience to behold. Guns were such superior weapons that the Sioux had little choice but to 'up and move'. For the Chippewa, with their Cree allies and French guns, the tide changed: the Dakota/Nadowessioux advance into what is now Northern Minnesota became a retreat down from the headwaters of the Mississippi to the Minnesota River valley and the area of present day Minneapolis. A Sioux named body of water, Lake Minnetonka (Great Water or Big Water) lies just west of Minneapolis. In a matter of 10 years, an eyewink in historical terms, most of the Sioux had vacated out of northern Minnesota.

The migrating people realized that the land of Minne-ahtah was also a cold, inhospitable place to live. Far fewer artefacts are found within this region, a fact that suggests that most tribes avoided the area to some extent. Several artefact collectors I have known related that an unusually long warm period accounted for most of their collections. Deep snows, cold winters can indeed be fatal. Further south-east, in the Kentucky area for example, numerous artefacts - stone axes, arrowheads and spear points — are still found to this day by collectors. This simple fact illustrates that the more conducive the land was for productive agriculture, the more population the land attracted and sustained. Productive agriculture typically does not grow as abundantly where the winters are long and the summers are short. Being comfortable was another main reason that tribes would be drawn to an area. Extreme cold, dangerous deep winter snows and a shorter agricultural season were generally avoided; unless, a smaller tribe was being crowded by potential enemies and did not have a choice. Often these tribe's settlements would be temporary: until better locales were scouted or they joined together with another smaller tribe for mutual survival and movement onward.

The Sioux, as I refer to as the general mass of individual Siouan speaking, migrating bands, would send out scouts and were always looking for what lay beyond the next bluff or river. The majority of the Dakota/Lakota were soon heading westward. The Yanktons and Yanktonai were the first to move. They drifted southward and came to the great elbow bend of the Minnesota River in the Swan Lake district. The Yanktons crossed the Minnesota River, separating from their tribal cousins, the Yanktonai, and settling in an area between what is now Blue Earth, Minnesota and the famous Pipestone Quarries near the Western edge of Minnesota. The Yanktonais went up the Minnesota River. Later the Oglalas and Brules (Sichangu) would cross the same area and occupy the Blue Earth River prairies westward, placing them west of the Yanktons. They would parallel the Yanktons and push on further west, gradually leaving the Yanktons behind them.

The Cheyennes were in front of the Teton Sioux, and already across the second largest river in North America – the Missouri River. Settling in the Black Hills which is now within the western border of the state of South Dakota, they were eventually pushed out eastward by the Crow Tribe on to the Great Plains west of the Missouri as the Sioux were steadily advancing westward. First, the lead tribes — the Oglala and their close associates the Sichangu (would later be called Brules),would have to get past the powerful Arikara to cross the Missouri, however. The Arikara was settled comfortably in bastion like earthen structured barricades: Native American forts along the Missouri.

It was a perplexing situation for the Sioux. Forty thousand Arikara, (northern and southern) including four thousand warriors and some mounted, were a bit much for the Oglalas who could not muster more than five hundred warriors, all of whom were on foot. A particular grouping of Teton bands, the Saones, would go up the Minnesota River, taking them further north.

This group included the Hunkpapas, whose chief would eventually be Sitting Bull. They too, were blocked by the northern Arikara at the Missouri River. Some Saone managed to cross the Missouri twenty to thirty years after the Oglala and Sichangu but it would be a half century (around 1825) before most all of the Saone would reunite again with their Teton relatives to the south (Oglala and Sichangu): to camp once again together during the annual Sioux Nation sun dance.

The last of the Sioux tribes to move would be the Santees, some of them settling down in Eastern Minnesota and the Twin Cities area (the Mdewakanton), where they remain to this day. The Santees were the last to leave the Wisconsin woodlands, and were possibly who Captain Carver wrote of when he projected the new name, Nadowessioux (or Sioux) upon the wandering People of the Seven Campfires. Of the Santees, the Sissetons would move the farthest west, settling in northeast South Dakota.

Tribes

All the tribes would face opposition and have to fight as they moved westward. The Iowa (Eeh oh wahs) and the Otoes claimed the Blue Earth River lands. The fierce fighting reputation the Tetons commanded sent the two tribes running southwest to join up with the Omahas. The Omahas had once held the Pipestone Quarries but the Yanktons had driven them out. Eventually the Omahas settled at the mouth of the Big Sioux River where it emptied into the Missouri. The Sioux had spent nearly a hundred years in Minnesota and now they would spend nearly a hundred years in western Minnesota and eastern South Dakota. We shall leave the Sioux as they progress westward toward what would later become the Dakotas.

French Guns

In retrospect the French guns (and cold weather), which drove the Sioux westward out of Minne-ahtah, were a blessing from a cultural standpoint. The Chippewa would spend at least a century more in close contact with the Europeans, losing much more of their culture than the Sioux. Up to the date of this writing, the Sioux have but a century of close contact with the white man, whereas the Chippewa have at least two centuries of contact and resulting cultural disintegration. Many modern day Chippewa, who now prefer to be called Anishanabe (Ah nish ah nah bay), have embarked on a great effort of preserving their past and incorporating their ancestral roots into their daily lives. A majority of the Sioux, eastern tribes primarily and the post war generation, were also thoroughly indoctrinated into the white man's beliefs. Nowadays, many language programs are underway and the old religion is being practiced openly. The Canadian Chippewa have been successful in maintaining their language connection and fewer have succumbed to the white man's religion. The Sioux, like the Canadian Chippewa, were aided by the shorter duration under the white man's rule. The Sioux' geography also became a blessing, as the Sioux reservations are vast. The Pine Ridge Reservation is close to one hundred miles square; an area larger than some states. The Standing Rock and Cheyenne River Sioux reservations are also vast. The two adjoin one another, their combined land reaching into both the Dakotas.

Tetons

The Tetons were one of the original Seven Council Fires of the Sioux. They increased in population when they found the horse and the vast buffalo herds in the Dakotas which is now part of Nebraska They evolved into the seven sub tribes - seven bands of the Teton Sioux. Chief Sitting Bull, Chief Gall, Chief Red Cloud and Chief Crazy Horse would soon become their leaders. They were all members of the Teton Lakota Nation. Three of these tribes stand out and are listed first below. (Referring to the Sioux as a Nation, we can confer tribal status on the seven tribes. If one refers to the Sioux as a Tribe we would name each of the seven as bands.) They are:

1. The Oglala (Red Cloud, Black Elk, Crazy Horse).
2. The Sichangu (Spotted Tail).
3. The Hunkpapa (Sitting Bull and Gall).
4. Minicoujou.
5. Sihasapa (Blackfeet).
6. Oohenumpa (Two Kettles).
7. Itazipco (No Bows).

The last five representatives of the Tetons, including the Hunkpapa, would be referred to as the Saones. The Tetons would soon be the most numerous of the Sioux, more numerous than the other two divisions put together.

Exodus West

To refresh our memory, the Sioux migrated down the Ohio River Valley to a once pristine Mississippi. The Kansa and Arkansa were among the migrating Sioux and broke off when the tribe came to the confluence of the broad Missouri and Mississippi Rivers. The Arkansa and Kansa generally remained in this area, although some Kansa and Arkansa headed across the river and southward. The main Sioux group started upstream to the headwaters of the Mississippi. On the northward journey other Siouan speaking bands broke off. The Mandan left to cross the big river and eventually head up the Missouri. The Crow soon parted at the mouth of the Wisconsin River and headed north-eastward toward Lake Superior. The Sioux were in three major groups while in the Wisconsin/Minnesota lands. The Tetons, particularly the Oglalas, would emerge as the principal leaders in the expansion westward.

Chapter 5

Crossing the Wide Missouri

In the extension of kinship to the Siberian tribes and the Uighur, Genghis Khan was not merely making alliances between his family and their ruling families. He was accepting the entire tribe or nation into his empire as familial members, since in the political idiom of the tribes, granting kinship to the khan was tantamount to recognizing family ties with the whole nation. In this way the idiom of kinship had expanded into a type of citizenship. Genghis Khan continued to use that form in the coming years, it came to be a form of universal citizenship based not on a common religion, as among Christian and Muslim people, or just on biology, as in traditional tribal culture. It was based on allegiance, acceptance and loyalty. The Lakota speaking Oglala and Sichangu would employ similar allegiance methods when they expanded westward and upon crossing the Missouri and finding a richer lifestyle were joined by many of the Dakota and even intermarriage with their new allies, namely the Cheyenne and Absaroke.

Teton Oglala

The Sioux had spent at least a hundred years in Minnesota and Wisconsin and now the Lakota-speaking Tetons would soon cross the wide Missouri. Of the two major divisions, Dakota, and Lakota, only the Teton Lakota would cross the Missouri with the exception of some Yankton and Yanktonai (Dakota).

Arikara Tribe

Along the eastern bank of the Missouri River the Arikara were a formidable obstacle to further expansion. The whole Sioux nation could not muster as many warriors. The Arikara had log and earthen villages, large villages up and down both banks of the Missouri River, strongly fortified with ditches, earthen walls and cedar log stockades. Some of these forts were tremendous in their size. One great fortress, about seven miles south of Pierre was built on a high plateau. The Arikara lived mostly by corn planting and raising other vegetables and had hundreds of acres under cultivation growing a variety of crops. Since they had horses, they would also supplement their diet with buffalo hunts. The Sioux who had spent some years near the James River were about to face some troubled times and initially accepted charity from the Arikara.

In the ancient Native American tradition of sharing, they had no hesitation to beg from the Arikara, who gave them food and even a few horses; other accounts say it was the Cheyenne. In the beginning the Sioux were on fairly good terms with the Arikara and would visit with them in their villages. To the rear of the Tetons were the Yankton. Feeling hemmed in they feared crossing the Missouri however for there were too many mounted Arikara warriors carrying Spanish saber blades tipping their long buffalo spears. An unfortunate Spanish exploration expedition met their fate against the mounted and taller Arikara. The Spanish blades were evidence of the battle. On the open plains they could easily ride down and kill any bands that were on foot, as the Sioux were. Sioux westward drifting movement was essentially stopped for at least 25 years. The Tetons balanced this threat by periodically raising large war parties of several hundred men and driving the Arikara into their fortified villages, so well fortified that the attackers could not storm them. After taking a few scalps and maybe a few horses, the Tetons would plunder their corn patches and go back home. Then disaster struck the Arikara that changed everything. A steamboat paddling upstream would bring disease for the Arikara and westward freedom for the Teton Sioux - the Oglala and their close counterparts, the Sichangu (Burnt Thigh) who later would be called Brule in French.

As the Oglala chiefs and medicine people looked on, they recalled their history from the now far away Atlantic coastal tribes beset and vanishing from the White Man's disease – mainly small pox and cholera. 'The White Man is powerful. He can come in his tall canoes and trade you knives and pots, for your fresh water, good meat and smoked fish, but in a moon, you will be dead from the sickness he also brings. He will not have to be present when he kills you. Such is his power.' Between 1772 and 1780, three great epidemics of small pox and other steamboat borne diseases hit the southern Arikara. Their population was reduced from 20,000 to 4,000. The strong fortified villages on the east bank of the Missouri could no longer hold out and were destroyed. As a result the Arikara withdrew to the west bank and consolidated all of their people in four to five villages just below the mouth of the Cheyenne River.

Pushing Westward

The way was now open for the Tetons to cross over and push westward. The Oglala led the way. They were reminded by the older generation who remembered the warnings handed down of the sailing ships which brought death to the coastal tribes and were no doubt the primary catalyst for the up and sudden move out of the East and westward by the Dakota/Lakota. The Sioux leaders, remembering well the fates of the coastal tribes, mostly now extinct, wisely warned their people to not approach the 'death ship'. Within a moon (month) Sioux warriors would liberate several thousand Arikara horses, staying well shy of the villages where helpless Arikara lay dying by the thousands. They were the first of the Sioux to pass over the Missouri, the first to reach the Black Hills and the first to turn south to reach the Platte River in Nebraska. It was the year 1775. Far to the east a new nation was about to declare its independence. The American colonists desired freedom and control of their own destiny. The

Declaration of Independence would bring a new era of freedom unknown in Europe.

The next one hundred years saw an incredible expansion in territory and an explosion in population that would make the Sioux the most powerful tribe on the Great Plains. The strength for this expansion came not only from physical strength and endurance but also from an inner spiritual strength that gave them supreme confidence and pride in themselves and a conviction that they couldn't lose. It would seem that this inner spiritual strength came from their intense awareness of their union with the Great Spirit, with themselves and with this Creator's Nature. There was a thrust to the people that made them recognize no odds. This same strength gave them the force to adapt to anything in changing their way of making a living because they were about to change from a food gathering and planting people to a people constantly on the move, hunting the buffalo for subsistence. Adaptability was a key word for the success of the Sioux, especially the Oglala and their almost constant partners the Sichangu (Brules).

From a small band of foot traveling rovers that straggled to the Missouri between 1750 and 1775, carrying their belongings mostly on their backs and begging food and horses from the Arikara, in just a few years, they were to be swarming over the plains from the Missouri to the Rocky Mountains and from the northern border of Kansas to the Canadian border. The very name Sioux, not as much the terms Lakota or Dakota, but Sioux, would strike terror in the hearts of other Native Americans and non-Native Americans alike. Obviously they retained their identification as Lakota or Dakota but as the Tetons went westward and became more successful the other tribes, especially those who were in front of them and had to fight or flee from the advancing Lakota, were referred to by opposing tribes as Sioux. The name obviously stuck and in time, even the Tetons got used to it.

Horses and Leadership

Essential to the southern Tetons' expansion at that time were two ingredients: horses and leadership. They were soon to have both. Accounts vary as to how the Tetons first got their horses. Some accounts state that they received their first horses from the Arikara and some accounts hold that they got them from the Cheyenne. The largest acquisition no doubt came from the doomed Arikara whose defense was severely reduced by the White Man's deadly diseases, small pox and cholera mainly.

As to the actual crossing of the Missouri, the following is one of the traditional stories of the Tetons. One day the Oglala were traveling along the Missouri right below the great bend in the river, some say Crow Creek and others say near Platte Creek. There were about 30 to 40 lodges in the group and they were afoot and nearly starving. It was wintertime and the Missouri was frozen. Suddenly the Eyapaha, the camp crier, called on the men to go after buffalo that had been spotted out on the frozen Missouri. Instantly the whole camp got involved hunting down and killing as many buffalo as possible. Since the buffalo could not run on the ice very well and kept falling down and thrashing around, the people were able to kill a great number of them. When the slaughter was over they found themselves much closer to the west bank than they were to the east bank (from where they had come from.). They set up camp on the west bank and began skinning, cutting and preparing the meat which took them a number of days and before they were finished, a warm wind came up and melted the ice on the river, leaving them stranded on the west bank.

Buffalo Meat

An interesting note on buffalo meat: Scientists have had a difficult time growing cancer cells in it and cancer was a rare disease among the buffalo-dieting Sioux. Modern dieticians consider it a prime nutritional source especially for those afflicted with diabetes. Many tribes, most all of the western Sioux, are now raising their own buffalo herds and the reservation inhabitants readily proclaim the merits of buffalo meat. Long ago, diabetes was almost an unknown disease among the early Sioux. Now it runs rampant among most of the western tribes. It is so prevalent that conferences are being held and the buffalo diet is seriously being discussed along with other safer foods which lead back to the old traditional fare basically and away from the modern diets and canned soft drinks which are referred to as 'junk foods.'

First Horses

One day the stranded Oglala saw two scouts approaching on horses. They turned out to be Cheyenne and fortunately were friendly. Since the Cheyenne had horses to drag their long tipi poles, their tipis were very tall and impressive. The Cheyenne took in the Oglala and treated them fine. At the end of their visit, the Cheyenne gave the Oglala a number of horses, which, according to this account, along with the Arikara horses was the beginning of the vast herds that the Tetons were going to have. Maybe it was this particular happening that occasioned the on-looking Sioux to name the horse – Tah Shuunka Wakan. It is said that upon the first sighting of mounted warriors the Sioux were on foot. The mounted warriors were approaching the Sioux in a zig zag fashion; this was an indication of peaceful intention and presumably, they were Cheyenne seeking to become allies. 'Ehhh, Ahtaah, Tah Shuunka' (They are big dogs) (Tah - big, large, Shuunka - Dog). Tah Shuunka Wakan - (Wakan - holy) 'It is a big dog holy because the man is steering it.' 'It is letting the rider steer it, therefore it has to be holy.' Later Crazy Horse would become a famous chief. 'Tah shuunka wakan Witko' would be the formal way to say his name. Horse Crazy. (Witko ko lah is the formal way to say crazy, or highly unusual action.)

The horse was the catalyst that released the tremendous

energies of the Sioux. In a few hours now they could travel distances that took them days to travel when they were afoot. For one thing, this meant game and buffalo could be spotted, run down and killed, all within a few hours. Before, when they were afoot, it would take days and every tribesperson engaged to organize such a hunt successfully, Now, a few hunters on horses could do in a few hours that which it took all the people many days to do. As a result of this increase of food, the people grew stronger and more vigorous. Babies that would have lost their lives by the constant travel and shortage of food were now being saved, and the people increased in number. Daring leaders were not lacking to raise exploratory parties and war parties to increase the range of their territories.

One result of these early successes was that other Tetons and some Yankton, still on the east side of the Missouri, heard about these exploits and added provisions and came to join the Oglala, bringing their families. Like the Mongolians of old under Genghis Khan, they would become Oglala based on their loyalty, acceptance and allegiance to a new tribe. This increase of people made the people stronger than ever and gave added force to their expansion. The Oglala became so numerous and strong that it was not very long before they, in turn, had to divide up into seven sub-bands, as they swept the western prairies as far west as the Powder River in Wyoming. The 'powder' that made up this explosion of people and territory was made up of:

a) daring leadership.
b) the horse.
c) the tremendous inner spirit and pride of the people themselves.
d) and of course their Natural Way Spirituality.

Although the Native American values had been operating in the people for centuries, it was during this period for about the next hundred years that these values can be seen most clearly, propelling the people to greatness and generating the immediate historical forces that shaped the behavior of the Native American people living today. The noted Native American value of sharing and generosity, for instance, is seen most clearly in the two areas in which they shared: food and shelter, and praise and shame. Now that they had horses to bring game, this meant fewer hunters could bring in even more game. Yet, although fewer were participating in the actual getting of the game, the whole group still shared in the increased game that was brought in. Whatever a few did, they did for the whole group.

What is remarkable about this in the case of the Oglala is that such a vast territory could be taken over by a people who were so small in number in the beginning. After the first 25 years since crossing the Missouri, when they were gradually acquiring horses, they still had the incredibly small number of only around 500 people. This was the estimate of Lewis and Clark in 1804 although I suspect it was an under estimation. Only twenty years later, in 1825, this number had quadrupled, i.e., made the amazing increase of four times its original number. This quadruple increase brought the number of people up to around 2,000, with about 500 warriors. This increase was not all birth rate related, however. This increase was caused, as was mentioned earlier, by other Tetons and some Yankton people coming to join the Oglala and Sichangu as well.

Other Tribes

This great expansion of territory caused, of course, conflict with other tribes, which required other tribes to move. People in those days moved either because they were looking for better places to live in order to eat better, or they moved because they were pushed out by other bands of superior size and force. It is hard for us today to realize that the peoples in those days saw no particular injustice in this practice and accepted it as one of the laws of life. They saw all the land in the whole world as belonging to everyone. As to who roamed over this particular territory at this time depended upon this particular tribe's size and strength. This was a law of life that they all accepted. Again and again, one sees examples in Native American history in which a given tribe would be pushed out by another larger tribe. Some years later, the pushed out tribe, now grown larger than the tribe that pushed them out, would come back and push out the original 'pusher-outers.' Throughout Native American history, there was a constant shuffling of territories. For instance, one can find a given tribe on a map from a certain period and when one looks at the map again a hundred years later, that tribe is not there, but hundreds of miles away in another direction. When a strong tribe would push out a small tribe, the smaller tribe would, in turn, push out someone yet smaller, and so it would go down the line, causing another reshuffling of the territory. As we said, this was one of the laws of life in those days, and everyone accepted it.

The Brules were soon to follow. Farther north, on the eastern side of the Missouri, the other bands of Tetons—the Saones—were held up for about another 20 years (about 1795) because the remaining Arikara had gathered themselves together and in this way, resisted for this length of time the westward movement of the Teton Saones. The Hunkpapas and the Blackfeet Sioux were held up until about 1825 and were the last to come across.

Chapter 6

Democracy - The Great Gift

President Obama made a trip to China and was criticized by the right wing media in America for his reluctance to take issue with the so-called 'Lack of Religious Freedom' in China. Little do the 'right wing', mostly Republican Party members and platform followers realize the serious danger Organized Religion is posing to inflict damage to our own country's existence while completely negating what Nature is demonstrating and most often exponentially, which history will eventually bear out. America has a separation of Church and State clause in its Constitution which is not followed in its full and intended entirety established by Colonial drafters. This chapter will bear my claim out but first let us explore another world change, one of tremendous magnitude much in line with the solid precepts of fairness and real truth implemented by Genghis Khan. This Gift owes its beginning to a later tribe of Chino/Mongol descended people with some Viking (Scandinavian) blood in their veins as well.

Varied Democracy

Democracy can and has to vary among countries which it certainly has, mainly due to geography, weather, agricultural productivity, resource availability and other varying factors notably past regimes and former rulers. There is no trademark or copyright on a country's version of democracy. The Americans seem to forget that they began their borrowed democracy in a land of seemingly untapped abundant resources, an unbroken land never touched by a steel plow; containing acres of rich black soil, millions of acres. They rode that crest for several centuries while highly touting to resource-poor countries (or depleted) how exemplary their democracy was but now the balloon 'has burst' so to speak especially when we note the lack of or depleted resources. Some serious alterations to American democracy have to be implemented by a government that will yet admit our exponentially increasing dilemma. They are now turning to China for economic aid but they need to adopt more than just Economic Aid to successfully survive. The Peoples Republic of China has far more freedom for its citizens now than when Mandarin China ruled and/or the aristocracy which Generalissimo Chiang Kai-shek allowed. It is rather foolish and unworkable for a government to attempt to allow so-called 'freedoms' when such allowances would be extremely detrimental to the realistic needs for the nation as a whole. Tremendous change and sacrifice had to occur obviously for such an immense country (China) to endure after WWII. Had it remained a weak vassal state, beset by endless famines and epidemics, who knows what form of the 'Boxer Rebellion' era would have returned under the direction of foreign powers; ready to establish their colonial regimes to exploit the country's resources; led by a puppet, corrupt regime under the command of whoever was supplying their arms and ammunition to keep them in power. This did not happen and now their country is a respected world leader. Economically China is financially sound in comparison to those governments who falsely tout their often unrestricted 'Freedoms' which have become detrimental for the Common Good of the populace. For example: Over population is the major cause of planetary heating which affects all of us let alone fostering extreme poverty. The Chinese government has wisely implemented much needed over-population controls while the rest of the endangered planet's residents foolishly standby and do nothing. Mexico is a prime example of over population to the extent that they have to migrate to other lands because they are controlled by a powerful church. This is not a corrective solution. 'Mexico is a poor man sitting on a gold mine,' an apt description. The richest man in the world is a Mexican citizen; Mexico is loaded with resources, namely oil. It must be admitted by all countries looking on that China's government has now brought them to world leadership primarily through needed disciplines and courageous, patient and intelligent foresight. I doubt if China's government would allow Mexico to migrate freely into its borders but rather would urge Mexico to take corrective action regardless of a controlling church. It is Mexico's only solution unless the United States is folly enough to let it keep pouring into its borders which it is doing. I doubt if Mexico will be able to see through the designs of its controlling church. The easy way out is for Mexico to take advantage of a weak political system in America who have little foresight for future generations of Americans. Eventually, America will be a Spanish speaking; over-populated, church controlled nation if one believes and respects one simple word - Math! Here again, the right wing is loath to admit the controlling danger Organized Religion fosters even though their resolute religious blindness spells doom for their country.

Note: To the Chinese/Mongolian People. If you happen to read this, some of you may complain of certain Freedoms and/or their lack thereof within your own parent country. I must advise you that your government has had to implement difficult but needed controls because of the serious factors that could and would lead to disastrous calamity if these measures were not implemented. Historically, the old China experienced tremendous fatalities, famines, disastrous floods and no Freedoms at all. Prior to World War Two, China was not far removed from the conditions within the feudal state of Tibet described earlier, except for a controlling religious authority in league with the ruling Chinese Warlords and Mandarins, of course. A tremendous infrastructure to promote commerce; mainly for agricultural goods to market had to be built. First it was the interchange of agricultural goods to feed the nation then the bridges, roads, electrical power, dams, rail that led toward massive shipyards which would then carry out her overseas commerce. Such a massive enterprise had to be accomplished for China to arrive where she is today. Discipline was first and foremost, to survive and break away from the feudalism of the past.

True Roots of Democracy

American democracy comes from the Iroquois tribal confederacy, a Chino/Mongolian descended tribe and not from Judaea/Christianity honed from Greco/Roman eras which American history so errantly proclaims. Two American Colonial period citizens and drafters of our early Constitution, Ben Franklin and Thomas Paine deserve most credit as to the further advancement of their findings and emplacement of democracy into American society, their politics, history and law. George Washington also deserves plaudits by not choosing to become another European king which he could have quite easily done. Paine & Franklin's discovery and related work on initiating True Democracy no doubt strongly influenced the first president (George Washington) and later President Jefferson. It was Jefferson, prior to becoming president, who encouraged the two to make a special trip to the then powerful Iroquois to join our side for the battles of Independence when we were fighting the British who were then controlling the early American settlers migrating out of Europe mostly from England. The British foolishly did not honor their very effective Native American allies against the Continental Army under General Washington. For this Eurocentric British mistake, the Iroquois went neutral. The Colonials were fast to seize upon the opportunity to keep the powerful Iroquois out of the war by sending two special envoys to visit with the leaders of the Iroquois Confederacy.

In England, the King controlled all aspects of government and there existed no Freedoms for the common man who was usually termed - 'the King's Subjects.' The wealthy land owners who were termed the 'nobility' moved about freely and swore their loyalty to the King or royalty, which was the term used for the King's family and heirs. They came to the King's side with their hired mercenaries when any form of insurrection or threat from foreign or local powers occurred. Such loyalty won them certain Freedoms granted by the King. The common man or British subject dared not travel about freely and could not even supplement his diet by harvesting deer and other species of wild game from the abundant forest. Outside the villages wherein the common man barely survived, the forest holdings were teeming with deer, wild boar and a type of forest cattle which would have provided adequate supplementary food as the American Native American enjoyed. No one owned or controlled the western hemisphere forests and consequently the inhabitants of those lands went to sleep every night with an adequate meal. The European's basic diet was gruel in those times, made from grains while little meat protein found its way into their basic diet. Hence, the early European was considerably smaller than the Chino/Mongolian descendants when they first arrived upon our land. This was a protein deficient dietary trait that led to a tremendous combat advantage for later Sioux warriors fighting the smaller sized U.S. Army several centuries later. Simply ask the American National Football League if size helps considerably regarding close sports combat. Only the royalty and nobility were allowed this hunting and movement privilege and for those of the common realm (also referred to as commoners) the penalty for hunting was to have their bow shooting fingers amputated. Needless to say, this procedure curtailed severely any ideas about 'freedom of movement.'

Franklin and Paine

The original Principles of Democracy in America - freedom of elected leadership, freedom of assembly, freedom of movement (you could wander on out to the surrounding (un-owned by barons & kings) woods and hunt and fish freely,) freedom of speech - all this and even suffrage (women's rights), came from the Iroquois; and initially copied, mainly by the Continental envoys, Ben Franklin and Thomas Paine who if not successfully at least encouraged the large Iroquoian Confederacy to remain neutral. Franklin was amazed after visiting the then powerful Iroquois. Americans are loath to admit the raw truth however: the pilgrims and the latter colonists knew absolutely nothing nor practiced any form of true democracy during this time period nor would they evolve to give honest credit to the Native American.Obviously, early Americans knew nothing of democracy. Iroquois women were voting when the unknowing pilgrims landed. Human's greatest gift to humanity was democracy and it came from - here - not there - the Greek or Roman slave states where only a very few, privileged wealthy few (all males) - voted. This Judaea Christian attempt at origi-nating ownership never worked in Europe where the mass of immigrants came from. For centuries democracy never rose under the controlling, non-democratic, woman subjective, Nature disrespecting, nobility backed by a collusive power/fear mongering king in league with an Organized Church. Odd, is it not, that democracy should suddenly flower from New World roots completely devoid of Organized Religion? Egotistic and Eurocentric America settlers however, just could not admit to the true source. Jack Weatherford's *Native American Givers* explains this Iroquoian source. The book is a must read for any of you who can hold back your false ego and explore some honest history. Two books by Weatherford have been very influential in my writing besides a personal friendship which I have enjoyed: *Genghis Khan, and Native American Givers*. Where did the Iroquois discover it (democracy)? By studying, observing Creator's Created Nature - of course. Their legends tell of Deganawida and Hiawatha, two brilliant and Nature observant Iroquois. They certainly did not discover such an important milestone for man from a man-written book composed by a world view ignorant human not long removed from living in a cave. The animal world is very democratic if one is observant. Their values are obviously placed within by a benevolent maker or maybe it is pure evolution that evolved to design which methodology works best for modern survival and to also live it as harmoniously as possible. Whatever, Nature has a much more successful track record if we compare to ever-warring, subjugating, fear controlling, corruptible, superstition spawning man. To the Native American - all lifestyle philosophy and spirituality lies within Nature, of course, as 'the' major teacher. Ours is an 'Unprinted Green Book' (Mother Nature) and not some black book,composed 3000 years ago, initially by Arabs and re-edited down through time according to who was in power to alter, add or subtract and worse declare foolish, binding statements heretically claimed to be direct words of Creator itself. Note: The Sioux lived in the Northeast and readily adapted to what they perceived as a better form of government (Iroquoian Democracy) and religious outlook, theology and ceremony as well. Eventually, in medieval times the controlling church created a Man-God from a man who existed in so called 'Biblical times'. In the past millennia, in the midst of the church sanctioned Great Inquisition, these followers declared that man was now God. These self-appointed 'Declarers' also backed the murderous Inquisition which rampaged through Europe, lasting into the 1800s. It was initially sponsored by the Roman Church and later the Protestant Church. This Absolutism murdered and tortured thousands of innocent victims, mostly defenseless women. Another 'Black Book,' the Koran was composed by Arabs in the first millennia. Their Koran does not declare mere man as a god but recognizes a special human as Creator's direct messenger. Neither of these two leading world religions attribute anything spiritually worthy emanating from Creator's direct and obvious work - Nature. Should those that gave the greatest gifts be followed? The greatest harmony to the Earth Mother which we all live on? And to humanity as well? What about the Wamaskaskan (the Animal Relatives)? The gift of democracy is indeed a great gift contrived and shaped by man ... and it came from indigenous spiritual based man! It did not come from what is generally accepted as 'civilized' Organized Religion Man!

Someday, maybe centuries from now, humans will finally arrive at an honest conclusion but only after truthful admittance, truthful introspection (as if Creator's communicative power was directly confronting them) and of course a shedding of the preventive ego which they find so difficult to be rid of. Possibly then humankind can make a true democracy work far more efficiently and fairly. We can only hope!

Chapter 7

Leadership

Before we look at four Sioux leaders, all of whom were born in the nineteenth century, let us look at a leader of the twelfth and thirteenth centuries. This man was Genghis Khan who is reviled by many European writers as a brutal, conquering warrior chief (Khan). However author, Jack Weatherford went to Mongolia numerous times and not unlike James Carroll and British author John Cornwell who dug through Vatican archives briefly made available, Weatherford discovered entirely contrary information. Granted, the thirteenth century was not a time when nations gathered to promote ethics, reason and humanitarian conduct. No such slogans like 'Political Correctness' or a United Nations existed back then. It was a harsh world and battles were fought with no quarters asked. Entire cities were often burned to the ground along with the occupants. Slavery or death for the conquered Caucasian or Asian, was often inevitable. Genghis Khan, however, was highly unusual, he forbade torture and habitually offered peaceful terms, even joining his forces to avoid warfare and share with the spoils of war, which many did. Until only recently has he been finally given due credit as the architect for commerce from India to Western Europe besides initiating early democratic principles. Not formal democracy, admittedly, which is little changed to this day as practiced by the Iroquois but Khan's contribution was more in the order of promulgated laws and conduct demanded from his occupying armies and later administrators. Thus he did emulate and shape toward such a government unheard of in his time span. Indeed, I consider this chapter as one of the most important in the book, for it gives 'moderns' in America, some semblance of hope that somehow a similar leader can or will rise up from utter 'nothingness' and lead us out of the virtual slavery the '1 percent' is locking down upon us. Our children, grandchildren and beyond are mortgaged. Isn't that proof enough? The (European) knights at their tournaments, in their finery, armor and emblems of ancestry, believed they were the foremost warriors in the world, while shabby appearing, un-uniformed Mongol warriors thought otherwise. Mongol horses were small, but their riders were lightly clad and they moved with greater speed. These were hardy men who grew up on horses and hunting, making them better warriors than those who were raised in agricultural societies and cities. Their main weapon was the bow and arrow. And the Mongols of the early 1200s were highly disciplined, superbly coordinated, could endure for days on scant rations and their combat leadership brilliant in tactics. In a span of just 25 years, Genghis Khan's horsemen conquered a larger area and greater population than the Romans did in four centuries.

Fire Power

Like the Sioux, horse riding began at an early age, usually from four to six years. Mongol youths, rode swiftly toward a swinging tethered buckskin ball, a foot or less in diameter, to release children's arrows in rapid succession; equestrian style, guiding their ponies, significantly smaller than the captured U.S. Cavalry mounts Sioux warriors would ride centuries later, and brandishing Winchester repeating rifles, but the training was the same. The Mongolian bow, fired rapidly from mounted archers decimated the foot infantry of the Europeans after the European knights were dispatched, usually taunted out of their ranks for a fatal chase. A common Mongolian tactic was to taunt the heavily armored knights by feinting retreat and fear. This was highly effective bait for the egocentric European. Safely away from the enemy archers and most usually a longer chase the Mongolian ponies were better conditioned in comparison and able to speed far ahead where fresh mounts would be waiting. Riders would then return to the chase of tiring European war horses carrying a burdening load of European armor on the horse as well. Knights would be tumbling from their mounts before closure of the two forces. The rapid fire from the archers won every battle except one, and that battle was a numerical loss rather than a failure of Mongol combat effectiveness. Likewise the Sioux would have the same success utilizing similar Mongol battle tactics against the U.S. Cavalry.

Spiritual Beliefs

'The Mongols were illiterate, religiously shamanistic and perhaps no more than 700,000 in number.' Thus is a commonly found description when 'Googled' (Genghis Khan). A more accurate term is that the Mongols were religious/spiritual followers who believed in a Supreme Higher Power, quite indescribable but ruling all things it created. Genghis Khan, not unlike the Sioux and especially, Chief Crazy Horse, would isolate himself in vast nature and beseech to this Ultimate Mystery which the Sioux would later term similarly; Wakan Tanka, Great Mystery, Great Spirit, Benevolent, All Providing Creator of All. Accepting and recognizing one's Higher Power/Ultimate Creator as sheer Mystery most often prevents disharmony or non-acceptability of other beliefs and faiths quite unlike the non-tolerant adherents of Organized Religion which too often demands that its 'Way' is the 'Only Way.'

Mongol language today is described as Altaic, a language unrelated to Chinese, derived from inhabitants in the Altay mountain range in western Mongolia. They were herdsmen on the grassy plains north of the Gobi Desert and south of Siberian forests. Before the year 1200, the Mongols were fragmented; moving about in small bands headed by a chief, or khan, and living in portable felt dwellings. The Mongols endured frequent deprivations and sparse areas for grazing their animals. They frequently fought over turf, and during hard times they occasionally raided, interested in goods rather than bloodshed. They did not collect heads or scalps as trophies and did not notch wood to record their kills.

Early Life

Records of the Great Khan's early life are sparse and contradictory. He was likely born in 1162, though some sources give it as 1155 or 1165. He had a hard childhood losing his father at nine and spent several years in slavery. His mother and siblings had a difficult time subsisting on roots mainly and small game that he and his brother had to hunt in order to survive. These difficult times did not make him hard and cruel however, but instead made him respect the needy and even pass future laws for their protection as long as they were not enemies. Following a series of raids against his small band, one in which his wife was kidnapped but later rescued, he began to accumulate followers. From his late teens to age thirty-eight in 1200, the Mongol named Temujin (Temüjin) rose as *khan* over various families. He was a good manager, collecting people of talent. He was vassal to Ong Khan, titular head of a confederacy better organized than other Mongol clans. Temujin joined Ong Khan in a military campaign against Tatars to their east, and following the success of this campaign Ong Khan declared Temujin his adoptive son and heir. Temujin delegated authority based on merit and loyalty, rather than family ties. He would even have his mother adopt orphans from a conquered tribe, bringing them into his family. These political innovations inspired great loyalty among the conquered people, making Temujin stronger with each victory. Ong Khan's natural son, Senggum (Senggüm), who was known for his cruelty to the conquered; horse dragging captives and boiling them alive, had been expecting to succeed his father and plotted to assassinate Temujin. Temujin learned of this, and those loyal to Temujin defeated those loyal to Senggum. Later Ong Khan's plot to assassinate Temujin failed leading to his defeat. Temujin was now established as the head of what had been Ong Khan's coalition. And in 1206, at the age of 42, Temujin took the title Universal Ruler, which translates to *Genghis Khan*, he addressed his joyous supporters thanking them for their help and their loyalty. His treatment of those he subdued led to swelling ranks of loyal followers. The united Mongols soon defeated the neighboring Tatars and Jurkins, and Temujin Khan assimilated their people rather than following steppe custom of looting them and leaving. Such was the key to the so-called 'Mongolian Horde' which would eventually sweep into Europe.

Yassa – The Body of Law

Like peoples elsewhere, Genghis Khan's subjects saw themselves at the center of the Universe, the greatest of people and favored by the gods. They justified Genghis Khan's success in warfare by claiming that he was the rightful master not only over the 'peoples of the felt tent' but the entire world. Genghis Khan continued organizing. He improved his military organization, which was also to serve as a mobile political bureaucracy, and he broke up what was left of old enemy tribes, leaving as ethnically homogeneous only those tribes that had demonstrated loyalty to him. He created a body of law that he was to work on throughout his life. As an incentive for absolute obedience and following his rule of law, the Yassa code, Temujin promised civilians and soldiers wealth from future possible war spoils. As he defeated rival tribes, he did not drive away enemy soldiers and abandon the rest. Instead, he took the conquered tribe under his protection and integrated its members into his own tribe. The kidnapping of women had caused feuding among the Mongols, and, as a teenager, Temujin had suffered from the kidnapping of his young wife, Borte. After devoting himself to rescuing her, he made it law that there was to be no kidnapping of women. He declared all children legitimate, whomever the mother. He made it law that no woman would be sold into marriage. The stealing of animals had caused dissension among the Mongols, and Genghis Khan made it a capital offense. A lost animal was to be returned to its owner, and taking lost property as one's own was to be considered theft and a capital offense. Genghis Khan regulated hunting, a winter activity, improving the availability of meat for everyone. He introduced record keeping, taking advantage of his former move years to have his native language put into writing. He created official seals. He created a supreme officer of the law, who was to collect and preserve all judicial decisions, to oversee the trials of all those charged with wrong-doing and to have the power to issue death sentences. He created order in his realm that strengthened it and his ability to expand. As stated earlier, he was far ahead of other.

Conquest, Collaboration and Consolidation

In 1210, the Jin dynasty, sent a delegation to Genghis Khan demanding Mongol submission as vassals. The Jin dynasty controlled the flow of goods along the Silk Road, and defying them meant a lack of access to those goods. Genghis Khan and the Mongols discussed the matter and chose war. Genghis, according to the scholar Jack Weatherford, prayed alone on a mountain, bowing down and stating his case to 'his supernatural guardians,' describing the grievances, the tortures and killings that generations of his people had suffered. And he pleaded that he had not sought war and had not initiated the quarrel. In 1211, Genghis Khan and his army attacked. The Mongols had an advantage in diet, which included a lot of meat, milk and yogurt, and they could miss a day or two of eating better than Jin soldiers, who ate grains. Genghis Khan and his army overran Beijing and pushed into the heartland of northern China. Military success helped as people acquired the impression that Genghis Khan had the Mandate of Heaven and that fighting against him was fighting heaven itself. The Jin emperor recognized Mongol authority and agreed to pay tribute. After six years of fighting, leaving one of his best generals in charge, Genghis Khan returned to Mongolia with engineers who had become a permanent part of their army, there were also captive musicians, translators, doctors and scribes, camels and wagonloads of goods. Among the goods were silk, including silken rope, cushions, blankets, robes, rugs, wall hangings, porcelain, iron kettles, armor, perfumes, jewelry, wine, honey, medicines, bronze, silver and gold, and much else. Goods from China would now come in a steady flow. The Mongols were happy to be back from China, their homeland higher in elevation, less humid and cooler. As eaters of meat and sparsely populated they felt superior to people in northern China, but they liked what China had to offer, and at home there was change. The continuing flow of goods from China had to be administered and properly distributed, and buildings had to be built to store the goods. Success in war was changing the Mongols - as it had the Romans and the Arabs. Tribes as far away as Kazakhstan and Kyrgyzstan heard about the Great Khan, and overthrew their Buddhist rulers in order to join his growing empire. By 1219, Genghis Khan ruled from northern China to the Afghan border and from Siberia to the border of Tibet. He sought a trade alliance with the powerful Khwarizm Empire, which controlled Central Asia from Afghanistan to the Black Sea. Sultan Muhammad II agreed, but then murdered the first Mongol trade convoy of 450 merchants, stealing their goods. The sultan there claimed that spies were in the caravan. Genghis Khan sent envoys. The sultan received them by having the chief of the envoys killed and the beards of the others burned, and he sent the other envoys back to Genghis Khan. Before the end of that year, the wrathful Khan had captured every Khwarizm city, adding lands from Turkey to Russia to his realm. In retaliation the Mongols rode across the desert to Transoxiana with no baggage, slowing to the pace of merchants before appearing as warriors in front of the smaller towns of the sultan's empire. His strategy was to frighten the townspeople into surrendering without battle, benefiting his own troops, whose lives he valued. Those frightened into surrender were spared violence. Those who resisted were slaughtered as an example for others, which sent many fleeing and spreading panic from the first towns to the city of Bukhara. People in Bukhara opened the city's gates to the Mongols and surrendered. Genghis Khan told them that they, the common people, were not at fault, that high-ranking people among them had committed great sins that inspired God to send him and his army as punishment. The sultan's capital city, Samarkand, surrendered. The sultan's army surrendered, and the sultan fled. Genghis Khan pushed deeply into Afghanistan and then Persia. It is said that the caliph in Baghdad was hostile toward the sultan and supported Genghis Khan, sending him a regiment of European crusaders who had been his prisoners. Genghis Khan, having no need for infantry, freed them, with those making it to Europe spreading the first news of the Mongol conquests. Genghis Khan had 100,000 to 125,000 horsemen, with Uighur and Turkic allies, engineers and Chinese doctors - a total of 150,000 to 200,000 men. To show their submission, those his army approached offered food, and Genghis Khan's force guaranteed them protection. Some cities surrendered without fighting. In cities that the Mongols were forced to conquer, Genghis Khan divided the civilians by profession. He drafted the few who were literate and anyone who could speak various languages. Those who had been the cities' most rich and powerful he wasted no time in killing, remembering that the rulers he had left behind after conquering the Tangut and Jin had betrayed him soon after his army had withdrawn. While Genghis Khan was consolidating his conquests in Persia and Afghanistan, a force of 40,000 Mongol horsemen pushed through Azerbaijan and Armenia. They defeated Georgian crusaders, captured a Genoese trade-fortress in the Crimea and spent the winter along the coast of the Black Sea. As they were heading back home they met 80,000 warriors led by Prince Mstitslav of Kiev. The battle of Kalka River (1223) commenced. Staying out of range of the crude weapons of peasant infantry, and with better bows than opposing archers, they devastated the prince's standing army. Facing the prince's cavalry, they faked a retreat, drawing the armored cavalry forward, taking advantage of the vanity and over-confidence of the mounted aristocrats. Lighter and more mobile, they strung out and tired the pursuers and then attacked (with fresh horses from a pre-planned staging area); killed and routed them. In 1225, Genghis Khan returned to Mongolia. He now ruled everything between the Caspian Sea and Beijing. He created an efficient pony express system. Wanting no divisions rising from religion, he declared freedom of religion throughout his empire. Favoring order and tax producing prosperity, he forbade troops and local officials to abuse people. Soon again, Genghis Khan was at war. He believed that the Tangut were not living up to their obligations to his empire. In 1227, around the age of sixty-five while leading the fighting against the Tangut, Genghis Khan, it is said, fell off his horse and died. In terms of square miles conquered, Genghis Khan had been the greatest conqueror of all time - his empire four times larger than the empire of Alexander the Great. The Mongol nation believed that he had been the greatest man of all time and a man sent from heaven. Among the Mongols he was known as the Holy Warrior, and not unlike the Jews, who continued to see hope in a conquering king (messiah) like David, Mongols were to continue to believe that one day Genghis Khan would rise again and lead his people to new victories.

Torture

It is said that Genghis Khan's military did not torture, mutilate or maim. But his enemies are reported as having done so. Captured Mongols were dragged through streets and killed for sport and to entertain city residents. Gruesome displays of stretching, emasculation, belly cutting and hacking to pieces was something European rulers were using to discourage potential enemies - as was soon to happen to William Wallace on orders from England's King Edward I. Modern America's advocate for torture was the former Vice-President Dick Cheney who amassed a fortune through his insider buying as Secretary of Defense primarily. He was also a key 'Decider' in the Bush Administration. Egypt under, the un-elected 'President' Mubarak was a collaborator of American captured and detained 'Security Suspects' who were sent to Egyptian prisons for torture sessions.

Politics and Economics

The Mongol Empire did not emphasize the importance of ethnicity and race in the administrative realm, instead adopting an approach grounded in meritocracy. The exception was the role of Genghis Khan and his family. The Mongol Empire was one of the most ethnically and culturally diverse empires in history, as befitted its size. Many of the empire's nomadic inhabitants considered themselves *Mongols* in military and civilian life, including Turks, Mongols, and others and included many diverse Khans of various ethnicities as part of the Mongol Empire. There were tax exemptions for religious figures and, to some extent, teachers and doctors. The Mongol Empire practiced religious tolerance to a large degree because Mongol tradition had long held that religion was a very personal concept, and not subject to law or interference. Various Mongol tribes were Buddhist, Muslim, shamanist or Christian. Religious tolerance was thus a well-established concept on the Asian steppe. Modern Mongolian historians say that towards the end of his life, Genghis Khan attempted to create a civil state under the Great Yassa that would have established the legal equality of all individuals, including women. However, there is no contemporary evidence of this, or of the lifting of discriminatory policies towards sedentary peoples such as the Chinese. Women played a relatively important role in Mongol Empire and in family, for example Töregene Khatun was briefly in charge of the Mongol Empire when the next male Khagan was being chosen. Modern scholars refer to the alleged policy of encouraging trade and communication as the Pax Mongolica (Mongol Peace).Genghis Khan realized that he needed people who could govern cities and states conquered by him. He also realized that such administrators could not be found among his Mongol people because they were nomads and thus had no experience governing cities. For this purpose Genghis Khan invited a Khitan prince, Chu'Tsai, who worked for the Jin and had been captured by the Mongol army after the Jin Dynasty was defeated. Jin had captured power by displacing Khitan. Genghis told Chu'Tsai, who was a lineal descendant of Khitan rulers, that he had avenged Chu'Tsai's forefathers. Chu'Tsai responded that his father served the Jin Dynasty honestly and so did he; he did not consider his own father his enemy, so the question of revenge did not apply. Genghis Khan was very impressed by this reply. Chu'Tsai administered parts of the Mongol Empire and became a confidant of the successive Mongol Khans.

Commerce

Genghis Khan emerged to alter the then civilized world significantly in the field of commerce which became his primary vision - opening up commerce by removing severe superstitious restrictions often generated by the various Organized Religions; Jewish, Nestorian Catholic, Buddhist, and Islam which were then prominent. He was democratic however; all of these faiths were represented as generals or commanders of his various army units. His other passion was unifying Mongolia with the domain his thousands of warriors captured all the way to the gates of Western Europe. In Eastern Europe, his armies defeated the many adversaries they confronted. According to Jack Weatherford's book, *Genghis Khan*, based mostly upon material offered to him from modern Mongolia's archives, he discarded the idea of invading Western Germany, France and Great Britain primarily because they had little enough wealth (commerce), in his estimate to be worthy of engaging his army in the field. His mounted archers riding equestrian style upon their swift ponies with both hands free easily dispatched the bit and rein holding Hungarian, Russian and German knights in Eastern Europe. Firepower, most often wins! Some of the new commercial laws Genghis Khan enforced were the rights of women to work as merchants, removal of religious based restrictive selling and buying taboos, tariff removal, and outlawing restrictions and impediments enforced upon certain classes of societies within his realm. A concerted attempt to eradicate caravan banditry was no doubt one of his greater commercial accomplishments for that era. The merchant class became elevated and artisans were free to travel and work their arts and crafts outside of their birthplaces. Caravan routes were policed and bandits hunted down and executed. Courts were created to hear and settle disputes. Mongolian law was applied equally from the lowest herder to the nobility. Religious clerics, mullahs, clergy and priests were considered exempt from capital punishment. Lawbreakers were punished but torture was forbidden. Organized Religion was allowed but it could not subvert or claim first allegiance over the Domain of Mongolia. He emphasized to his generals and field commanders of various faiths, that their first allegiance was to Mongolia and then to their God concept! Obviously such a command was not disputed. God or the Higher Power was revered and respected but Genghis Khan, who remember; went out in solitude to beseech the Higher Power as did the American Native American leaders of Mongolian extract; the Supreme leader held an attitude that such a Higher Power didn't need human's worship. It was obviously the Supreme Provider of all and so powerful; what benefit could mere humans convey upon it? Thoughts of allegiance in this world, therefore, was to

Mongolia as a whole - all dutifully working together for greater harmony which cultural characteristic has carried into present China today. I find myself not adverse to such a pragmatic consideration and would much rather have a leader so devout that they would go out for several days alone spiritually respecting much more deeply, in my opinion than an hour's charade on the seventh day. Our sun dances last for four days without food and water while we beseech to our Higher Power concept thanking IT that we live. Needless to say, Commerce flowed freely in early medieval times, not only westward to Europe but south to the Chinese and on into the Mid-east and India.

As stated earlier, this chapter could be one of the most important for it offers us hope for our own country's future which is at a sorry stage at present. 'Legalized' corruption is rife and the term, '1 percent', controls the masses. A People's Congress needs to be spawned and a prudent, practical, pragmatic leader, much in the mold of Genghis Khan elected. Arrows and bullets however, need not be utilized. The great weapon communication can be employed far more effectively if True Democracy can return, much in the mode of the original Colonial era Founding Fathers' visualization, and of course with a strong flavoring of Iroquoian democracy which highly influenced our early governmental beginning. It goes without saying that Organized Religion can be extremely disruptive to a smooth running, efficient Democracy. G.K. would not tolerate its interference nor does modern China or present Mongolia today, yet citizens are allowed their religious/spiritual participation – as long as they do not proselytize. Wherein religion is truly 'Mystery,' fanatically, zealous human has proven repeatedly that religion is too often dangerous for the existence of True Democracy and spawns poor, narrow-minded political candidates. We can simply observe the political candidates in the 2012 primary presidential election process. Three candidates; a

Congresswoman, a former governor and a former Senator all elected to their office mainly through a single themed religious issue, were obviously ill equipped to administer a much broader form of direly needed policy making. Congresswoman Bachmann of Minnesota even called for Organized Religion to be a major portion of national policy making and an abolishment of church/state separation. Enough of this writing has and will cover further the horrendous damage such a political philosophy can wreak upon freedom seeking citizens.

Sioux Leaders

Why should one study Sioux leadership in order to seek Spirituality? Does the White Man not tell of his leaders back in biblical times? The lives of the Sioux leaders may be found to be just as interesting, and for many readers, more so. The caliber of a nation's moral and ethical leadership guidance should reflect the high or low degree of its respect for what code a Higher Power would possibly expect – would it not? Weatherford tells of the deep spirituality Genghis Khan held for his concept of his Higher Power. As stated earlier, Genghis Khan would at times disappear for several days alone into the high hills of a Mongolian hinterland to beseech to his concept of Creator. Obviously, such solitude helped create a democratic leader unusual for his time despite the false claims and accusations by the Eurocentric writers of later times.

By studying the four Sioux leaders, we will immerse ourselves deeper into the 'natural' living and nature blended mind and hence come closer to honing our own abilities. These men demonstrate honor, bravery, self-sacrifice, decision making and always kept a deep spirituality. Example - is a powerful teacher. In these perilous environmental times, our country is in dire need of such leaders. If we look at the political leaders in America they are at the bottom of the public polls that are often held. Why? Because Congress has a history of financial self-promotion and continues to pass such self-promoting laws besides absolving itself from certain taxing and duty burdens imposed upon the populace. None of them immerse themselves in creator's soothing, calming, mystical Nature.Life is not a pharmaceutical supermarket wherein one can purchase a quick-fix to serenity and happiness. At least not from what I have observed. Nature does not condone or allow the encapsulated, 'ready-made' approach to life's journey. Isn't it obvious that we are here to 'prove ourselves' over the long haul for hopefully a higher purpose in a Beyond? This holding is not my exclusive thought, by no means. It seems to be a universally accepted viewpoint. The danger laden attempts through drugs or alcohol and/or over-materialism, greed and selfishness demonstrate the futility of human's foolish short-cuts to real happiness, character building, exemplary track record and true confidence let alone striving to protect the planet. We do have a planet to save!

Warrior Chiefs

Warrior chiefs' bravery upon the field of battle was unquestioned. That means that they were willing to risk their very lives in the field of combat to protect their tribal constituents. Very few of the Congressional members in Congress are combat military veterans despite the many wars America becomes involved in allowing them many opportunities to volunteer for the military and go out into the field of battle. The presidency rarely has a leader who has been a combat experienced veteran. The Sioux leaders sun danced, vision quested, sweat lodged and smoked the sacred pipe to beseech to their Creator and Creator's Six Powers. Chief Red Cloud was known to pull back his troops in the midst of a military engagement and ride away to participate in the annual sun dance. Obviously his commitment to God was more important than fighting with other men. No American or European military leader would ever think of doing such an act. Their culture would not condone it.

Chief Red Cloud, Oglala-Teton Lakota Sioux, (1821-1909)

Red Cloud had an Army fort surrounded and was starving out the occupants. It was in the hot summer of the 1860s out on the Great Plains. The occupants were out of water and suffering from dehydration. No re-supply was able to rescue the doomed occupants and they were planning to surrender and capitulate. The next morning Chief Red Cloud's warriors were gone. Yes, simply vanished. The fort commander sent out a rider upon the strongest horse to summon help and supplies. A detachment hurriedly went to a water point a creek that still bore precious water with containers to bring back water to the fort. The soldiers rejoiced and lived. Years later, Chief Red Cloud was asked why he left a sure victory. He calmly stated, 'I had a date with God. That is more important than killing men.' A Sun Dance had been scheduled to meet with other tribal bands to hold a Thanksgiving ceremony to their concept of the Higher Power.

Sun Dance

The primary ceremony for the Sioux was the annual Sun Dance which is mentioned by almost all past writers in regard to Chief Red Cloud, Chief Crazy Horse and Chief Sitting Bull. I do not believe any of these writers had the depth to explore why this was such an important event to stop fighting their campaigns or at least placing their combat on hold. Something this important would certainly seem to bear some scrutiny, some curiosity, some probing; would not one think? Did not any of these leaders go into the Sun Dance before their Creator concept and ask Wakan Tanka to spare them one more time, one more battle, feed them one more winter, bring the Wah shi chu to the treaty table? Would not these issues be heavy on their minds? I have participated as a Sun Dance Pledger in six sun dances. Many sun dancers have taken part in many more sun dances than I but as a writer, I believe I have taken part in at least six more sun dances than almost all the rest of the related subject writers of Native extraction, with the exception of my fellow authors, Manny Two Feathers and Dr. Chuck Ross.

Chief Red Cloud was born in 1821; therefore he bore the brunt of the major fighting with the Army during the turbulent 1860s. He was the Commander-in-Chief for five years of constant battle from 1862 to 1867 although he began fighting the American Army while in his thirties. His superb fighting tactics were dependent upon well-conditioned, well trained mounts whose riders repeatedly defeated the U.S. Cavalry culminating in his winning the famous Treaty of 1868. He had his warriors train their mounts to be ridden equestrian style. This meant that the rider guides the horse with his knees and weight shifting, allowing both hands to be free: Such an advantage for aiming a rifle. The U.S. Cavalry clumsily tried to aim their rifles while mounted with only one arm free while the other had to guide the horse with bit and reins. No wonder Genghis Khan swept through the armies of Europe with his mounted archer cavalry letting loose a hail of arrows at close range. Hence the name, 'Mongolian style': to ride a horse with both hands free. Maybe it was the Mongolian blood within the Sioux that allowed them to readily adapt to the horse and use the Mongolian battle tactics so successfully in less than a hundred years of experience with the horse. Why the American generals could never adapt to this proven strategy is easy to understand: sheer, foolish, disastrous Eurocentric ego. Eventually the Army had to submit to the burning down of their three forts on the Bozeman Trail because of Red Cloud's leadership tactics and strategy. Sioux horse herds grew significantly under Red Cloud as did their weaponry and ammunition supply which was mostly captured from the U.S. Cavalry. This solid fact, historians are loath to admit. How else could the Sioux mount so many warriors and effectively arm them?

The signing of the Treaty was supposed to guarantee to the

Native Americans that the land west of the Missouri River to and including the Black Hills of South Dakota whose western boundaries include the state of Wyoming; North to the Cannonball river (North Dakota); and as far south to the Nebraska Sand Hills; would remain to the Sioux: for as long as the grass will grow, for as long as the rivers will flow and for as long as the Sioux dead lie buried. This meant forever to the Native American and was thus their battle won grant under Chief Red Cloud for ceasing to fight (and thoroughly beating) the U.S. Army. At this point I have to add one more battle tactic of the highly skilled chief. He had Sioux youth ride the warrior's battle mounts every day to keep them in top physical shape. Army horses were no match for such firmly conditioned Sioux mounts, many of which were captured Army horses; no doubt probably the majority of them. These horses were also well adjusted to gunfire from the many buffalo hunts they experienced (and enjoyed, no different than the energetic reaction we experience with good hunting dogs in modern day shooting of pheasant and quail.). Native mounts did not throw their riders, bolt and run at the first volleys of attack as did many of the inexperienced Army mounts. Red Cloud took an oath that he would not fight again; believing that the U.S. Government would keep their word regarding the Treaty of 1868.

Chief Sitting Bull, Hunkpapa-Teton Lakota Sioux (1831-1890)

Sitting Bull of the Teton Saones (Northern Lakota) was born 10 years later after Red Cloud. After many battles with neighboring tribes, mostly Crows, his bravery and daring led him to become chief of the Hunkpapa tribe of the seven tribe Tetons. The Oglala and Sichangu were also members of the Teton group but further south upon the Great Plains, yet teeming with buffalo. Sitting Bull was so brave, notably his specialty was to crawl daringly into enemy campsites at night trailing his own mount where the horse herds were and steal many of them if not driving the whole herd off. This feat would result in a sure death warrant, should they become discovered and/or captured by patrolling night sentries.

Among the old-time Sioux, there were two kinds of chiefs. The Nacha was a war chief who was in command of the group of warriors only when they were outside the camp on a war party. While in the camp, he was just one of the boys like anyone else. The other kind of chief was the Itanchan, or camp chief who ruled in the camp and was responsible for the welfare of the people. Sitting Bull was both kinds of chief in one. A chief, Itanchan, or camp chief, had to have a great heart. He had to be generous, always understanding, and above all spite or selfishness. He had to keep his temper always and had to constantly share with those who, he knew, could never repay him. Sitting Bull was all of this and more. He was a spiritual leader as well as a military leader. Stanley Vestal (author) said Sitting Bull was:

A man who was a peacemaker in the camps, and never quarreled. A generous man, who was always capturing horses from the enemy and giving them away, a man who constantly shared his kill with the poor and helpless when hunting, a man who could not bear to see one of the Hunkpapa Lakota unhappy. An affable, jocular, pleasant man, always making jokes and telling stories, keeping the people in a good humor, a sociable man who had tried to please everybody all his life, and was not in the least haughty or arrogant—in spite of his many honors. A man who … was devoutly religious, whose prayers were strong, and who generally got what he prayed for. Toward the end of his days, he was to write in a letter one of his convictions that he had carried all his life, '… all Native Americans pray to God for life, and try to find a good road, and do nothing wrong in their life. This is what we want, and to pray to God … who made us all.' He was known to state frequently, 'I pray to God every day.'

In the beginning, the idea of making war against the non-Native Americans and the non-Native American soldiers never entered his mind. It was only later when the military became a threat to the land he had fought to take and a threat to his people that he did turn his fighting forces against the soldiers, and this was out of sheer self-defense. It was, to his way of thinking, the only way to solve his problem of protecting his people and his country. The time would come when he would have not only his traditional Native American enemies to hold off, but strong military forces of soldiers.

General Sibley

In 1863 Sitting Bull had his first skirmish with the Army. After a Mormon cow incident wherein some Sioux killed and butchered a wandering cow belonging to some Mormons, a migrating religious sect; U.S. soldiers over retaliated by killing some Native Americans over the incident. These were Oglala and they promptly retaliated by killing the lieutenant commanding and his men. The Hunkpapa usually gave the Army troops a wide berth afterwards and fought only in self-defense. The chief ranged from northern Wyoming across northern South Dakota to the Missouri River and had been relatively free of contacts with the emigrants and military. Because of drought conditions, he had to hunt east of the Missouri in 1863. General Sibley who had put down the Dakota Sioux in the Minnesota uprising was out patrolling the same area. Sibley, without warning, opened fire on a Hunkpapa hunting party. In retaliation, Sitting Bull attacked Sibley's wagon train at Appel Creek. To show Sibley he was unafraid of him, Sitting Bull rode in within easy range of the Army rifle fire and returned with a government mule.

General Sully

In 1864, the Hunkpapa again faced the U.S. Army under General Sully who was in Wyoming attempting to run down a large group of Yanktonai and Santee Sioux fleeing Minnesota. This group attached themselves to Sitting Bull's warriors and attracted a running battle wherein the Hunkpapa had their first taste of cannon fire. They wound up having their camp, including the tipis and winter's supply of meat, destroyed. The soldiers then turned back eastward leaving the Hunkpapa the task of working extra hard to get in a new supply of meat, clothing and make new tipis for the coming winter.

The following year, Sitting Bull made General Sully pay dearly by chasing him all the way across Wyoming, this time westward from the Little Missouri River crossing clear to the Yellowstone River. Sully lost hundreds of horses and mules due to the extreme drought and grasshoppers destroying the grass at the time. It came out later that the soldiers had thought that none of them would survive the hunger, thirst and attacking Sioux. They barely survived by reaching the Yellowstone River where steamboat supplies saved them. Sitting Bull broke off his attack and went home feeling some retaliation against Sully for destroying his tipis the year before.

Sitting Bull's skeptical; wait-and-see attitude after the Laramie treaty in 1868 was fully justified only four years later. In 1872 Colonel O.S. Stanley commanded a military escort for a surveying party of the Northern Pacific Railroad. The survey placed the railroad on the south bank of the Yellowstone River, in clear violation of the Laramie Treaty. Stanley promptly had a run-in with Chief Gall and his warriors, and when word of this reached Sitting Bull at his camp on the Powder River, he immediately rode out with a large party of his Hunkpapa, accompanied by Oglala, Minicoujou, Sans Arc, and Blackfeet Sioux warriors. He tangled with Major E.M. Baker and his four hundred men in the valley of the Yellowstone below Pryor Creek on August 14,

1872. Losses were relatively light on both sides, but Sitting Bull had made his point that no one was to come into his territory without being hit.

The most notable feature of this battle occurred when Sitting Bull got off his horse, gathered together his war pipe and smoking equipment, and calmly walked up to within easy rifle range of the soldiers. Here he sat down, lit his pipe, and smoked the tobacco all the way down to the bottom of the pipe, with the bullets of the soldiers whizzing past his ears and kicking up dust all around him. When he had finished, he quietly cleaned the pipe, put it back into its bag, and sauntered back to his own lines. Having shown his lack of fear of the soldiers, he called his men together and went home.

Lt. Colonel Custer

The years of 1873 and 1874 were relatively quiet, as far as fighting was concerned, but Sitting Bull was busy, hunting and supplying food for his people. He kept a wary eye toward the east, however, because he still had his wait-and-see attitude. Again, his suspicions were justified when Lt. Col. George Custer led a force of over 1,100 men and 110 wagons to explore the Black Hills in 1874. This was in clear violation of all the treaties and resulted in large numbers of non-Native Americans filtering into the Black Hills area - many of them lured there by the reports of gold that Custer had brought out. Sitting Bull knew that the non-Native Americans were closing in around him and that a showdown would have to be coming soon.

The Unrealistic Order

The next year, 1875, found Sitting Bull and his people in their winter camp at the mouth of the Powder River. He and his Hunkpapa had camped here for years during the winter, but further treaty modifications had placed the western boundaries of Native American Territory just east of the Black Hills which is now in Western South Dakota. For this reason, Sitting Bull and his people, in the eyes of the military, were off reservation boundaries and were, therefore, 'hostile'. The government had long been annoyed that the various tribes would wander off reservation boundaries in order to hunt. On the basis of a report filed with the Commissioner of Native American Affairs by a U.S. Native American Inspector named E.C. Watkins, in the fall of that very year, November 1875, the Secretary of the Interior issued an order that all the bands had to return to their respective reservations by the end of January 31, 1876 or the Army would come after them.

This was an unrealistic order. No one including the Army could move during that very brutal winter. Most bands never received the message because no one dared travel or rather could not travel once the winter snows came fiercely in December and way into March. General Crook attempted to march his troops out of Ft. Laramie in that month and barely made it back by eating his mules and horses let alone receiving a severe mauling from Crazy Horse and Cheyenne allies.

Sitting Bull's Little Big Horn Battle Dream

Sitting Bull had been far to the north of the Oglala and Sichangu during the heavy fighting in the 1860s. He would stay out of the '60s era conflicts in the southern Dakota Territory and North Platte/Powder River battles but he would be as mentioned, fighting his own with the Army, first General Sibley and then General Sully. It would be after the signing of the Treaty of 1868 and the breaking of that treaty's agreements that the northern Tetons, Hunkpapa and Minicoujou mainly, would rise up with the southern Oglala and Sichangu. Sitting Bull's spirituality is highly exemplary; he prayed almost daily and had powerful prophetic dreams. About a week before the famous Little Big Horn battle, at the huge encampment where the attack would soon take place, Sitting Bull had a powerful dream of soldiers falling into the camp upside down. This vision predicted that enemy soldiers would come and be defeated as the dream symbolized by having them fall upside down. The Battle of the Little Big Horn was fought. Sitting Bull's powerful dream, the prediction, was quite accurate. After that battle, Sitting Bull and many of his Hunkpapa finally ended up in Canada in 1877, but they were very unhappy there. The Canadian Mounted Police (the red coats) watched them too closely and, in 1881, after four years there, Sitting Bull decided to return to his reservation. He became a friend of Buffalo Bill Cody and even joined his Wild West show that toured the East for a period of time.

Chief Crazy Horse, Oglala-Teton Lakota (early 1840s)

Twenty years (approximately) after Red Cloud's birth, Crazy Horse, also an Oglala would be born. Crazy Horse was renowned for isolating himself in Creator's Nature for days and nights. I would assume that Crazy Horse was Vision Questing to Creator. He shunned publicity or the public limelight despite his fame and military prowess. Hence, no photographs exist of him unlike Chief Red Cloud and Sitting Bull. During the '60s era fighting with the Army, Crazy Horse would be a young warrior under Red Cloud's command. He counted over eighty coups during the earlier era of tribal combat. His rise to acclamation as one of the greatest of warriors was culminated with his victories in his last three battles with the Army during the spring and summer of 1876. A coup can be described as one committing a brave deed or action during the heat of battle. Often, a coup would be an act of extreme bravery as in reaching out and touching an enemy and not killing him.

The Battle of the Little Big Horn in what is now the state of Montana is regarded as the greatest battle of the Sioux. Several thousand warriors fought back against a foolish attack by an egocentric George Armstrong Custer, commander of less than 700 soldiers and Crow Native American scouts. Many historians believe he had his sights set on the Presidency of the United States. By 'Riding through the Sioux Nation' which he occasionally proclaimed, he thought such an act would send him through politics to eventual Commander in Chief of the Nation.

Military intelligence predicted that a large gathering of the Sioux would take place during the late spring/early summer of 1876 in the Big Horn plateau country where the last of the once enormous buffalo herds were still ranging. This area is to the east of the Rocky Mountain range and referred to as the Big Horns. Three military forces were dispatched to encircle the encampment, attack and force the surviving Native Americans back onto their reservations, mostly in the States of North and South Dakota. General Crooks would set out from Ft. Laramie with approximately 1,440 cavalry mounted soldiers and Crow scouts. General Terry and Custer would come from a fort in what would become North Dakota and Colonel Gibbon would come down from a fort farther west in what would eventually be Montana. This was called the Three Pronged Attack strategy.

Tongue River Battle

This battle was far more 'famous' in my opinion because it displayed the superior fighting ability of the Sioux. Less than half as many warriors easily defeated the advancing forces of the White Man. Just over a week before the Custer battle, General Crook was advancing northward toward the Big Horn Mountain range. Sioux scouts reported he had a contingent in excess of a thousand men including Crow Native American scouts advancing upon the large Sioux encampment along the Little Big Horn River which was also bolstered by their allies the Northern Cheyenne and the Arapaho. U.S. Army records list Crook's forces at 1,440. Chief Crazy Horse was selected to stop the invading force, and he picked less than 700 younger warriors, blatantly avoiding over a thousand of the older, more experienced ones. Before he left, Chief Sitting Bull approached him to chastise his selection. 'Why are you picking such few warriors, less than half than the approaching enemy and leaving out most of the veterans?'

According to the warriors whom Dr. Bryde interviewed in Lakota when he was a young Jesuit priest, they told him that Crazy Horse laughed and picked up a Winchester rifle. 'I pick young men because they do as I tell them!' He aimed the weapon and pretended that he was mounted on a horse. 'I do not like to waste men. Why should I take too many and have their women crying after the battle? I will stop him,' he remarked confidently. 'You will see.' Which he did! In less than two days of his encounter with Crook, the General's badly mauled forces were sent fleeing back to Ft. Laramie. Even the Army's records admit this defeat.

Note: Crazy Horse's preference for young warriors was also because most were yet unmarried as it was Sioux custom that a man would not marry until well after he had been a proven warrior and a meat providing hunter. Usually it would not be until a man was in his thirties before he would marry and begin to raise offspring.

Battle of the Little Big Horn

About a week later after the Tongue Battle which is also termed, 'Battle of the Rosebud,' Lieutenant Colonel George Armstrong Custer foolishly neglected to utilize reconnaissance when he set out with his 650 mounted men along with pack handlers and Crow scouts. Fearing that General Crook was in the area and would reach the Sioux encampment ahead of him and steal his imagined glory, he hurriedly marched his troops on tiring horses. The night before the battle he marched all night which would spell doom for later chance to escape. All in all, approximately almost two thirds of his command would be lost.

After sighting a portion of the huge Sioux encampment, Custer split his forces sending Major Reno and Captain Benteen toward the river in separate forces. Major Reno would attack from crossing the river. Custer would attack the opposite end of an encampment much larger than they could imagine and teeming with warriors within quick reach of loaded rifles. These rifles, when not carried, were always within easy reach from rifle racks outside each tent made from a pair of supporting twigs holding a cross branch for the standing rifles; Winchesters and the single shot '45-70'. As he approached, the encampment remained mostly hidden by the rolling bluffs until he came over the last crest when it was too late to make a wise retreat for later arriving forces. Likewise at the same timing, Custer had waved to Reno to begin his charge across the river. Reno was also blinded by the sloping and shielding view of the opposite river bank his horses would have to ride over. As soon as the Native Americans reacted to the short lived attack, the immensity of tremendous Sioux, Arapaho and Cheyenne fire power would bring such a foolish move to an abrupt end. The battle was quickly over. Custer was one of the last to die with his men behind a hasty makeshift barricade of dispatched horses. Most reports state that he received two gunshot wounds, either of which could prove fatal. Despite his ignorance and many flaws; both character wise and military deficient, he is buried in the U.S. Army cemetery at West Point Military Academy near the Hudson River, New York.

Dr. John Bryde

Bryde was a former Jesuit priest who could speak fluent Lakota Sioux. My mother spoke the language fluently as did my father. Both grew up speaking Lakota. She stated that he spoke the language well after conversing with him. For over 15 years Bryde interviewed the last of the remaining warriors mostly from the Oglala reservation where I was born. These men, mostly in their eighties and nineties were anxious to talk to a White Man who spoke their language. According to Bryde, they had the unusual ability to reflect back upon their past with clarity and would not speak of battlefield events unless they had a fellow 'verifier' to add to the accuracy of their recollections. The Sioux lifestyle provided a healthy environment indeed compared to our present modern day living. Bryde stated that the mind debilitating diseases of Arthritis, Parkinson's and Alzheimer's were rare among the old time warriors.

The Time it Takes to Eat a Meal

The Battle of the Little Big Horn was over within less than an hour; closer to a half hour if Dr. Bryde's combat experienced Sioux interviewees were listened to. 'In less than the time it takes for a man to eat a meal,' is the way they described its duration. Most 'Custer Battle' books, they are numerous; both non-fiction and fiction have the battle advancing into flanking movements and time consuming battle strategy, all obviously made up by the authors of course; primarily for Hollywood fomented enter-tainment is my suspicion and hence – selling of the books. Two Sioux Native American authors have also joined those ranks. One is a non-fiction writer and the other more popular, a fiction writer and both quite patterned after the most notorious error filled story teller of them all - Maria Sandoz. In my historical non-fiction book, *Crazy Horse and Chief Red Cloud*, I quote Author Larry McMurtry eight times who points out Sandoz' writing deficiency. I honor and respect McMurtry's writings. He criticizes other writers as well for not bothering to quote from the only sources surviving to truly and reliably report the main portion of the battle. These sources were the Native Americans who were there! He no doubt would criticize just as severely the two Sioux Native American writers as well.

Black Elk

Black Elk (born 1863) was a powerful visionary who outlived all of the leaders mentioned above. He remained basically unknown throughout his life time, except among his own people where he was regarded as a powerful healer. His healing abilities took place while the Sioux were in containment on the reservations after the turn of the century. In just one lifetime, these leaders were upon the planet at the same time period. It is needless to doubt that the Natural Way produced equivalent selflessness from other leaders before them who were elected and led selflessly. Such contrast, their exemplary contact compared to the greedy selfishness that modern elected officials now display. Simply look at the list of benefits the American Congress has provided for itself compared to the laws they have cast upon the populace. This was said earlier but the gravity of the lack of true leadership in America and the majority of other countries as well make it well worth repeating. It seems that the White Man's religion has not produced comparable leaders - has it?

Congressional Reform Act of 2012

1. No Tenure/No Pension. A Congressman/woman collects a salary while in office and receives no pay when they're out of office.
2. Congress participates in Social Security. All funds in the Congressional retirement fund move to the Social Security system immediately. All future funds flow into the Social Security system, and Congress participates with the American people. It may not be used for any other purpose.
3. Congress can purchase their own retirement plan, just as all Americans do.
4. Congress will no longer vote themselves a pay raise. Congressional pay will rise by the lower of CPI or 3%.
5. Congress loses their current health care system and partic- ipates in the same health care system as the American people.
6. Congress must equally abide by all laws they impose on the American people.

7. All contracts with past and present Congressmen/women are void effective 12/31/12. The American people did not make this contract with Congressmen/women.

Serving in any political office is an honor, not a career. Envisioned were citizen elected legislators. They should serve their term(s) for the greater good of their people, then go home and back to work.

The Example

Genghis Khan's empire connected and amalgamated the many civilizations around him. At the time of his birth in 1162, the Old World consisted of a series of regional civilizations. As he smashed the feudal system of aristocratic privilege and birth, he built a new and unique system based on individual merit, loyalty and achievement. His was not an empire that hoarded wealth and treasure; instead, he widely distributed the goods acquired so that they could make their way back into commercial circulation. He created an international law and recognized the ultimate supreme law of the Eternal Blue Sky (his concept of a Higher Power) over all people.

At a time when most rulers considered themselves above the law, Genghis Khan insisted on laws holding rulers as equally accountable as the lowest herder. He granted religious freedom within his realms though he demanded total loyalty from conquered subjects of all religions. He insisted on the rule of law and unlike our country under the Bush/Cheney regime, he abolished torture, but he mounted major campaigns to seek out and kill raiding bandits and terrorist assassins. Why do I quote such a leader from the past that European writers vilify?

Simple, the 'warrior veterans' were at the battles and not behind an academic desk at some University composing highly inaccurate John Wayne entertainment. Need I say more? Genghis Khan was a leader that changed the world far more positively than negatively. Such a leader needs to rise up again in this perilous time in which we are all living and suffering now! Impossible? You might be right. I guess that we all will have to suffer the consequences then. Possibly, America will erupt. The new communication can be powerful. In time a new form of democracy will have to happen. Economics, population increase and the environment will demand needed change. At least some will have clear minds when we reach the Spirit World. What did you do?' (Or did not do?) We will be asked. 'Why did you lack observation? Why did you lack courage?

Chapter 9

Black Elk's Vision

In December. 2004, an earthquake struck off Indonesia's Sumatra Island and triggered a devastating tidal wave that cost 230,000 lives. 131,000 lives were lost in Aceh Province alone. The outer island people, those who were first exposed to the deadly onslaught, were mostly not members of Organized Religion. The island folk were Nature based in their beliefs and readily noticed the unusual actions of the birds and other animals that took to the high ground immediately when the earthquake happened. The outer Island people reacted to Nature's warnings and survived. Thousands of Organized Religion's adherents did not.

The Vision

We have experienced some powerful Natural Way ceremonies and now know the history of the people who kept their Natural Ways alive, even to this day. Now let us explore a powerful happening that is most revealing of the words 'Spiritual Imagery.' Bill Moyers, noted American interviewer of those exploring the various realms of life experiences, philosophies and championing environmental causes, interviewed William Campbell who explored worldwide the various tribes and Indigenous who still follow their Natural Way. Moyers asked Campbell, 'You speak of Spiritual Imagery often. What is the best example, in your opinion of it?' Without hesitation, Campbell replied, 'Black Elk Speaks!' (*Black Elk Speaks* authored by John Neihardt, published in 1934.)

Religious Prophet

Do Native Americans have religious prophets? I would consider the Oglala named Black Elk as more of a visionary than as a prophet upon which the White Man, both the Christian and the Islamic, seem to place a greater reliance. Native Americans I have known, mostly Sioux, shy away from all-knowing prophecy because they truthfully admit that when dealing with Mystery there are simply too many unknowns. I say that, not looking for argument. It is simply the way and how we have observed upon our own life journeys. It is all that we can offer; what we have experienced and are too respectful, even now, to try and embellish and change its direction.

1873 or 1874

It is now the 1800s, around 1873, 1874. Having migrated westward from close to the Atlantic Ocean, the Sioux Native Americans entered the vast grasslands of the Great Plains and now followed the buffalo and often the buffalo followed a great circle of their own. A river coursing through the eastern plateau of the Big Horn Mountains' country, just east of the higher Rocky Mountain Range, the Greasy Grass wandered and meandered, bound and obedient to Creator's gravity, silently flowing its powerful course eventually toward the Yellowstone, the Missouri, the Mississippi River and hence to the sea. But a few years later a great battle by two-legged (human) would be fought by those who respected the teeming herds which grazed its meadows and those two-legged in blue who did not. Newspapers would soon make this river as historically immortal as Bastogne, Kasserine Pass, Guadalcanal and the Chosen Reservoir, terming it – the Little Big Horn River. The Battle of the Little Big Horn would soon echo worldwide. But for the moment, the winter counts would term the slow paced river as the Greasy Grass. A young boy named Black Elk, a Teton Oglala, had a powerful vision here on its banks as would a great chief named Sitting Bull, but a few years later. His vision, Sitting Bull's, however was for the moment; the men in blue would be falling, helplessly head first, down, into a great Sioux, Cheyenne and

Arapaho camp and they would be swallowed up. Considering these two visions that happened there, maybe this Greasy Grass like Bear Butte Mountain or the Pipestone Quarries is a special place for those who quest. I would have to consider the boy's vision as the more profound however. Maybe one could claim that it held more of a world view. For Sitting Bull, his vision or dream soon bore truth. The soldiers did 'fall' fatally for them, into the Sioux camp. In 1876, Colonel Custer lost his entire immediate command when he foolishly attacked the large, well armed Sioux encampment supported also by Cheyenne and Arapaho warriors. Black Elk's vision is indeed puzzling, yet thanks to Neihardt's book, millions have become aware of what the boy experienced, after he journeyed into a strange Spirit World. The boy was innocent and it would have been difficult for him to make up such a vivid portrayal. His lifelong actions following this great event insured this vision as surely as the river's journey would end at the sea.

This event occurred several years before the famous Custer (Little Big Horn) battle, no doubt in the very camp of Oglalas, the Wahshasha Lakota Band (Oglalas) under Chief Crazy Horse's command. It was a time when the tribe enjoyed the freedom of the Great Plains. The boy named Black Elk was a young boy when he had such an open, understandable vision as it pertained to all of Creator's Nature which surrounds us. It began with the Wamaskaskan, the animal creations, finned, flying and four-legged, all in a myriad of gracious display. Yes, whatever was responsible for such a powerful vision did include the Wamaskaskan (the Animal Brothers and Sisters). His vision took him into a Rainbow Covered Lodge of the Six Powers of the World.

The Vision

Two spirit men carried this young boy upward to the spirit world. On a cloudy plain, thunder beings leaped and flashed. A bay horse appeared and spoke: 'Behold me!' Twelve black horses appeared showing manes of lightning and nostrils that rumbled thunder. The bay horse wheeled to the white north and there Black Elk saw twelve white horses abreast. Their manes flowed like a blizzard wind and their noses roared. White geese soared around these horses. The bay wheeled to the east and there, twelve sorrels (red horses) appeared abreast. Their eyes glimmered like the day-break star and their manes were like the red dawn of morning. The bay wheeled to the south and there, twelve buckskins (yellow horses) stood abreast bearing horns and manes like living trees and grasses. The horses went into formation behind the bay horse. The bay spoke to Black Elk: 'See how your horses all come dancing!' A whole sky full of horses danced and pranced around him. Black Elk walked with the bay and the formation of horses marching four abreast in ranks. He looked at the sky full of horses and watched them change to other animals and winged. These fowl and four leggeds then fled back to the four quarters of the world from where the horses had come. He walked on toward a cloud that changed into a teepee with a rainbow for an open door. Within, he saw six old men sitting in a row. He was invited to go into the rainbow door lodge and told not be fearful.

He went in and stood before the six old men and discovered that they were not old men but were the Six Powers of the World. Of the powers, the West Power, Wiyopeyata, spoke first. When the West Power spoke of understanding, the rainbow leaped with flames of many colors over Black Elk. The West Power gave him a wooden cup filled with water and spoke. 'Take this, it is the power to make live.' The West Power gave him a bow and spoke. 'Take this, it is the power to destroy.' The West Power then left and changed to a black horse but the horse was gaunt and sick. The second power, Waziya, the Power of the White North, rose and instructed Black Elk to take a healing herb to the black horse. The horse was healed and grew fatter to come back prancing. The horse changed back to Wiyopeyata and took his place in the council.

The North Power spoke again. 'Take courage, younger brother,' he said, 'on earth a nation you shall make live, for yours shall be the power of the white giant's wing, the cleansing wind.' When the North Power went running to the north, he became a white goose wheeling. Black Elk looked around and saw that the horses to the west were thunders and the horses to the north were geese. The third power, the East Power, Wiyoheyapata, spoke. 'Take courage, younger brother,' he said, 'for across the earth they shall take you.' Wiyoheyapata pointed to two men flying beneath the daybreak star. 'From them you shall have power,' he said, 'from them who have awakened all the beings of the earth with roots and legs and wings.' The East Power gave Black Elk a peace pipe that bore a spotted eagle. 'With this pipe,' the power said, 'you shall walk upon the earth, and whatever sickens there you shall make well.' A bright red man appeared standing for good and plenty. The red man rolled and turned into a buffalo. The buffalo joined the sorrel horses of the east. These horses then changed into fat buffalo. The fourth power to speak to Black Elk was the yellow South Power—Itokaga, the power to grow. 'Younger brother,' he said, 'with the powers of the four quarters you shall walk, a relative. Behold, the living center of a nation I shall give you and with it many you shall save.' In Itokaga's hand, the power held a bright stick that sprouted and sent forth branches. Leaves came out and murmured and birds sang in the leaves. Beneath the leafy stick, in the shade, Black Elk saw the circled villages of people and every living thing with roots or legs or wings, and all were happy. 'It shall stand in the center of the nation's circle,' Itokaga said, 'a cane to walk with and a people's heart; and by your powers you shall make it blossom.' Then when he had been still a little while to hear the birds sing, he spoke again. 'Behold the earth!' Black Elk looked down and saw the earth and in the center bloomed the holy stick that was a tree, and where it stood two roads crossed, a red one and a black one. 'From where the giant lives (the north) to where you always face (the south) the red road goes, the road of good,' the South Power said, 'and on it shall your nation walk. The black road goes from where the thunder beings live (the west) to where the sun continually shines (the east), a fearful road, a road of troubles and of war. On this also you shall walk, and from it you shall have the power to destroy a people's foes. In four ascents you shall walk the earth with power.' Black Elk thought that an ascent was a generation and that he was seeing the third ascent (generation) when he revealed his vision in the fourth decade (1930 to 1940) of the twentieth century. Itokaga rose and stood with the buckskin horses (yellow horses) at the end of his words. The South Power became an elk and the buckskin horses changed to elks. The fifth power, the Sky Spirit, which was the oldest of the Six Powers, was the next to speak. Makpiyah Ate, Father Sky, became a spotted eagle hovering. 'Behold,' he said, 'all the things of the air shall come to you, and they and the winds and the stars shall be like relatives. You shall go across the earth with my power.' The sixth power, the Earth Spirit spoke, 'My boy, have courage, for my power shall be yours, and you shall need it, for your nation on the earth will have great troubles. Come.' The Earth Power rose and went out through the rainbow door. Black Elk followed, finding himself on the bay horse that had appeared at the beginning of his vision. The bay faced the black horses of the west, and a voice said: 'They have given you the cup of water to make live the greening day, and also the bow and arrow to destroy.' The bay faced the sorrels of the east, and a voice said: 'they have given you the sacred pipe and the power that is peace, and the good red day.' The bay faced the buckskins of the south, and a voice said: 'They have given you the sacred stick and your nation's hoop, and the yellow day; and in the center of the hoop you shall set the stick and make it grow into a shielding tree, and bloom.' All of the horses now had riders and stood behind Black

Elk, and a voice said: 'Now you shall walk the black road with these; and as you walk, all the nations that have roots or legs or wings shall fear you.'

Black Elk rode east, down the fearful road and behind him came the horsebacks (horses with riders). He came upon a place where three streams made a river and something terrible was there. In the flames rising from the waters a blue man lived. Dust floated all about him, the grass was short and withered, trees were wilting, two legged and four-legged beings were thin and panting and the winged were too weak to fly. The black horse riders shouted 'Hokahey!' and charged down to attack and kill the Blue Man but were driven back. The white troop riders shouted 'hokahey!' and charged down but were driven back; then the red troop and the yellow. When each failed they called to Black Elk. Black Elk's bow changed to a spear and he charged on the Blue Man. His spear head became lightning. It stabbed the Blue Man's heart and killed him. The trees and grasses were no longer withered and every being cried in gladness. Black Elk thought that it was drought that he had killed with the power that had been given to him. At the time that he related the vision, he was probably unaware of the great environmental dilemma that the Blue Man was symbolizing.

John Neihardt

Black Elk intended that the world should know of his vision. Several writers had earlier attempted to secure Black Elk's story but he was not satisfied with them. When John Neihardt came to his cabin, he told Neihardt that he was the one he was waiting for. 'Where have you been? You should have been here earlier.' It was in the fall. Black Elk said that it was too late that year to relate his vision. 'You come back when the grass is so high,' the holy man held out his hand to indicate the height of spring grass, 'and I will tell you my story.'

Ben Black Elk interpreted between Neihardt and the holy

man, who the missionaries would later give the name, Nicholas Black Elk. Ben was well satisfied with the finished writing, Black Elk Speaks. His satisfaction should dispel the false accusations which have been heaped on John Neihardt as self composing. Here we have the interpreter being very satisfied. Wouldn't one who had ordinary common sense and a bit of intelligence easily discern that a son is generally, usually going to know which are his father's words and which are those of someone else? Especially when he interpreted a long conversation both ways - in English and Lakota! Ben always spoke glowingly of the finished work as, 'My Father's book!' I personally knew Ben, beginning as a child. He gave me my child's name, 'Wanblee Hokeshilah – Eagle Boy'. Later he was instrumental in changing my name to Wanblee Wichasha - Eagle Man, after I returned from war in Vietnam and was in the sun dance when my name was changed. The book was published in 1932, but at that time there existed so much prejudice and ignorance that it went into remainder and copies were sold for 45 cents apiece. It wasn't until thirty years later that the importance of such a profound vision would be rediscovered, thanks to the interest of Carl Jung and Dick Cavett. The book has now sold well over a million copies and has been printed in many languages, including Japanese. But now it has been severely altered as mentioned earlier.

With Our Own Kind

The reservation missionaries made a strong attempt to dislodge Black Elk's vision and were almost successful. Why? All that I can surmise on their behalf is that it intruded on their belief system as this writing will be judged. It was also quite convincing if one would rely on direct observance of what surrounded us all. Many Sioux know little about it, or they believe the detracting dogma perpetuated against it. That is their loss; my opinion. I harbor little remorse for those who deny direct observation. It is the choice they made while on their Earth journey; a foolish choice; my opinion. Hopefully, there exists a Spirit World in which we can be with our own kind. That categorization, also hopefully, will not be a separation by race or worldly accomplishment, but one of how well we utilized our mind while here upon this journey. How much did we place into this greatest of gifts which Benevolent Creator has designed specifically just for us? Courage, bravery, generosity and sharing - the four cardinal virtues of the Sioux may also have their importance toward our final destination. I deeply hope that when one enters the Spirit World, one will be able to go or be placed with one's own kind. 'According to your truths!' This could be the real 'Heaven or Hell' most of us wonder or ponder about, if we are at all truthful. We will seriously elaborate upon this theme in a later chapter. There are many from all walks who are taking a serious look at this vision. Joseph Campbell's remark that this vision is the best example of spiritual imagery is very appropriate. There are many people who have discovered the visible Six Powers of this earth and who are now relating these daily entities in balance, acknowledgement and kinship to their everyday lifestyle. Black Elk lived at a time when Chief Crazy Horse, Chief Red Cloud and Chief Sitting Bull were alive and in power. As I said earlier, I believe that these three leaders we have studied were spiritually respectful men who believed that it was the Six Powers (Shakopeh Ouyea) who regulated the known world to the Sioux under the laws, actions and powers of the Creator, Wakan Tanka, as those leaders understood it.

The Six Powers: There are many of you who will want a greater depth to explore regarding this powerful happening; this Spiritual Imagery; so I will continue with it. West Power. We acknowledge the life-giving rains as the power to make live. The thunder and the lightning are the power to destroy. As the sun goes down in the west, darkness comes to the land. The color for the west is black. The spirits who enter ceremony appreciate less distraction in the darkness when two leggeds seek to communicate with them, therefore the spirit beseeching ceremonies are usually held when the west power has allowed darkness to come forth. The spirit world is associated with the west power in this regard but is not confined to a direction.

North Power. We think of endurance, cleanliness, truth, rest, politeness and strength as associated with the North. The cold north has Mother Earth rest beneath the white mantle of snow. She sleeps and gathers up her strength for the bounty of springtime. When the snows melt, the earth is made clean. When native people wintered over, often confined to a small area for a lengthy time while they waited for the spring thaw, they learned to be extremely polite, to be truthful and honest with each other. They kept clean by using the sweat lodge to take winter baths and to beseech to the spirit world. The power of the cold white north taught them to endure. The cleansing white wing within Black Elk's great vision emphasizes endurance and cleanliness. East Power. The third power brought him the red pipe of peace. Peace begins with knowledge. To have peace, one must first become aware of knowledge, which comes forth out of the red dawn, the east, with each new day. When you have knowledge and it is discussed and considered, it can become wisdom. Others share their thoughts, their observations and their needs. A widow can add much wisdom to a council that is deciding to make a war, or planning to send out a war party. She can tell of the loneliness of the children and her own grief when they learned that their father and her husband were slain on the last war party. When lands are to be taken from a people by financiers or politicians the people's voices should be heard. Communication and knowledge of what is happening can lead to the wise decision that the people's interest must be seriously considered and they must be adequately compensated, or the project may be halted. Especially when sabers rattle and threats are being made, wisdom can lead to understanding and understanding can bring peace to the land. The pipe of peace and the red dawn that brings new experience each day is symbolic of knowledge, wisdom and communication coming together in this day and age.

This is the beginning of the age of communication. We have seen great progress from communication that allows new knowledge to come into people's lives. The red dawn rises to bring a bright new day in which we can add knowledge to our lives on a daily basis as long as we walk this planet. Now we have modern communication that is allowed by the mystery of the radio waves, the television waves and other mysterious gifts. These created and allowed forces, put here for our use, give us optimism that our planet can be saved from past practices of destruction. We have no choice. We have seen in Rawanda and the 'ethnic purity' cleansing of Bosnia what can happen when humans refuse to communicate.

South Power. Medicine from roots, stems, herbs and fruits are associated with the south power. Today, many species are beginning to disappear and these medicines can soon be lost. The sun rises higher and higher as the South Power advances with summer. Eventually plants such as corn and wheat will bring forth yellow or golden kernels that will sustain much life through the long winter. Abundance is the primary gift from this power, for it makes all things grow and we are allowed to take that which grows. During the summer buffalo fattened on endless grasses. During the heat of summer, buffalo hunts provided meat to cure in the hot, blowing wind for long winters. During this time of plenty, dances and gatherings of thanksgiving would happen. To be thankful for what you receive adds strength to your search for sustenance, provisions and shelter. Sky Power. Father Sky spoke and said the things of the air would be with Black Elk to help him in his struggle. He warned that a time would come when the Earth Mother would become very sick but the 'things of the air' would be there to help her. Could these 'things of the air' also be the open space of communication which now can transcend across the globe? Can it also be the satellites—'things of the air,' beaming back video and radio waves so we may see and talk directly across the skies? Communication is a powerful tool to bring understanding and prevent costly, wasteful and polluting wars. If so, Truth will be more difficult to distort. Now we have modern communication that is allowed by the mystery of the radio waves, the television waves and other mysterious gifts. No doubt there are new mysterious waves yet to be discovered. The computer stores vast information and transmits volumes in an eye wink. None of this could so perform were it not allowed by a Powerful Vastness! These communicative forces, created for our use, foster optimism that our planet can be saved from past practices of destruction. I perceive that what the Sky Power said could be closely associated with the advance of more communicative people upon the earth because the things of the air are helping to promote peace and harmony. Distortion, lies, falsehoods mainly over greed can be combated with immediate, exposing communication. It is happening right before us. Earth Power. Mother Earth, the Sixth Power, spoke and took Black Elk to the danger that was confronting the earth. This danger was the Blue Man of greed and deception that was already harming the living things. This Blue Man symbolizes the corruption, insensitivity, greed and ignorance upon the Earth. The Blue Man would wreak great destruction using lies and untruths and would have to be addressed or else all creatures including two leggeds would perish. Untruth is the Blue Man. In America, every day we observe much deception by those who lobby our political leaders in Washington with disregard for the environment and the ongoing dilemma. As the situation worsens, more eyes will be opened and eventually the old ways of real Truth will have to be accepted in order to finally destroy the Blue Man. Hopefully, it will be in time for the planet to have a chance to regain the old harmony. Two leggeds will discover that there is no other choice. Religious fundamentalists will no doubt keep on praying and waiting for miracles but the realistic and workable solution will be to return to the values that actually worked. The ozone layer and the population spiral will not wait for miraculous curing. Some tragic consequences will be learned along the way.

They all were mounted on horses. Black Elk himself sat upon a horse and carrying the bow gifted to him by the West Power. Down below three rivers flowed toward each other. Where they met a man stood in the confluence of waters that grew foul and putrid. Fish were dying and floating in deathly form. Water birds suffocated as they flew through the putrid haze. This danger was the Blue Man of greed and deception that was already harming the living things in more ways than just drought which the rains could cure as always, down through time. This Blue Man symbolized the corruption, insensitivity, greed and ignorance which are now upon the Earth. The Blue Man would wreak great destruction using lies and untruths and would have to be addressed or else all creatures including two leggeds would perish: Perish through their greed and over consumption. 'Come,' cried Mother Earth. 'We must charge this Blue Man! Hokahey!' With that call, the Six Powers flew down upon their mounts and attacked the Blue Man but he beat them back. After a furious battle they stood panting. They called up to Black Elk, exhorting him to join in the fray. His bow turned into a spear giving him confidence. The bay horse beneath him reared and snorted fire. Horse and rider charged down and killed the Blue Man with the spear.

The Blue Man. The Six Powers attacked the Blue Man but were beaten back. They called on Black Elk for his help, which was the knowledge he had received and had the power to communicate, now that he had learned of the Six Powers. His bow changed to a spear and when he attacked, he killed the Blue Man. The Six Powers demonstrated the need for two leggeds to destroy the corruption, lies and greed of humankind which in turn is destroying our environment. His bow changing to a spear and thus giving him the ability to destroy the Blue Man, I interpret as symbolic that he now had new knowledge and it was a very powerful knowledge, which enabled him to kill the Blue Man who was causing unnatural and chaotic suffering and destruction. Is it the Natural Knowledge from his vision that is really the spear which can save the world environmentally and give it a more peaceful perspective, free from war-fomenting greed and wasteful detraction which is not working? By learning to be peaceful, two leggeds can devote their energy to the environment.

Interpretation

Everyone is free to their own interpretations, even Raymond DeMallie's, whom the Neihardt foundation's new Director, Coralie Neihardt, has now designated to add his narrations within the very pages of the new re-printing of the book after the death of her Mother, Hilda Neihardt: such an sacrilegious insult to the Spirituality of the Lakota Sioux People who revere the Great Vision. My interpretation vastly differs from Professor Raymond DeMallie. DeMallie has never Sun Danced, never Vision Quested, never conducted a Sweat Lodge, never visualized a Yuwipi Ceremony nor personally knew the real narrator of Black Elk Speaks - Ben Black Elk as I have known since I was a child and participated within the aforementioned mind and culture expanding ceremonies. What belief system is DeMallie? I highly doubt that he follows or champions the Way of the Traditional Lakota! DeMallie was also severely criticized by Hilda Neihardt before me and her son Robin, one day when I paid her a friendly visit in Nebraska. Thankfully I believe in a Spirit World where all Truth shall reign and we all will be called 'upon the carpet' so to speak for the ignorant and wrongful actions we have imposed on others. In this case it is a serious insult upon an entire nation - the Lakota people. It is also long overdue that the Neihardt Trust compensates the descendants of Black Elk and Ben Black Elk's descendants in particular. Yes, long overdue for a book that could never have been printed without the words of Old Black Elk, translated by Ben Black Elk which hence reaped thousands of dollars in royalties. This is typical greed employed in America against Native American people.

The Six Powers are quite observable but yet it is almost impossible for Dominant Society folks including their converted Native Americans to understand them. This is merely my perspective and we shall wait and watch how the succession of new political administrations worldwide shall deal with the Blue Men that surround them daily. I expect little from them and I hope that they prove me wrong. I have more faith in the people rising up with a renewed spiritual imagery and consequently destroying the Blue Man, along with the corrupt politicians and their supporters. Organized Religion will never admit that too often, it was their backing and support that has allowed too many Blue Men to rise to such control and power. Organized Religion supported more than one decadent dictator such as Francisco Franco of Spain. In time, if Real Truth does not come from humankind, Mother Earth will act. Nature based people assume that Creator has endowed Mother Earth, the Sixth Power, with far more corrective power to survive than that which mere two-leggeds can employ. Real Truth will return one way or the other when Mother Nature severely reacts. It is possible, that supreme suffering occasioned by the 'Four (Nature-based) Horses of the Apocalypse' will finally bring humans to a true reckoning of their situation and hence, dramatic change, politically, socially and even religion-wise! These Four forces are beginning now, though an inadequate few are recognizing them. They are: Heating of the Planet, Water Shortage, Gone Resources and Too Many (Over Population): quite possibly we should add - Uncontrolled Water as well (floods, wasted water)!

Note: Had America not wasted her resources on the Vietnam, Iraq and Afghanistan wars and instead built a massive pipeline/aqueduct from the Minnesota, Mississippi or Missouri Rivers to transport water at least at flood stage, the Western United States would bloom with fertility toward needed crops for a hungry world. And while they should have been at it, they could also have diverted the Red River (notorious for its flooding in North Dakota) toward the Missouri. Such a waste however, which man will someday realize. A detailed plan will be offered in the last chapter.

The colors to be remembered as representing the four directions are; black (west) and following clockwise, white (north), red (east), and yellow (south). Blue, for the life giving rains, also often represented the west. These are Black Elk's colors. So many tribes, including Sioux bands, know nothing about this arrangement or ignore it.

Untruth is the Blue Man. Every day we observe much deception by those who lobby our political leaders in Washington with disregard for the environment and the ongoing dilemma. As the situation worsens, more eyes will be opened and eventually the old ways of Nature's Truth will have to be accepted in order to finally destroy the Blue Man. Hopefully, it will be in time for the planet to have a chance to regain the old harmony which was there in the first place. Traditional Sioux hold that two legged will discover that there is no other choice. Religious fundamentalists will hold to their beliefs and no doubt keep on praying and waiting for miracles. It would be extremely convenient if their beliefs work out as they vehemently proclaim. The movies, tales, and fiction literature most often have satisfying endings. Scientific proclamations however, do not always paint a rosy rainbow covered ending or bear chocolate covered results. Being told one has cancer is not a pleasant revelation. Barring some miracle by Creator, if Creator is so inclined, the realistic and workable solution will be to return to the values that actually worked. The ozone layer, water depletion and the population spiral will not wait for miraculous curing, it seems. Some tragic consequences will be learned along the way. As I have said earlier and aside from Black Elk, I hope that the wishes of Dominant Society's Organized Religion come through but in my own opinion, I consider that highly questionable if I am to remain honest. It is still a democracy and one should be allowed their views, should they not?

Canton Asylum

The Canton Native American Insane Asylum was created in 1902 while Red Cloud was in his eighties; a time when the United States' official Native American policy was assimilation. The Federal Canton Native American Insane Asylum was built out of brick at Canton, South Dakota, in the eastern part, south of Sioux Falls, the largest South Dakota town. I even have a picture of it sent to me by a Canton township person. It demonstrates how brutal and primitive the mindset of the government officials was as well as the church people who lobbied for it. Leonard Bruguier says whatever the intent behind the asylum; it was a convenient tool for reservation agents. Bruguier is a member of the Yankton Sioux and Director of the Institute of American Native American studies at the University of South Dakota. Many Native Americans who went into Canton, simply disappeared. A large graveyard is now part of the Canton golf course. 121 bodies of, former patients are buried between the fourth and fifth fairways.

So in order for the agent to feel more comfortable being surrounded by yes-people, it would be very easy for him to say 'This person's insane,' and have him shipped to Canton to be administered by a whole different set of rules. Basically you'd just be able to get rid of 'em.' It is alleged that medicine men were also incarcerated with no symptoms whatsoever of 'insanity.' This too was a method to wipe out the old religion.

Black Elk's 'Conversion'

After the Custer battle Black Elk settled on the Red Cloud Agency. He was a part of the short-lived Ghost Dance and had been in Europe with Buffalo Bill Cody's 'Wild West' shows. Returning to the reservations he took up his call once he found that he had strong healing power. His reputation grew and he had many Tetons coming to him for various afflictions.

In 1902, Black Elk had an experience with a Jesuit missionary. Father Aloysius Bosch, who came upon Black Elk innocently conducting a healing ceremony and was promptly set upon by the angry priest from Holy Rosary Mission. The yet young visionary and practicing medicine man had his altar dismantled and sacred objects (peace pipe) thrown on the ground. The burly priest yelled at the Native Americans in attendance and told them to go back to their camps. This account is partially recorded by Raymond DeMallie and the negative portions (from an Native American's point of view) have been excluded or told not according to Neihardt's notes. Hilda Neihardt told me personally she was quite set out against DeMallie whom she had given permission to see her father's notes and primarily by this omission to offer the full story. She was extremely disappointed that he omitted key materials in the so-called 'conversion' controversy that modern academics are constantly bringing up regarding Black Elk. What was omitted was that Aloysius Bosch returned to the mission, and under a clear blue sky, lightning hit the priest's horse and he was thrown from it, his leg broken. One account holds that he died. The Native Americans naturally believed that the priest should not have been so disrespectful to the Native Way and went on happily with their healing ceremonies. Within a few years, along came Father Lindebner and did the same thing. Black Elk was grasped by the neck and yelled at, 'Satan Get Out!' Black Elk was a slight man and not a typical Sioux warrior whom a priest would have a hard time in so subduing. He was also in the throes of despair at the time.

After thrown physically into a wagon by the overreacting Lindebner, and hauled to the Holy Rosary Mission to be exorcized by one Father Joseph Zimmerman, S.J.; Black Elk was converted. He was issued a pass for his compliance and now could travel freely upon the reservation. In time, as long as he did the bidding of the missionaries, he could travel to other reservations as well, which he did.

Canton Asylum was in operation at the time and the Sioux 'Grape Vine' certainly knew of it. Numerous books clamor regarding this superior-istic 'conversion', egotistically championed by the likes of Raymond DeMallie, Clyde Holler, and the Jesuit writers, Steltenkamp and Steinmetz. Oddly these men offer little focus on the profoundness of the Vision despite the reference to it from Joseph Campbell to Bill Moyers; 'the best example of Spiritual Imagery!' none of these academics mention in their writings the foreboding asylum which waited for medicine people who would not toe the missionary line. More than one holy man was 'converted' to avoid this horrid place, and more than one medicine man who would not comply was forever doomed behind the restrictive bars at Canton.

Vine Deloria, well-known Yankton Sioux writer, never mentions it (Canton) in his extolling of the 'Big Four', Episcopal breed missionaries, one of whom was his Grandfather. His Great Grandfather had to kill four Sioux; the white man's God told him so, regarding conversion and the book is thus dedicated. I have to be honest however, and admit that the victims of his first and last killings definitely deserved their fate. The breed priests, Lambert, Deloria, Ross and Walker; their pictures are in his book, Singing for a Spirit, are dressed in their missionary finery wearing those 'Mickey Mouse' hats that we also saw the Diocesan Catholic priests wear. That is what we Native American youth used to call them. By 1900, '12,000 (Native Americans) were converted', he proudly states. Evidently the 12,000 disappeared for the Wakpala mission became a ghost church; its cross bearing steeple had broken in two and lay fallen at an angle into the grass, sage and sun flowers. Chief Eagle Feather and I used its abandoned basement over a quarter century ago to hold a Yuwipi Spirit ceremony heavily attended by spiritually hungry Hunkpapa. DeMallie disrespectfully refers to the Yuwipi as a 'conjuring' ceremony. If my Great Spirit told me to go out and kill four Native Americans to join some new religion, I doubt if I could do it although I have to respect, the great-grand father, Saswe, as I said, for taking out the two who definitely deserved their fate. Would Great Spirit issue such an order? Judging from the white Man's track record of inhumanity especially toward the Indigenous, why didn't Ultimate Creator say, 'Go out and kill four White Men!' I am highly dubious that Creator would issue either order: 'Kill four Whites or Four Native Americans'. I certainly would not dedicate any book of mine to any man that did so especially when some victims were purely innocent. I can't help but think of the old traditionalist however, bleakly attempting to hold onto the old Sioux Way at that time or the ones doomed at Canton Asylum. Reservation missionaries had strong influence on the government agents. Yes, it is interesting how some so-called scholars can omit some hard-core evidence that does not support their egotistical, religious superiority. I must remind the reader: 'My spirituality is my choice for myself, but I do not hold it out as superior for your needs or your mindset.' I know that sounds highly unusual in this proselytizing I-know-everything world. My tribe is still intact. Possibly, that is the reason it works for me. Most readers are not specifically from a tribe. Nature will take care of everything, eventually, one way or another, is my reassurance. Simply carry on, care for your offspring, appreciate and be good citizens. If you increase your knowledge base as you are presently attempting to do, then that is well and good, (wasteh aloh) my opinion. Leave it at that. Mystery is mystery and we should definitely not be fighting or arguing over it. Wah- steay- ah- loh!; spoken firmly, it is a very pretty word, and we use it often as a compliment.

Prior to Canton being investigated and soon afterwards shut down, Black Elk boldly told of his powerful vision, Standing Bear standing beside him to verify; every word passing through his interpreter son, Ben, while Enid Neihardt, John Neihardt's daughter served as stenographer. John Neihardt listened to every word and often broke into the old man's running conversation to ask a question to verify a particular point. The old man would frequently lapse off into a deep nap, revive, and continue on. The missionaries were greatly disturbed when they discovered they had been omitted from the telling and demanded from Neihardt a copy of his manuscript. When asked, by Neihardt, 'On what grounds do you make such a demand?' The Jesuits replied that they indeed had a right to such information since Black Elk was now, 'one of theirs'. They also believed that they could then 'edit' on behalf of Black Elk. John Neihardt not being of any particular white man's faith, simply scoffed and refused to deliver. The Jesuits were highly incensed and not used to being rebuffed on what was 'their Sioux reservation' but little could they do about it. Such was the accustomed pomposity of the reservation missionaries over the Sioux. Later, the writers previously mentioned, came along to seriously distract from this simple yet deep discourse given beside a log cabin in far out Manderson, South Dakota. Julian Rice should also be added to the list of 'conversion squabblers'. All have neglected to explore what I presume to be the major issue of Black Elk - his Vision! The academic writers however, have tied themselves in knots as to what degree Black Elk agreed or did not agree to be converted! Shouldn't a religion stand for God's ultimate objective; that we sincerely cultivate and practice Truth? I mean, real, real sincerely as if the Creator was right before you and you were about to divulge what you genuinely observed with no alteration, no ulterior motive or just to please someone. Wouldn't a man, about to tell a powerful happening held up inside of him for decades and along with much supporting evidence and a personal friend right there to help verify, and your very own son, to serve as an interpreter: wouldn't this be sufficient enough evidence to pass on to a narrator or a recorder who has the immediate opportunity to question or have repeated what he did not at first comprehend or understand fully? Why would religious outsiders be needed to further the truth of the relating? Why would they want to 'edit' this work? Is that how organized religious history has been explained or verified down through time? Is this what they call the 'sanitation process' or 'political correctness' in order that the control of the people comes first? This thought process is what the Native Americans faced when they had to deal with the treaties to a high degree, is my opinion. The white world and the Native American world indeed were very separate when it came to basic human understanding and carrying out the full meaning of the word – Truth!

As I have said repeatedly in many of my works; I firmly believe that Mother Nature is about to deliver some very ultimate Truths. Why? Because human has allowed himself to be so misguided by some ultimate un-truths which are highly incompatible with Mother Nature's environment is why. It is as simple as that. Time will certainly tell. In Oklahoma, few of the tribes kept their language; fewer kept their religion, the old spirituality of their forefathers. One tribe even referred to itself as a civilized tribe whatever meaning that meant. For we Sioux, we were always an extremely 'civilized' tribe, in my opinion. The reservation boarding schools were used to make the Native American children into white children. Hair was cut. Long hair meant manhood to the Native American men. And one day Red Cloud found his own daughter scrubbing a floor with a white woman threatening her. This and other episodes turned him against education for a while. These were not the promises promised in the Treaty of 1868.Toward his last days he did praise education and saw it as the major means to adjust to the demands of the dominant world surrounding his people. Half the day the students labored in the fields, or scrubbing, cleaning and maintaining the boarding schools. Far too much time was spent on religion in the Christian boarding schools. In the end, the Native American student received very little 'formal' education as was received by the white students off reservation. When it came time to compete for college they were ill prepared and not until after WWII, was there hardly any enrolment into the colleges and universities.

I had six brothers and six sisters. I was the last. The old traditional Sioux family was much smaller in size compared to the reservation families after the missionaries spread their influence. My parents, both Oglala with some Cheyenne blood as well which was not recorded on the tribal rolls; both went to boarding school - to the sixth grade; my mother an eighth grade, my father, respectively. Our Oglala blood line was registered or as some say, enrolled. Neither parent ever learned to drive a car but certainly knew horses. All of my brothers and sisters, except the one sister next to me, went to reservation boarding schools. None ever walked into a college except when a few sisters attended my graduation from a Catholic men's University, years later. My father did not own a suit so was too reluctant to attend. I attended a public school when my family moved off the reservation due to the War Department confiscating the northern end of the Pine Ridge reservation for an aerial machine gun and bombing range for WWII training. We had 30 days to vacate our property and were fortunate to get jobs at the new military air base being hastily built in Rapid City. In those days there was no such thing as protest. A World War was on and we actually were proud that our land was helping fight the war in an indirect way. Five of my brothers saw combat. My father worked at the military base. Prejudice existed in Rapid City but the war effort was first and foremost. Every one hated the 'Germans and the Japs' during that conflict. Since so many Native American men were in the service and most volunteering for front line units, prejudice abated considerably. Had I not gone to public school, I seriously believe I would never have had the confidence and mainly the preparation to pursue a higher education after high school let alone become a jet fighter pilot. Few of my age group went on to graduate from college and I know of only two other Sioux to become military pilots.

Chapter 9

Vision Quest & Sweat Lodge

'How much of my created world did you actually observe?' Will God ask us this question, once we enter the Beyond - the Spirit World? I have my doubts as to any such ultra-special greeting but do supposition that a Spirit or some 'supernatural' entity may ask the same.

Vision Quest

Two ceremonies can be performed by the lone individual – Vision Quest and Sweat Lodge. Most often, the sweat lodge is performed by a group of individuals but usually no more than a dozen or so. Too many participants in one lodge is not recommended as it makes for a lengthy, uncomfortable ceremony. Vision Quest, however, is endeavored by the lone individual although a supporter or helper, often a medicine man or holy man will go with the individual to an isolated butte, mountain top or high and remote place where solace and isolation can be enjoyed. What I saw in Spain were many such places, no different than in America, where complete solitude can be found to undergo two, three or four days of isolation for undistracted prayer, contemplation and spiritual communication to take place.

Why does a questing one go to a high place? Do Spirits or God (Gods) prefer high lofty places? I doubt it. It is back to plain common sense again. Yes, plain common sense which Creator has given you such an intrinsic mind for – providing you use it and not let it get cluttered up with foolish man spawned orientation. Most people I have met seem to lose this guidance; simply look at the results of our lawmakers. Somewhere in this writing I think I mentioned the word focus. Spirits are everywhere and which no doubt Creator is also. A high place is often breezy and usually devoid of any distraction or annoyance by mostly the flying ones

- the insects. A swarming mosquito breeding marsh is definitely not a place to quest. I once knew a woman named Judy who tried it (Vision Quest) in a marshy Minnesota camping area. She could not emerge out of her tent which she fortunately had provided for herself without being attacked. Obviously she was severely distracted.

For those of you who are afraid of reptiles and hopefully have a strong respect for the poisonous ones let me assure you that snakes have to eat too and usually dwell where there is much more abundant food in lower altitudes that provide for more quarry to hunt and hiding cover is more available for them to escape the predators (hawks, owls) that seek to eat them. I have never encountered a reptile upon a sparsely vegetated mountain top or Badlands butte. Chief Crazy Horse, Oglala Lakota would often go out alone after a successful combat mission and isolate himself on a lonely butte or remote hill and contemplate to his concept of the Higher Power, no doubt, in Thanksgiving for coming back alive and/or losing few or no warriors under his command.

America has many wars and many Native American men join the military, most often the Marine Corps or the Army paratroopers. There are few jobs on the Native American reservations and the military allows one to seek a form of employment, enjoy adventure and leave the reservation with some degree of security awaiting them. Plus, we Native American people are fearless warriors so we most often are readily sought by military recruiters. None of my six brothers ever met much opposition. Four saw action in World War II and all came back alive. Two of us were in Korea and one got hurt in basic military training and was the only one who did not experience actual combat. I did my first Vision Quest after I came back from combat in Vietnam. Many native warriors conduct Vision Quest to simply thank Creator that we were allowed to endure and return.

The actual mechanics of Vision Quest (Hahnblacheeyah) are quite simple. Two of the medicine men that were my mentors simply told me to carry four colored clothes with me to the top of Spirit Mountain. You do not take any water or food with you, even if you are going to stay for as long as four days and nights. To be honest, many participants will endure for a shorter period of time but longer than any detractors who do not go up on the hill or mountain at all. I was told to place the four colored cloths around me. I arranged them in the pattern that I term 'Black Elk's colors'. I use Red for the East, Yellow for the South, Black for the West and White for the North. I cut some finger thick twigs with my jack knife and tied the cloths onto the twigs with string I brought for the occasion. I sharpened the opposite end and pushed the small flags into the ground to form a square large enough for me to lie within.

Far to the South I watched a thunderstorm rumble and flash lightning as it slowly approached. I fell asleep and it was raining on me when I woke late into the night. Between lightning flashes I could see a cliff and tall pines slightly below me. I ran for cover to escape the rain. I squeezed up close to the slanted cliff where it was still dry and stayed there until the storm passed over and red dawn slowly crept from the Eastern horizon. An eagle hovered when it was much lighter and I took that as a good sign from Creator's Nature. It actually made several low passes over me which they rarely do. It was the first time that I ever viewed one so close in flight. I have been fairly close to them while they were on land however, surprising them while feeding on a kill, a jack rabbit or prairie dog usually. In the fall you have a better chance of surprising one while pheasant hunting as they come down from Alaska and feed on the pheasants that are crippled or shot by the many hunters that come to the Dakotas.

I went back to my four colors and reset myself within to contemplate and enjoy the serenity all around. Being totally alone in Nature is very comforting. After a while you forget about water and food unless you are a Diabetic then the medicine men encourage you to at least bring a large bottle or two of water and not stay out too long which I have to agree with. I have to mention that I was instructed by my two mentors to stay within the four flags I had set out. Common sense told me to obviously leave the rectangular pattern I had made for myself when my body demanded to relieve itself. This also I had done when the rain had come earlier and the slanted cliff wall had kept me dry. A cold wind blew during the storm and took its time subsiding. Had I been soaked with the falling rain I would have experienced a great deal of discomfort, even dangerous exposure. Hence, never give up what is simple common sense. I hold 'Rules' as simple guidelines but always hold in reserve certain chance adjustments if needed. I had remained fairly dry and could continue with less diminishment of needed focus for my Vision Quest.

What does one think about? I imagine that we all are a bit different from each other because of the myriad of differing experiences we all have. I simply think about my life and when one is younger, 'Where am I going with my life?' should be a prominent question. I also want to be appreciative for the life Creator has allowed me. One must always be appreciative. I think that one should always acknowledge that Creator (God) is All Powerful, is All Knowledge and of course, All Truth. I often wonder about the Spirit World beyond. I have to think that it is much different than what we have here on this planet. I certainly hope that nothing but All Truth reigns supreme in that Beyond World. If Creator is all powerful and all Truth, then it seems quite reasonable that it would be a place of pure Truth.

What does one want to bring with him other than the clothes upon one's back? Plains' Native Americans mostly carry a peace pipe with them when they go to Vision Quest. I used to but recently I have given away my two peace pipes. One I made myself and the other was given to me by Chief Fools Crow. A while back, there were some serious ongoing arguments about who should possess a peace pipe and which groups of people, mostly white people, should be forbidden to have a peace pipe. I was mentored by Chief Fools Crow and Eagle Feather and both did not mind sharing our Spirituality, including the peace pipe with all races of people. Fools Crow stated: 'This Way is for all. We should not exclude others.' Many medicine people agreed with him but a significant amount of others disagreed. When it got too argumentative, I decided to simply give up my pipes and continue onward, believing that Creator was not exclusionary as Fools Crow meant. I simply carry a 'wotai' (Woe tye) stone that is made by Creator and get on with my beseechment without further distraction.

I also dislike the taste and smell of tobacco. I played many sports as a youth and hence avoided tobacco. I still play one particular sport similar to tennis that is popular among the elderly in America. You play this sport for several exciting hours and you build up a healthy sweat. My lungs are still healthy and allow me to play with enjoyable vigor. If you wish visit www.pickleball.com, it allows you to view this wonderful pastime which is now sweeping the older communities with close to an addictive rage. I and a partner won a 'gold,' first place medal in one of the state's annual 'Senior Games Tournament' recently; which of course we are quite proud of. Had I been a 'smoker,' we never would have won.

Wotai Stone

A special stone often comes into a person's life some time after one chooses to travel the Natural Way. Many have told me of this experience, therefore I find it difficult to not believe otherwise. Stones are everywhere. Many have images upon them. When you find yours you will discover these images. You, yourself can beseech, acknowledge, respect or seek to the Spirit World beyond. Most people now use a simple stone which they carry.

When I want to use it, I hold my stone outward at arms' length or hold it up in an offering posture as though I am presenting. I face a direction and call upon what I contend is the power or the representation of that direction. 'Oh, West Power, Oh Wiyopeyata,' I call out. 'I thank you for the life giving rains. I thank you for the fluid, the motion you allow me while I am on my journey across this planet.' I have thanked and recognized a gift from God through one of its creations. 'Oh spirit world that I associate with the west; Oh spirit world look on and be with us in our small ceremony tonight. We will beseech and acknowledge to the Great Spirit through that which it has created and you are welcome.' I have extended a pleasant welcome and in this scenario I would be in an evening ceremony. If I was alone in my home, I would probably say, 'I thank you, Great Spirit, for letting me enjoy this day.' I might point out something in particular that I learned or experienced that day.

Sun Dance and Spirit Calling

You are now becoming familiar with Sioux ceremony, dear reader. The Sun Dance is a gathering of many tribal members. They gather to annually express their Thanksgiving to the One above. It is a ceremony of human's appreciation but also a time for those who have been granted a special favor. Many will camp out in tents for four days and nights to support a relative or close friend who has pledged to endure the grueling Sun Dance. Most Pledgers will not eat or take water for four days besides suffering the piercing of their chest skin and then eventually breaking their bond to go free, usually on the fourth day of the ceremony. In the Spirit Calling ceremony you have witnessed the communicative power of a Sioux holy man. He or she has the ability to call in Spirit Helpers from that outer world, the place where traditional respecting people believe everyone goes after they pass on from this world. I think that Vision Questing and/or participating in a Sun Dance make for strong ties to the Spirit

World, Creator and all of its helpers (Spirits).

Who are the Spirit Helpers?

No one knows for sure is my opinion. I do strongly suspect that they were once former humans that led positive moral and ethical lives while here. I also believe they seriously made themselves aware of Creator's creations while here. They did not waste their attention on foolish, distracting, addictive pursuits.

Sweat Lodge

A sweat lodge is built quite easily from saplings which abound throughout the world. A circle is drawn upon the ground that will accommodate ten to fifteen people sitting comfortably facing each other within the circle's perimeter and outside of a pit or depression dug in its center. The pit is a bit less than an arm's length in diameter and about two hand length's deep. Five sharpened saplings approximately 30 mm at their base are implanted into the ground across from each other. The north sapling is bent to connect to the southernmost bent sapling and tied together. The east and west saplings are also bent and tied in the same manner. The fifth large sapling is placed about a shoulder width beside either the east or west sapling and also bent forward to the connecting sapling.

I personally do not prefer a particular direction the doorway will face as there are differing preferences among the various Indigenous tribes. Smaller saplings are then placed into supporting holes equidistant along the lodge periphery. These are all connected together to form a frame work along with longi-tudinal saplings utilized to afford added strength to support the covering for the lodge. Among the Plains' tribes buffalo hides were used for covering of the frame but in these modern times blankets or tarps are used. The interior of the lodge should not be too high as the steam may not lower if too high and needed heat from pouring water onto heated rocks brought in may not be adequate enough to induce a refreshing sweat.

In a sweat lodge, a group gathers together in a small igloo-shaped construction, usually large enough for five, ten, or twenty people to sit in a circle and beseech or pray. I do not recommend more than twenty participants. Too long a ceremony can become dangerous for some who cannot endure too much heat. If thirty people wish to participate then I recommend that two separate ceremonies of equal size are held. The lodge is covered and hot stones are brought into the lodge so that the people will sweat and become very clean. Steam will be generated by pouring water over the heated stones from a ladle. The stones are brought in by a metal pitchfork and deposited into a pit dug into the lodge center. A bucket of water is placed beside the one who will be conducting the lodge ceremony. I must warn that a sweat lodge can be dangerous if the conductor makes it too hot, does not open the door often to let in fresh air and makes foolish rules such as not letting anyone leave the ceremony if they feel uncomfortable or panic from claustrophobia. A greedy White Man in Sedona, Arizona, *James Arthur Ray; charged an enormous price to each participant which they stupidly paid and conducted a sixty person lodge. It was stifling within the hot lodge. They were told they could not leave before completion and three died from asphyxiation. This is not what sweat lodge is about.

I bring one up to a gradual sweat and do not overdue the heat by using more rocks than necessary. I also raise the entry flap considerably so that fresh air comes in. Above all, I tell all within that they can leave at any time. I have conducted many lodges and have had no ill effects happen to any participants. I also do not charge any fee. Unlike Organized Religion, most Spirituality leaders charge no fee; their 'medicine' is not for sale. I may add: Unlike Native American university academics, I do not charge an honorarium for my public speaking either. I only ask for my travel expense and a roof over my head.

Eagle Feather's Four Parts of the Sweat Lodge

Usually, there are four parts to the sweat lodge. The lodge that I have seen Chief Fools Crow and Chief Eagle Feather conduct was in four parts. I am influenced strongly by Black Elk's vision; therefore I conduct a sweat lodge as following:

The first endurance or some say 'door' is a greeting to the Spirit World. A 'Fireman' who tends the fire heating the rocks will bring in a number of heated stones and place in the depression or pit in the center of the lodge. The lodge entry door is then closed and the darkness within is broken only by the glow of the red hot stones. The conductor often uses a drum to break the silence and a song or chant may be offered. Afterwards, each participant will address a greeting to the Spirit World beyond; most often calling out their own name, introducing themselves. Water will be poured onto the stones, the lodge will completely darken and steam will begin to bathe the participants. The greeting circle will complete. This done the flap will usually be raised and cool air will come into the lodge. Light from the fire outside the lodge will also enter.

The lodge leader may call for a heating stone or two and the second round, endurance or door will begin. I term this event as the Contemplation Round. One will be praying or beseeching in earnest in the third round so it is time to contemplate what one will soon be speaking out loud to the Spirit World. Several songs by the conductor or knowledgeable individuals may be sung. Often, the participants may all sing some simple yet beautiful songs that are easy to learn has been my experience with 'first-timers'. The third endurance, each participant prays or beseeches in turn.

The fourth endurance is the Ending. I usually have four parts to this endurance as taught by Eagle Feather. The first part is to yourself. Thank yourself for bringing yourself to ceremony. The second part is a short period of silent contemplation for a loved one. The third part is for a particular nation or world issue. The environment is most often regarded in this calling out or address. Lastly, we all put out our right hand to touch an imaginary mystical tree in the center of the lodge and state in unison - 'Mitakuye Oyasin' - We are all related. The lodge is now over and the Fireman is called to raise the entry flap.

A More Definitive Description

The first door or endurance is to the West Power and acknowledges greetings and welcome to the spirit world. The second endurance is to the North Power and acknowledges truth, cleanliness and meditation. The third endurance is to the East Power and acknowledges knowledge, wisdom, understanding and peace. The individual prayers are often said during this endurance. The fourth endurance is to the South Power and acknowledges healing, honoring yourself, family members, special friends and the commitment to protect Mother Earth.

The most important part for me is when the people each say an individual prayer to the Great Spirit. I think that a lodge should be held wherein people are allowed, without fear, to pray individually and from the heart with a minimum amount of distraction or discomfort. The darkness certainly precludes distraction. A more detailed account of this ceremony and other related ceremonial descriptions are found in *Mother Earth Spirituality*. John Fire offers his sharing of the sweat lodge ceremony in the chapter, Inipi—Grandfather's Breath, *Lame Deer, Seeker of Visions*. Mikkel Aaland, *Sweat;* is also a very informative book.

Organized Religion terms their formal beseechments to their Higher Power concepts as 'worship'. To me, Native American ceremony is more of a calling out to the Spirit World than a worship service. Before a ceremony begins, the people participating usually gather together in a circle or stand facing the leader of the ceremony. If sage or sweet grass is available, this offering is lit and the smoke bathes the participants (smudging). Sage, especially, has a very definite, pleasing odor, more so when lit and the smoke permeates the area. Certain items such as a drum or a peace pipe, if present, are also smudged with the pleasant smelling grass or sage.

A welcome is extended to the spirits to enter the ceremony. It appears these spirits are simply former humans who were once here and understand what our ceremony is about. Except in a Yuwipi spirit calling, we do not address a specific spirit but assume that they are indeed attending our calling. Possibly, we ourselves will become observing spirits once we pass on to the spirit world. The leader will then beseech to each cardinal direction, west, north, east and south. Most often, the people will also face each direction as it is called upon. I usually hold up my personal wotai stone to use as my portable altar when I beseech to each direction. I hold it outward to the direction I am calling upon and recognizing. Bear in mind that each direction is an entity created by the Ultimate Creator in order for us to live here upon this planet. If the life-bearing sun did not rise from the East direction we would have no life. If the life-giving rains refuse to come out of the West upon this hemisphere, then we would not have our life-sustaining crops. The cattle and grazing ones would have no grass. White man takes all of Nature around us for granted and refuses to acknowledge or realize what reality is in a spiritual way. Therefore he remains extremely ignorant as to unlocking Nature's door and can never access the Code to save the planet, by such an attitude.

I always turn to my right in a clockwise manner as I go from one direction to the other. In this northern hemisphere, water spirals in this manner when it drains through an orifice. Therefore, I want to reach into an encompassing harmony or at least recognize this. In New Zealand and Australia, indigenous people turn ceremonially from right to left to be in their harmony.

A medicine wheel ceremony or a power of the hoop ceremony recognizes the meanings of each of the four directions and often is a recognition and connection with Father Sky and Mother Earth as well. Bear in mind, these entities are considered as extensions of the Great Spirit because they are created by the Great Spirit. Throughout this work, this theme has been often repeated in one form or another. At the conclusion of the beseechment to the Six Powers, the Great Spirit is often formally invoked. I usually make a statement thanking the Great Spirit for giving us the Six Powers which allows us our life.

When a peace pipe is used in connection with this ceremony, tobacco is placed in the pipe after some has been placed back to Mother Earth from where it came. We do not place any form of hallucinogens in the tobacco. This is absolutely contrary to natural harmony and extremely disrespectful. The mind is inhibited when hallucinogenic products are so used. This result is, no doubt, very displeasing to the spirit world to which the beseechment is being directed. The pipe is then the portable altar and pointed to each direction as its (the direction's) power, teaching and meaning is recognized.

I do not recommend that non-Native Americans use the peace pipe in respect to Arvol Looking Horse's request that only Native American, tribal Native American pipe carriers so do. Chief Looking Horse is the Keeper of the Sacred Pipe. A long list of Lakota practicing medicine men who have signed a statement are in disagreement however, with this edict. For harmony and avoidance of needless argument, I recommend that the wotai stone can just as efficiently be utilized. As mentioned earlier, I personally have been gifted a peace pipe by Chief Fools Crow himself and also made a pipe myself. Both have been given away even though I am as qualified a pipe carrier as any. I base this statement on the fact that my teachers were Chief Fools Crow and Chief Eagle Feather in the six sun dances I have been a participant under their direction. I loathe religious or spiritual argument however and am quite comfortable with my wotai stone. The spiritual results of my ceremony are no different than when I used the pipe. That is what truly matters.

Before a sweat lodge, Chief Bill Eagle Feather would open with a pipe ceremony. When he was teaching me this lodge ceremony, he would often have a woman formally open the Sweat Lodge. One of his reasons was that we all come from a woman. Another reason was that the Buffalo Woman was a powerful figure in our history. He also recognized that Mother Earth is very powerful and that we are all made from Mother Earth. Bill was a practical holy man. It seemed that just about everything that he taught me or spoke to people about made a lot of common sense. He was a 'no-frills' holy man and did not take long to make his point. He also had a strong sense of humor which he was not afraid to employ, even in ceremony. He definitely was not an angry man. He was a great teacher from my perspective. When Bill would conduct a sweat lodge, he would address each of the four directions at separate times within the Sweat Lodge ceremony. Everyone within the lodge would have their special time to pray out loud and individually. This procedure, he pointed out to me, was highly important.

Six Powers and the Spirits

Because the West is where the sun goes down, darkness comes and there is much less distraction. In the daytime, most of us are busy making a living. Our focus is elsewhere. The night is not something to be feared. Why should you be afraid of what Benevolent Creator has created, the dark (Earth's shadow)? Darkness and night are created by the Great Mystery. It allows one to concentrate more and be less distracted, especially in a group. In a dark sweat lodge, you are not distracted by what someone is wearing. You are able to concentrate on the prayer you will be speaking out loud. Don't you like to have someone's attention and focus when you make a special effort to go and visit them? Many of us believe that the spirit beings listening in want our attention without distraction.

By praying to or including spirits in a ceremony, am I praying to another entity and not God? Considering where these spirits are, I believe that they are much closer to the Great Mystery than I am. I also think that it is the 'higher planed' ones, those who are becoming very highly evolved, who are able to have the 'spiritual intellect' to observe our ceremony or beseechment. Their conduct while they were here as a human probably allows them to understand what we are doing because they were more observant, more focused, less distracted by those who were far from Creator's blessed and revealing nature teachings. Maybe they placed more information, which they gathered daily, on their 'Disks of Life' – their conscious minds. It wouldn't seem practical that the 'blank disks'; those that settled for soap operas or were beer guzzling, non-balanced 'couch potato' individuals will evolve to such a level or spiritual plane.

Like the spirit guides that enter the foretelling ceremonies to help the holy men make accurate predictions, these on-looking spirits that we hopefully cultivate are familiar with what we are doing. Those with 'blank disks' have no knowledge of what we are doing therefore they are not present and we are spared their ignorance. To put it bluntly I feel more confident in beseeching through these 'Spirits' than I would through priests, bishops, sky pilots, evangelists, mullahs, clerics and popes.

I get in touch with my concept of the Higher Power mainly through my everyday thoughts. The Native American, no doubt, had this very same informal basis. I believe that this informal reaction of thinking about and relating to Great Spirit was almost automatic. They believed that the Great Spirit was always around them and was constantly revealing itself through its creations which were so highly visible to these people. Consequently, most of them were very reverent and harmonic people. Go out into Nature. A butterfly suddenly floating before you or a tiny waterfall made by a fallen tree across a stream can make you think about God.

Do not leave out the animals, finned, winged or four-footed in your beseechment. The Wamakaskan are already in communion with Wakan Tanka. I would say that they have some 'direct connections.' Even if you live in a city put out bird food or water. The winged will soon stop by and become your friends. Talk to them. Did not the Wamakaskan appear in the great vision of Black Elk? Did not the animals play an important part in Chief Eagle Feather's finding ceremony of the lost students in the airplane crash? Prayers are usually personal but some songs are structured and for those who are familiar with Black Elk's vision, there is a clockwise structure within the beseechment. In a group ceremony such as Sweat Lodge or a Yuwipi ceremony or the tribal Sun Dance there exists a definite structure, however an 'official' or a fearful atmosphere does not (seem to) emanate. Respect is very apparent but it is not cast in a demanding or fearsome tone.

Power of the Hoop

I often perform a semi-formal ceremony which I call a Power of the Hoop ceremony when I want to get in touch with the Higher Power, or whatever mysterious spirit forces there are around us, that seem to be concerned about our earth journey. I also use this means when I want to center toward or focus on a particular area or need. Often when I rest or sit in a place to contemplate, I draw a circle in the air with my hand and draw two intersecting lines in the circle. This act signifies the four directions and the circle of life. It also can be called the Power of the Hoop and can stand for the Six Powers of the World. I am simply emphasizing at that moment that the Six Powers are all around me and that I am an extension of these powers which were put here by the Creator. I believe that these Six Powers are extensions of the Great Spirit and so in a more remote sense, we two legged are extensions of the Great Spirit through these powers. Regardless, your life, how you conduct it, is your ultimate prayer.

I would like to point out that we are physically made up of three of these six powers; the Sun Power, which is within Father Sky, provides our energy, our electronic ability; the Earth Spirit, which gives approximately 20 percent material for our bodies, and the West Power, which takes up approximately 80 percent of our bodies in the form of water and henceforth gives us motion and fluid for our physiology. Some of my information will be repetitive as are other aspects within this writing. It is intentional because I believe that it is that important and establishes a strong base for you to become established within the Natural Way. You do not learn a song, how to hunt, fly fish or become good at a sport if you do not follow some repetition. The other three powers that I observe, sense and feel are within my spirit. They are not as physical as the first three (West Power, Mother Earth and Father Sky) that I have mentioned; they are more from the mental aspect or a part of our decision making.

From a standpoint of personal prayer; the North Power helps us to recognize endurance, cleanliness, truthfulness, honesty, removal, independence, provision, preparation and politeness. Once learned and recognized, this power is within us. Native peoples often wintered over in the cold, north climes. Their survival depended upon their ability to endure and prepare for the long winter. Polite manners, quietness, respect for space and truthful conduct were virtues to live congenially within confining space limited by restricting snows and cold. The sweat lodge was used to keep clean during the winter. Little water was needed and snow was often used to make cleansing steam. When the snows melted in the springtime Mother Earth was washed clean. The virtue of cleanliness comes through very strongly if I think and identify in this manner.

The East Power reminds me to always appreciate a new day. When the red dawn appears in the east, new experiences, new happenings will accumulate more knowledge upon my Disk of Life. I will strive to be cognizant of what is unfolding before me. After the sun has coursed across the sky, I will contemplate what I have learned. In time I will discourse with others and weigh their opinions where this new information might be relevant. When we share new knowledge, wisdom can come into being. Wisdom leads to understanding, and peace can follow. Understanding, wisdom and peace were strong words which Black Elk identified in his vision. Wisdom associated with spiritual contemplation becomes Grace. These were the gifts from the East Power. I believe the thoughts, memories and deeds related to these virtues carry over into the spirit world.

Growth, medicine, healing and bounty are from the South Power. We all have to make a living. We have to provide, especially if we have dependent children or relatives. If you wish to hone your ability to provide, then beseech to the South Power. Ability, determination, interest, skill, improvising and perseverance are traits that I associate with this direction because they are needed to provide food, shelter and clothing. Itokaga (South Power) was manifested by the Creator specifically for provision. It is an extension of the Creator. Why shouldn't we beseech in a specific manner to it?

Medicine is made from the plants; their stems, roots and fruits. The South Power causes these plants to grow and all of our foods as well. Even the buffalo was a result of the gift of Itokaga, because it fattened and lived from the grasses that grew tall as a result of the summer sun causing all things to grow. If I was unemployed or was unhappy with my occupation or situation, I would beseech to the South Power. If I was physically sick, I would beseech to Itokaga. If I did a ceremony for a person who was physically sick, I would face that person to the South Power. Those who are very compassionate and seek to help and to heal will be helped greatly if they explore the medicines and herbs and also seek spirit helpers that have gone on with their knowledge of medicine and healing. Naturally, they should seek knowledge from those who are yet living. These kind and loving people will be very pleasant to be around in the spirit world, like butterflies and flowers.

So, these three powers, North, East and South, are of the mind when they are ascribed to humans. The characteristics, the traits and virtues of The North, East and South Power; we can implant upon our Disks of Life. They will then become a part of us. The application of endurance, truthfulness, seeking of knowledge, ability to share wisdom and understanding, along with our own example of bravery or courage, all help us to harmonize and fit in with our surroundings. Do not forget and I repeat; the West Power is our fluid, the life-giving rains. Fluid allows our bodies to have motion. The fifth power is the sun's energy which flows through us and of course, the sixth power, Mother Earth's elements and minerals make up our physical being. All of these entities are placed here by the Ultimate. Even the most ardent detractors cannot truthfully deny this fact.

Free Choice

The benevolent Creator has even given us free choice as to how we shall use what is symbolized and made obvious by these powers. If we want to avoid and ignore them, then we have that choice to do so. If we want to sit and detract, make fun of or be jealous and contribute nothing, we have that power also. It will be a long, cold time for this kind in the spirit world. Who will want to associate with them? What is upon their mind except empty, useless detraction? They have avoided the harmony that is so evident in Nature. I believe that jealous detractors are paid back severely in the Spirit World, especially those detractors who tell vile lies within their detraction. They will be in a foreign place when they enter the Spirit World. I believe strongly that the spiritual realm is so close to the Great Spirit that disharmony is absolutely not condoned, tolerated or allowed. Yet, their distractive habits and character will be with them as will be their former addictions. They will truly be miserable and have to look back with many regrets. Good, harmonic spirits will avoid them because they will have nothing in common to share. This is a much more practical supposition of the Beyond than that which the White Man has conjured for us. I suspect that his hell fire, brimstone and pitch fork carrying devils' major purpose was that of control.

Chapter 10

What Spirituality is Not

The old Lakota was wise. He knew that a man's heart away from nature becomes hard.
Luther Standing Bear, Oglala Sioux

Suppression of Truth

Very little has been written about the truth of the Holy Inquisition, which was an extremely important part of European history and oh so far removed from what we know of democracy. What Organized Religion committed upon civilization was far more atrocious even than what the Nazi Regime did to the Jews. Nazi atrocities lasted a decade - the Church's reign of terror lasted centuries. Such is the power of Organized Religion to suppress the truth. I received an 'A' grade in a Church History class taken at a prestigious Christian university and learned very little about the Inquisition. Why should this information be swept under a rug? It most certainly did have an effect upon history. We should allow this knowledge to fortify our intellect so that these events will never occur again.

Holy Horrors

James Haught, author of *Holy Horrors*, Prometheus Press, describes in detail the human sacrifice within the Great Inquisition which existed over 500 years and even reached into the New World to punish Native Americans who adhered to their beliefs. Efforts to establish heresy led to the establishment of the Holy Inquisition, one of mankind's supreme horrors. It paralleled feudal/pre-China occupation Tibet which you read earlier. In the early 1200s, local bishops were empowered to identify, try, and punish heretics. When the bishops proved ineffective, traveling papal inquisitors, usually Dominican priests, were sent from Rome to conduct the purge ... *Pope Innocent IV authorized torture in 1252, and the Inquisition chambers became places of terror. Accused heretics were seized and locked in cells, unable to see their families, unable to know the names of their accusers. If they didn't confess quickly, unspeakable cruelties began ... Swiss historian Walter Nigg recounted ... So that the torturers would not be disturbed by the shrieking of the victim, his mouth was stuffed with cloth. Three-and four hour sessions of torture were nothing unusual. During the procedure the instruments were frequently sprinkled with holy water ...*

The victim was required not only to confess that he was a heretic, but also to accuse his children, wife, friends, and others as fellow heretics, so that they might be subjected to the same process. Minor offenders and those who confessed immediately received lighter sentences. Serious heretics who repented were given life imprisonment and their possessions confiscated. Others were led to the stake in a procession and church ceremony called the 'auto-da-fé' (act of the faith). A papal statute of 1231 decreed burning as the standard penalty. The actual executions were performed by civil officers, not priests, as a way of preserving the church's sanctity. Some inquisitors cut terrible swaths. Robert le Bourge sent 183 to the stake in a single week. Bernard Gui convicted 930 - confiscating the property of all 930, sending 307 to prison and burning forty-two. Conrad of Marburg burned every suspect who claimed innocence.

Haught includes numerous paintings and drawings from medieval artists which portray torture scenes to add further proof that these agonizing horrors did happen. The smaller, break-away sects were the victims of the larger Protestant sects and of course Roman Catholic. Later, these fledgling church organizations would grow and kept records, even museums of victim portrayal. Some illustrations exhibit a pope or a bishop looking on with their cortege and often wearing a halo. Examples of the descriptions are as follows: *Albigenses Christians, also called Cathari and Publicani, were burned by Catholic bishops in the late 1100s, before the Pope declared a military crusade against them ... About 2,000 Waldensian Protestants in Calabria, southern Italy, were massacred in 1560 by Catholic troops under Grand Inquisitor Michele Ghislieri, who later became Pope Pius V and was sainted ... St. Dominic wears a halo in a church painting as he presides over an Inquisition session deciding the fate of two accused heretics stripped and bound to posts ... Pope Pius V and his cardinals (background) watch the Roman Inquisition burn a nonconforming religious scholar, about 1570 ... Ceremonious burning of convicted heretics at a religious 'auto-da-fé' (act of faith) climaxed the Inquisition process. Engraved in 1723 by Bernhard Picart ... Accused 'witches' first were stripped and searched for 'devil marks' - then the torture began. The process usually ended in execution. This painting depicts an attractive woman in terror, bound and nude before two male torturers, one who is reading a manual on torture. Burning at the stake was the chief fate of accused witches, but others were hanged, drowned, or crushed ... Another portrait shows an accused woman repenting, holding a crucifix as she looks to the heavens while tied to a burning stake.* It is no wonder that so many Christians have a fear of their religion or their concept of God. The DNA blueprint which all beings have would surely carry over some of that fear implanted in such a horrible age of ignorance that lasted down through generations.

The Inquisition was divided into three phases: the medieval extermination of heretics; the Spanish Inquisition in the 1400s; and the Roman Inquisition, which began after the Reformation. In Spain, thousands of Jews had converted to Christianity to escape death in recurring Christian massacres: So, too, had some Muslims. They were, however, suspected of being insincere converts clandestinely practicing their old religion. In 1478 the pope authorized King Ferdinand and Queen Isabella to revive the Inquisition to hunt 'secret Jews' and their Muslim counterparts. Dominican friar Tomas de Torquemada was appointed

Inquisitor General, and he became a symbol of religious cruelty. Thousands upon thousands of screaming victims were tortured, and at least 2,000 were burned ... The Roman period began in 1542 when Pope Paul III sought to eradicate Protestant influences in Italy. Under Pope Paul IV, this inquisition was a reign of terror, killing many 'heretics' on mere suspicion. Its victims included scientist-philosopher Giordano Bruno, who espoused Copernicus's theory that planets orbit the sun. He was burned at the stake in 1600 in Rome ... The Inquisition blighted many lands for centuries. In Portugal, records recount that 184 were burned alive and auto-da-fé processions contained as many as 1,500 'penitents' at a time.

The Inquisition was brought by Spaniards to the American colonies, to punish Native Americans who reverted to native religions. A total of 879 heresy trials were recorded in Mexico in the late 1500s ... The horror persisted until modern times. The Spanish Inquisition was suppressed by Joseph Bonaparte in 1808, restored by Ferdinand VII in 1814, suppressed again in 1823, and finally eradicated in 1834 ... Lord Acton, himself a Catholic, wrote in the late 1800s, The principle of the Inquisition was murderous ... The popes were not only murderers in the great style, but they also made murder a legal basis of the Christian Church and a condition of salvation ...

Women were special targets of the Inquisition: During the 1400s, the Holy Inquisition shifted its focus toward witchcraft, and the next three centuries witnessed a bizarre orgy of religious delusion. Agents of the church tortured untold thousands of women, and some men into confessing that they flew through the sky on demonic missions, engaged in sex with Satan, turned themselves into animals, made themselves invisible, and performed other supernatural evils. Virtually all the accused were put to death. The number of victims is estimated widely from 100,000 to 2 million. Pope Gregory IX originally authorized the killing of witches in the 1200s, and random witch trials were held, but the craze didn't catch fire until the fifteenth century. In 1484 Pope Innocent VIII issued a bull declaring the absolute reality of witches—thus it became heresy to doubt their existence. Prosecutions soared. The inquisitor Cumanus burned forty-one women the following year, and a colleague in the Piedmont of Italy executed 100 ... Soon afterward, two Dominican inquisitors, Jakob Sprenger and Heinrich Kramer, published their infamous 'Malleus Maleficarum' (Witches Hammer) outlining a lurid litany of magical acts performed by witches and their imps, familiars, phantoms, demons, succubi, and incubi. It described how the evil women blighted crops, devoured children, caused disease, and wrought spells. The book was filled with witches' sexual acts and portrayed women as treacherous and contemptible. *'All witchcraft comes from carnal lust, which is in women insatiable,'* they wrote. Modern psychology easily perceives the sexual neurosis of these priests—yet for centuries their book was the official manual used by inquisitors sending women to horrible deaths ...

Witch-hunts flared in France, Germany, Hungary, Spain, Italy, Switzerland, Sweden, and nearly every corner of Europe - finally reaching England, Scotland, and the Massachusetts Bay Colony. Most of the victims were old women who roused suspicion of neighbors. Others were young, pretty women. Some were men. Many in continental Europe were simply citizens whose names were shrieked out by torture victims when commanded to identify fellow witches .... The standard Inquisition procedure of isolating and grilling suspects was followed - plus an added step: the victims were stripped naked, shaved of all body hair, and 'pricked.' The Malleus Maleficarum specified that every witch bore a numb 'devils mark,' which could be detected by jabbing with a sharp object. Inquisitors also looked for 'witches' tits,' blemishes that might be secret nipples whereby the women suckled their demons.

A profound irony of the witch-hunts is that they were

directed, not by superstitious savages, but by learned bishops, judges, professors, and other leaders of society. The centuries of witch obsession demonstrated the terrible power of supernatural superstition.

Modern Atrocity

It is now the 'Age of Communication'. In Ireland it now appears that modern man has had enough and is retaliating against such blatant injustice - often criminal injustice. Letter to Archbishop Dermot Martin read by Reverend Kevin Annett during a meeting with Archbishop Martin on May 4, 2012.

> *My name is Kevin Annett ... the Secretary of the five-nation body known as The International Tribunal into Crimes of Church and State (ITCCS). ... Our coalition represents over fifty organizations ... We have also been recognized by seven aboriginal nations in North America, and been authorized by them to recover the remains of their relatives who died in Catholic Native American residential schools and orphanages; and to bring to justice those responsible for the death of over 50,000 children in these church-run institutions. ...*
>
> *The Roman Catholic Church has imposed and is perpetrating a reign of terror and crimes against humanity on generations of children, ... Nevertheless, on behalf of the nations and survivors we represent, ... I have been authorized to give the Church a final opportunity to change, by presenting the following demands to the Roman Catholic Church in Ireland, ... and Vatican officials. ...*
>
> 1. *The Church must issue full reparations to all of its victims, ...*
> 2. *The Church must surrender for a proper burial, without conditions and at its own expense, the remains of all those who died in its institutions or while under its care.*
> 3. *The Church must return all land and property taken from its victims, ...*

4. *The Church must surrender without conditions all of the evidence of its crimes against children, and all of those persons responsible for committing these crimes and concealing them, including its highest officials. ...*

5. *The Church and its guilty parties cannot hide behind so-called diplomatic immunity or other privileges to evade justice and avoid prosecution. ...*

6. *The Church must immediately expel and defrock all known child raping priests, officials and employees in its ranks, ...*

7. *All clergy and Church officials must agree to be licensed and monitored as public servants, ...*

8. *The Church must forgo and withdraw from all of the tax exemptions, financial concordats and agreements, ...*

9. *The Vatican must agree to the annulment of its status as a so-called state, ...*
    All of the wealth accumulated by the Church and the Vatican Bank ... must be returned to its victims ...

10. *It is time for all people of conscience within the Church to choose who they will serve: a self-governing, criminal church system that sets itself above the law and God – or its suffering victims, ...*

The Vatican Bank is the top controlling bank in the world. The fact that the president of this bank was recently fired is very big news. The Pope is also in big trouble and it is said is set to resign. The resignation of this Pope is one of the last prophecies to be fulfilled and it is in the process of working out right now. The Catholic Church has controlled people longer than any organization in history. It is claimed that Peter-Hans Kolvenbach – coined the The Black Pope, is connected with the Vatican Bank, and so has huge influence financially, politically and socially. He is in charge of the Jesuits. There have been more people killed in the name of religion than for any other reason. Isn't it time for all that violence to stop? For more information check out http://itccs.org/2012/05/04/catholic-church-faces-disruption-and-banishment-as-irish-cardinal-set-to-resign/

Harmonic Balance

As I have said an elevated priesthood that does not recognize the balance of woman and her leadership can prove to be a very dangerous thing. Human sacrifice is a horrendous example of extreme zealousness. People get too carried away with 'knowing' that they are right and the others, the outsiders, 'are definitely wrong.' This idea—that God does not care if the zealous exterminate the victims of their choosing—has been a tragic part of human history. Pretending that this past did not exist or blaming it all on the Incas and Aztec Native Americans in the New World is not beneficial knowledge if we desire to seek balanced harmony amongst all creeds. Such history assures me that my mere perspective—'I do not know' and 'It is all a mystery,'—seems like a harmless butterfly flitting through the woods, in comparison. I believe there is a spirit world. Those poor medieval victims are quite possibly in that spirit world and they just might be reminding their tormentors for an eternity how wrong they were.

Personal Sacrifice

The Sioux had a personal sacrifice which was freely originated or initiated by a pledger of the tribe. It was your own choice and not some outsider's infliction upon you. A desperate hunter might take a vow to be pierced in the forthcoming Sun Dance if he would see a deer to bring back to hungry people. I personally took a vow to pierce in the Sun Dance if I would come back from the war in Vietnam. No one forced me to take this vow and the pain that I endured was of my own choosing much like a woman who gives birth to a baby. She chooses her own pain so that the people might live. The Sun Dance is a time when the people thank the Great Spirit. It is also a time, in Sioux culture, that certain men can and will fulfill their sun dance vows, usually for a favor or a request that was made in time of need. When the need or request was fulfilled, the pledger honored his promise.

Around the sun dance tree, which was a cottonwood tree placed earlier in the center of the tribal arena in Sioux custom, the sun dancer would dance. Singers gathered around a large drum to sing old tribal songs. For me, these songs are hauntingly beautiful. I can hear them as I write this description. A bed of sage would be placed beneath this 'tree of life' and the dancer would be taken to this spot and be pierced in the chest by the Sun Dance Chief, the intercessor for the ceremony. A pair of small slits would be made in the man's skin and a wooden peg would be skewered through; in and under the skin. The end of a rope would be brought down from the tree, and it would be attached to the wooden peg by a buckskin thong. The other end of the long rope would be attached toward the top of the tree. The dancer would rise after he was attached and would slowly dance backward, away from the tree's base to the end of his rope. Other dancers would be pierced and after all were pierced the piercing song would be sung and the dancers would dance inward toward the base of the tree to beseech strongly to the Great Spirit who was believed to be looking on. After the dancers touched the tree, they would go back, away from the center to the end of their ropes. Four times, this beseechment would take place. The on looking tribe would be in very serious prayer, with very little distraction. The tribe praying together in a concerted effort was considered to be far more powerful and beneficial than the drama of the sun dancers. This was the main focus of the Sun Dance—the tribe praying as a unit, praying together. The drama of the piercing assures an unbroken, undistracted spiritual focus. After the fourth time, the fourth beseechment, the dancers would be free to lean back and break themselves free by putting their weight upon their tether to the tree of life embedded into Mother Earth. The rope was their spiritual umbilical. When the peg would break through, their sun dance vow would be fulfilled. Such is a description of the Sun Dance, which is a personal and unlike medieval, Organized Religion torture, a freely chosen sacrifice. No one is required to Sun Dance and the majority of tribal members do not actually become pledgers or sun dancers. The Sun Dance is a minor sacrifice and also honorable when compared to the fearful ordeal of medieval human sacrifice. Our concept of God is one where we see and appreciate that It makes a simple thing such as flowers, beautiful waterfalls, eagles and wondrous life. We realize that we would be going way beyond our ego to take other two leggeds and kill them just because they do not share our beliefs; worse, to torture them to death. It is all mystery—a great realm of unknown.

Woman can also sun dance, but she does not pierce because she has given her pain so that the people may live every time she gives birth. Such also is the depth and recognition of Sioux ceremony. To this day, among many Native American tradition-alists, it is believed that one's medicine can have added power or a ceremony of healing can often end with favorable results if a pledge to do something honorable or a related personal commitment (personal sacrifice) is made. But it is always an honorable and a reasonable request.

Creation Denial

Odd, how the followers of Organized Religion believe in an all-powerful and all-knowing Creator, yet totally ignore what its Creation obviously displays in a myriad of knowledge, directly observable every day to human; if he or she wants to make an effort to observe. Man's ego can become so powerful and blinding. Neither of their Black books admits, relates or recom-mends wherein a treasure of rich, life style-applicable-knowledge abides outside of their man written proclamations. The Black books abound in man statements, mostly from men who knew little of science as modern man has progressed towards today.

There were no Hubble telescopes observing the Universe back in Biblical and Koranic fostering times. Nor did microscopes, computers, calculators, carbon dating, lasers and all other forms of modern scientific and exploratory tools probe vast Creation not only here upon our planet but those which reach out beyond our atmosphere.

Not many centuries ago, the Religious hierarchy forbid and even put to death early scientists who discovered physical laws that proved how errant certain church proclamations were in blatant error. In these modern times the extreme right of America is steering their politicians to introduce Adam and Eve as the first parents biblical concept (origination of Man) versus the more realistic (and more sensible) Darwinian Evolution theory, the dinosaurs existing but several thousand years ago, Noah's Ark, the Great Flood necessitating Noah's Ark, Jesus (a human) as God and, of course, not mere messianic man; are but a few of their demands to place upon a secular respecting America. Odd that modern human bases their religious declarations on a complete ignorance of observable Creation. One Biblical passage followed by the White Man is: 'Mutiply and subdue the Earth!' Meaning: 'Over population is OK'. Look at where the human race is at now with over population that is exponentially expanding into the billions upon billions with only so much tillable, crop producing land to sustain human. Therefore; a tremendous gap exists between the Red Man's World views in contrast to the White Man's.

The Ban

Freedom is a big word in so-called and self-acclaimed 'True' democracy yet the Christianity folks lobbied Congress back in the Grant Administration to have our Native American Religion/Spirituality banned which was totally unconstitutional yet Congress sided with a controlling religion. A half-century later the Judaea (Jewish) followers would find themselves severely persecuted in Europe with little support or sympathy coming from America before and during early WWII. Our Religious Freedom Right came back in 1978 when Congress finally woke up. (After we Native Americans faithfully served in WW1 & WW2, Korea and Vietnam). Incidentally, North American Indigenous has the highest military volunteer ratio of any nationality group.

Organized Religions especially have proven to be very non-supportive of True Democracy. It is called - Control! I do not need to spell out history going back a couple thousand years. Fanatics have killed or severely inconvenienced millions more down through time. Inquisitions, Holocaust, Manifest Destiny, Enslavement & now Jihad - it keeps on going. Organized Religion Man, thinks he has got the one true Path to the Higher Power and be damned and even killed if you do not believe his way. We know. We suffered under those zealots, controlling religious missionaries, specifically our youth sentenced to federal Boarding Schools.

Pedophilia ran rampant in the Boarding Schools, more so in the Organized Religious ones, especially those administrators and teachers who took the Vow of Poverty and Chastity. There was some mystery in that chastity vow that brought on a higher degree of pedophilia victims it seems. In Canada it was the Church of England that controlled the boarding schools that resulted in a pedophilia epidemic among the native youth. Only recently have the Boarding Schools been closed down and replaced by the same type of Day Schools that the white youth have. The State of South Dakota, lobbied by Organized Religion, namely the Catholic Church, however, has blocked law suits filed by Native American Boarding School pedophile victims utilizing the Statue of limitations time limit ploy which in the Natural Way Law is extremely untruthful. In the Spirit World, those victims will have their say for an eternity, however. Man does not control an all truthful spirit world.

Traditional believing Native North Americans do not hold out that all knowing premise - being much like the Jewish People - we do not proselytize. We will not come knocking on your door or burn a peace pipe image in your yard but we also request that you do not come knocking on our door to somehow 'Save' us from that boogie man devil character you have designed, invented and made up. Also, like most Jews we do not believe our Higher Power - The Benevolent and All-Providing Great Spirit has any need to allow such a thing nor would ever conceive of allowing any outside power other than what IT shows us daily. Have you ever observed one? (Devil or so called Satan). You never will! Once again - it is Back-to-Nature again for our primary teachings. To us it is rather an insult to Creator's providing generosity for such an obvious false belief within ITs Creation. Whatever, the Founding Fathers included a Separation of Church & State Clause in their attempt to secure True Democracy. (They were much more aware of the Great Inquisition and its horrible dangers than modern Americans today who have been insulated for several centuries.) The Great Inquisition was still fresh in colonial minds back then and they, no doubt, realized the danger of an all-controlling Church over the independent hearts and minds of a people who primarily fled the suffering, misery and lack of opportunity spawned by European conditions which were so heavily influenced by Organized Religion. This misery was alleviated and eventually obliterated by a free democracy primarily thanks to its early incorporation by the Iroquois - a Chino/Mongolian tribe who much earlier, like the Sioux, came across the Bering Strait long ago.

Chapter 11

Evolvement & Needed Change

A Spirit World lies beyond. Our tribe has pretty well proven that. Simply go to our ceremonies. Spirits exist! The Wah shi chu downplays our ability mainly because he does not have the preparation to call them in. He can't do it and therefore has to detour his followers away from such truthful communication. He loses a great spiritual value by his negative actions. Obviously he is not honest. Not a real seeker of Creator's (God's) Ultimate Truth. His religious leaders will not admit. Their false pride holds them back. Too long they have thought themselves so errantly superior, feasting on marketing, power and control completely oblivious to the Easter Island example encompassing all that is around them. They are no different than the opiated Tibetans, drugged and nullified with no courage or communication to urge them to rise up. The Wah shi chu is taught to never seriously introspect, no not until extreme environmental calamity will force him to awaken. Much suffering for all of humanity will happen before he finally awakens. The world is heating; overpopulating; thousands in Africa alone are starving. Eventually such tragedy will move to all countries. Environmental danger is everywhere. It is not the time to ridicule those who can help the most – the Spirits who are watching all this.

What Are You Doing to Progress Toward
the Spirit World?

It all starts right here: Your life, here, on this planet. Organized Religion lives for the 'now'. Spirituality-moved followers live for the Beyond. Beyond is a bit longer. There is far more discipline among the Spiritual regarding true ethics, morality and Creator's truth. Their lifestyle promotes a much higher degree of harmony in this life; simply look at the results of the not too long ago Indigenous who met the early European followers of Organized Religion with peaceful hospitality and not immediate warfare and enslavement. They were so encompassed with practicing Real Truth that when interviewed by historians the Sioux warriors would not comment about certain battles and battle strategies without being supported by a verifier who experienced the same. Dr. John Bryde noted this respecting characteristic in his many notes given to me for my book Crazy Horse and Chief Red Cloud – Warrior Chiefs.

Dragon Fly - Tusweca - Tuss We Kah

The Sioux point out Dragon Fly to tell you why they believe a Spirit World does exist. Remember: It is simply one of many ways Creator tells you; from what IT (not Man) has designed and created. Tusweca represents the colors of the Six Powers of Black Elk's Great Vision. It is white as an egg and black as a nymph hiding in the swirling waters under rocks from voracious trout. It knows nothing at that stage about life. All that it knows is light and darkness, hiding from hungry enemies and seeking its own food to live. It knows nothing of what is above that light above the swirling waters of the brook which turns to darkness in an endless cycle. Then one day it floats upward, sprouts wings and flies from the waters. Its eyes transform to look down and find out what life is about. Its wings are red - East Power, yellow - South Power, green – Mother Earth's colors and also blue for Father Sky. Black is the West Power and white is the North Power. The dragon fly has to be amazed at the new life it is now in. We two legged will sprout our wings to reach the Spirit World whether or not we have been truthful, honest and observant of Creator's creations and their workings. There, we will learn much more fully of the mysteries of life that surround us in this world. What is time? What is space among the many unknown, unfathomable mysteries?

Plato's Allegory of the Cave is very similar: *'Life is but a mere shadow on the wall compared to the complete reality of the life Beyond.'* The difference however, I have to assume from my observance while I have been on my life's journey is that; since Creator has placed so much of its Truth all around us, it seems quite probable that the more Truth that those who have strived to learn and hence – advance; their focus or endeavour can be a probability in that Spirit World beyond. The more clear and clean is the mind, the Spirit or the Soul, the more able, responsive or adaptable one will be to move further into that realm. I can imagine that it is a definite realm of such higher advancement of knowledge quite contrary to the fire and brimstone promised by Organized Religion. Those who have cluttered themselves with Untruth, so to speak, the unprepared, will be much less able to move on into that new realm. The allegory of the gold wire and the more efficient passage of the electrons therein comes to mind. Whatever, it is an interesting supposition.

Grasp the Spirits

How can one grasp the Spirits? How can one reach out and re-live the lifestyle of the old Native American; the old Celtic? How can one seek Celtic bardship in this modernized world which increasingly covers real Mother Nature every day with pavement, concrete, buildings and new dwellings due mainly to the exponentially increasing world population? Yes, exponentially! We have now experienced the role of the Native North American and we have read now of their ability to preserve their customs, values and real Spirit Calling ceremony little different than many of European lineages who have Celtic ancestors of old. Yes, a few tribes such as mine, managed to keep their language and their Spirituality despite the devious devices and attempts by Organized Religion to suffocate their Spirituality but fortunately did not succeed against a few of the tribes notably the Lakota Sioux. Thus the old Way was preserved for those tribes that did not lose this wonderful, direct-from-Creator, and not Man, connection; and hence, to re-learn from. We need not attempt to copy these people's ceremonies exactly however. I have portrayed, revealed, and explained them primarily to show that a people can preserve what is intrinsically Wahsteay - Good. You now must go on and attempt to bring out the principle spiritual fortification that emits from ceremony to benefit in accordance with the mode of your own background. Appreciation, thanksgiving within all that you do whether ceremony or lifestyle: This was the essence of Nature-respecting Man and in my opinion – it obviously worked for millennia and not just the few centuries that White Man has eradicated it – almost. It will come back. It has too if all colors, red, yellow, black and white want to survive. Recognition of all that Creator makes is the key point you must seek to absorb daily, if you can.

Discipline

With always the thought of an eventual Spirit World waiting beyond, Spiritual Man maintained a discipline to keep his life more fulfilling for both worlds – Here and There. His concept was to be as God would want one to be: To be a pure conductor of Truth as has been given in the example of the gold wire, so to speak. But there was no short cut, no avoidance of the necessary discipline needed, required to attain truthful, earned bliss to acquire higher knowledge and therefore truthfully earning a rewarding harmony in that world beyond. Nature illustrates that conception to two-legged (human) every day. Nature metes out discipline. She does not forgive. A false promise of sugar coated forgiveness dilutes, erases, avoids discipline and hence we see the world as it is today and soon to be doomed to the unbending, unforgiving laws of true, God created Environmental Discipline. How foolish for control attempting mere man to thwart and mock the obvious, observable laws of Created Nature. The results of Man's erroneous actions are unfolding now in our lifetimes. Misleading forgiveness is sheer marketing by Organized Religion and very effective. Not one Congressman/woman or State legislator in this acclaimed 'Christian country' is worried about having to eventually answer in some Beyond World. They have been brought up to become foolishly believing that they are somehow 'insulated' from any wrongdoing despite the far reaching effect of their decision making regarding the Earth's flora and fauna, the necessary health of the planet and the sheer survival of the human race eventually. It will be interesting to observe which side will be the most accurate once we reach the Spirit World. I do not hold that one should explicitly attempt to copy a tribe's ceremonies – per se. Yes! The sweat lodge is a universal ceremony, practiced even by the Celtics; is a belief by some scholars. A reviving, refreshing hot bath utilizing heated stones was as welcome and healthful in the medieval ages as well as it is today. Nature is nature and as equal across all oceans, I believe I stated earlier. By all means practice the sweat lodge; it is a perfect ceremony to bring one closer to Earth wisdom. Go up on an isolated area, I saw many such inviting areas on my trip to Spain. Scotland has numerous high remote hills. Vision Quest there for several days. Contemplate, Introspect, Wonder while looking out at vast God provided Nature.

Guidance Not Doctrine

This book is merely a guide. It is neither a bible nor an attempt at being so. I do not have 'all the answers' as others attempt to profess. If I am truthful, which I intend to be, I will only relate from my experiences or what trusted mentors that I could depend upon and possibly, the Spirits may have or may not have put into my life or upon my journey. No one man, no group or association of mere humans possess any such wisdom to falsely profess that they have life's answers. They go so far that they even attempt to offer the only salvation for a proper place in the Spirit World: Of course, through their man created Way only. The present environmental situation they have errantly led us to is sheer proof of their inability. Their self-claimed, 'All-knowing' professed bible states absolutely nothing of environmental prophecy! Wouldn't the tragic demise of our life providing planet deserve an intense revelation by its supposed prophets? I place little stock in what mere human could utter for me spiritually beginning some 3,000 years ago and knowing so little of what modern Science today reveals and explores for us - principally of nature. I place much more confidence and respect in and from science, its discoveries and revelations than from mere, basically scientific ignorant Man with all his myriad of superstitions, superstitious based pronouncements and edicts overshadowing real, revealed Truths to guide my journey. His track record is pitiful, most often disastrous for the entire planet if we weigh in his population disregard and include the actual ongoing planetary heating as evidenced by extreme weatherstorms, Tsunamis, record heat, record cold, etc. Simply look at Mexico. The extreme poverty, mainly brought on by their religious, bible oriented disregard and blatant ignorant insulation from needed knowledge as to what exponential over population can wreak upon a country.

'Suffer ye, to come unto me,' is not a statement that I can respect. Once I drove by a convent in Wisconsin. Off to the side of a road intercepting the highway was a sign advertising the convent. 'The Seven Sorrowful Sisters of the Sorrow-filled Heart'. It stated in bold lettering. Needless to say, I kept on driving, maybe a little faster to give me some distance. I am not into seeking suffering or sorrow. The more I can avoid - the better - my opinion! Again, and again, I simply state - It is only Nature that has the truly honest answers. Creator is All Truth and All Knowledge. Nowhere, other than Nature is that statement so truly reflected! She is the most accurate teacher, and Nature does not forgive! Where does nature tell you to enjoy or seek suffering. Quite the contrary; she teaches you to avoid such foolishness.

The Spirits and the Nine Life Cat

I have had many unique and seemingly 'Spirit induced' happenings. Often, I have faced near death too many times, more lives than a nine life cat to put it bluntly. I have been shot three times (It really stings but I do not suggest that you try it), crashed two jets, two helicopters (one a lost engine, not really a crash.). I safely auto rotated into a North Carolina cornfield; two *SAM missile survivals; that should cover the first nine lives and I could go on for another nine if I had to; mostly involving automobiles and of course the combat missions in Vietnam alone could fill several more 'nine cat lives'. The close air support a Marine pilot experiences flying protective cover for the embattled and endangered troops below and often within 500 feet of your attacking plane – the enemy shooting up at you - are also that close. On at least some of them it would seem that some Spirit activity may have been involved. *Surface to Air Missiles that were often effective in bringing down our Jet Fighter/Attack bombers. Mathematically, 100 missions is numerous times a Marine pilot carrying 12 bombs and dropping one at a time, would be exposed close to enemy fire well over a thousand times. Close Air Support for the ground troops below means coming in as low as 500 feet, repeatedly within the same mission, not once or twice but many times, well within the range of small arms fire including the 37 mm anti-aircraft weapons. Thankfully a Phantom F4 was very fast and obviously a bit difficult to hit. Mountains, especially at night and weather did take its toll on our fighter bombers. The Spirits must have been with me! Maybe they wanted me to write a few books!

Humor

I have to add that in the airplane crashes I was involved in, I was never charged with pilot error. I know that this statement has nothing to do with Spirituality but I do have a degree of professional ego and hence have to exonerate myself pilot wise. I doubt if we will get to fly airplanes in the Spirit World but in case we do I do not want to disqualify myself. Note: To the extremely serious among us, the preceding two sentences are simply stated in a half way joking manner. Native Americans are loaded with humor and I sometimes place a little in my writings but admit that I am quite devoid of such in this book and hence apologize. In England, my good friend Barbara and her many friends can attest to my humor. Many friends including my grown children will attest as well here in the U.S. By all means – cultivate and appreciate good, healthy humor. It is almost a life saver in itself in this day and world. Remember: God (Creator) allowed us, gave us our entire make up - including humor.

Utilize The Four Directions - Six Powers of Black Elk's Vision.

The Four Directions are not made up. I sincerely believe that they exist. They are here; right in front of you, put there by the Great Spirit for you to learn from. In the summer, the South Power is more obvious than the cold bringing North. The Red East Power does bring new knowledge every day. Wiyoheyapa – the sun (Wiyo) does rise and appears to travel across the earth (Heyapa) from a red dawn and brings new knowledge if one simply looks for it. Yes, I am well aware it is the Earth's rotation that makes such so. Wiyopeyata, the West Power stands for needed rest when the sun (Wiyo) goes down (Peyatah) and casts the long dark shadow of nightfall for needed rest. Why fear the night? It is Creator's making not so-called 'evil spirits' which are superstitious man creations. Also, in America, the West stands for the life-giving rains that come from the West. Provision and mobility are the life-giving rains. Most humans however, waste their minds on empty pursuits such as watching vacant, numbing television shows which in America are called 'soap operas'. Celebrity watch or celebrity gossip is also a consumer of much of America's leisurely, non-rewarding, non-knowledge producing pursuits. Little attention is shown toward Nature unless of course when she rages up with her tornadoes, devastating storms and earthquakes. Waziyah - the North Power can be very harsh and unrelenting. North Power demands that two-legged puts away adequate provision for the long winter months ahead. We learn confidence from enduring the winter. We become clean through the sweat lodge and rub ourselves down with sage to smell pleasantly when we return to the confines of the lodge as well as projecting courteously to our fellow lodge dwellers respecting each other's small space. We appreciate the budding spring and the disappearing snow allowing us the mobility to hunt once again. Freedom is dearly appreciated. All is not peril with Mother Nature's trials however. Itokaga - the South Power brings forth the rich bounty of harvest at summer's end and into fall. Many North American tribes schedule their annual celebrations of Thanksgiving to Creator – Great Mystery toward the end of Itokaga's reign.

Coming Together

I cannot visualize a non-tribal, non-indigenous searching people wanting to regain their Natural Way to utilize the Sun Dance other than coming to view it on the Native American Reservations or with the Canadian First Peoples. But I am not one to issue out rules, Spirit World forbid! A form of annual coming together which is the deeper meaning of the Sun Dance I would strongly suggest instead. Why not come together in a natural setting and express Appreciation to Ultimate? This I think should be arrived at by a people returning to their natural ancestry that protected and preserved the planet in a much higher and harmonic state. The Sun Dance can probably be studied possibly especially by those who would be quite devoted to the Return. Some tribes are a bit possessive, so to speak concerning this beseechment ceremony and even limit who can attend. Some sun dances are much smaller, attendance wise that are held which are purely family associated. Not even non-related tribal peoples not specifically invited are allowed to attend these four day thanks-givings to their Creator concept. On the other hand, which Sichangu Medicine Man Leonard Crow Dog holds, (Medicine Man of the Sichangu, Brules) his is a large annual summer sun dance. Several summers ago, close to 400 dancers, many from foreign countries were allowed to participate. Not at his sun dance but at the even larger Brule, Sichangu summer Fair and Pow Wow (Social Dancing event), Leonard Crow Dog led a spectacular honoring for me in which I was presented an Eagle Feather while wearing part of my Marine uniform with rank and aviator wings. I probably should include a picture of this event. Crow Dog regaled at our early attempt to revive the Sun Dance and explained the difficulties we had some 40 years earlier with the reservation missionaries and their supporting converted Native Americans who tried to prevent us with the help of government police (along with Native American academics) and how I and two other young sun dancers at the time, Buddy Red Bow and Sonny Larvie, adamantly stood up against them while supporting the two Sun Dance Chiefs, Fools Crow and Bill Eagle Feather. The huge crowd cheered and the women cried during my speech. I had to circle within the crowd and shake hands with the men who came forth and most of the women cried when they hugged me. They cried sadly but happily for the return of the Way that was now fast upon us – finally after a long time of being unconstitutionally banned, namely through the overzealous, ignorant, demanding, my-way-only Christian missionaries who then controlled us beginning with the U.S. Cavalry that they used to force us to give up our ceremonies and our own Way. I still do not blame the U.S. Army per se. It was the politicians that passed the laws after the missionaries success-fully lobbied them. The Army was only taking orders. In Spain it was the Romans who came and forced out the old beliefs – I understand. It is all the same modus operandi basically. It took quite a while for me to circle the entire arena shaking responsive hands. Yes the Sun Dance is indeed powerful. Many non-Native Americans have attended and felt the deep experience. There are now quite a few open minded, sharing medicine people who after getting to know certain, respecting, polite, not-in-a-hurry non-Native American folks are often invited. This seems to be a growing mode. Chief Fools Crow, famous Oglala medicine man made the statement, 'These ways are not for us alone, they must be shared.' There are other medicine leaders who still stick to a fairly closed format although admittedly the participants, many of them from what I have viewed have a high degree of non-Native American blood as our tribe does inter marry with the non-Native Americans considerably. Whether a medicine person is closed, somewhat open or brazenly open as is Crow Dog, is that person's option and should not be criticized is my opinion. Crow Dog has certainly 'paid his dues', so to speak. He was imprisoned for standing up for the Way back in my prime. No one can criticize a leader is the old Sioux tradition unless you have done what they have. Theoretically, I would not be criticized by another unless they have stood up bravely for the Way against real adversaries; been a Sun Dance Pledger (Participant) seven times (I have been in six Sun Dances) and flown over 110 combat missions or equivalent exposure to a real live enemy that was shooting at you or attempting to take your life. You cannot criticize Crow Dog unless you have 'served time' (been imprisoned for the Way). Such is the traditional answer toward undeserved, jealousy motivated or false criticism. Do not criticize a warrior unless you have done what he has done!

Mystery

Life is a mystery. No one can predict which way man will eventually seek, return, go onward or adjust to. He might even perish – bringing on his own demise and extinction and mostly from disastrous religious influence before the Sun (Wiyo) burns out several million years from now. Who knows, not even the 'All knowing Bible Thumpers!' No one knows and it is a wiser human who will respect Mystery. Indeed, Europe, and Australia as well, do not reflect much zeal toward Organized Religion if their dilapidated churches I have personally viewed and the several hundred commonality of chastising responses of citizens of each country visited are any indication. Actually it would be a majority of thousands if I took the time to interview that many. In Europe I rarely ran across the overzealous, extremist religious nuts so prevalent in America and now beginning to dangerously control our politics and worse – onward toward championing future holy wars. Odd how they support Israel primarily from the Arabs, yet a goodly many of them state in their major prayer to Creator that the Jews must be converted. I highly doubt if that 'Conversion' will be a peaceful one having known some determined Sabra Jewish folks who even invited me to speak in several of their synagogues. Aside from all this, slowly but steadily, the environment, Nature's principal teacher, is creeping forward with deadly accuracy and the Europeans are first to realize nature's spiritual magnitude once again. This is my observation.

What Will You Do Concerning the Environment?

We now have new insight to prepare ourselves for that journey Beyond, but what other rich task can we take upon ourselves while still traveling this road? Did you make yourself aware, at least, of the needed care you could have given to this planet that Creator made for us? Will you have a lasting memory, to proudly proclaim from that Spirit World to state, 'Well, at least I tried!'

Water Disaster – Too much Water. Fukuyama, Japan example. As I have said earlier, Water and Nuclear Power do not mix. And let us not forget the Tsunami disaster off the coast of Sumatra (2004) and how outer island Native peoples still close to Nature managed not to suffer the fatalities which their mainland,

Organized Religion folks experienced because they readily recognized Nature's warnings and safely retreated to higher ground immediately after recognizing unusual activity - the birds taking flight and animals scurrying to higher ground. Water Shortage - This subject is worldwide, even in the United States it is happening. Uncontrolled floods take trillions of gallons out to the sea and most often carrying needed soil sediment from land erosion. America spends billions on wasteful wars and a bloated Defence Department (actually a War Department) when that expenditure could have been spent on blossoming the vast desert areas of the west with much of the floodwaters of the Missouri and Mississippi rivers. In my home state of South Dakota, man again is playing with disaster by seeking to build a transcontinental pipeline across the largest of the countries aquifers which has its beginning in the Black Hills. This pure water is primarily snow mass runoff. This aquifer extends down under Nebraska, Oklahoma and into Texas; supporting farms and ranches and of course, many small towns mostly. It does not flow into the sea. One oil leak on that proposed pipeline and agriculture in many states will experience disaster. Oil pipe lines have a history of leakage. Water and oil do not mix either. After a recent major leakage that has polluted and killed many Montana fresh water trout, the oil companies claim to run their pipelines beneath and not over major rivers. Oil floats to the top of water should an underground leak occur.

General Eisenhower

President Eisenhower is regarded as the key strategic planner. During the European theater conflict, he picked capable subordinates and was not adverse to replace Division commanders who were not as effective, talented or dedicated. His selection of General Patton was a crowning achievement to carry the brunt of the fighting chasing the German Army back across the Rhine River and on into Germany. General Patton earned his promotion through his tenacious ability to subdue German opposition earlier in Italy. An indication of his (Eisenhower's) character is reflected at a slave labor prison camp in Western Germany his troops encountered. The conditions there were the extreme of man's inhumanity to man. The surviving conscripts, mostly Jewish, were either bed ridden waiting to die or barely moving and mostly weighing less around 70-80lbs. Photographs were ordered to preserve such tragic suffering for history's sake. Eisenhower then ordered the nearby German villagers to view what atrocity was taking place in their own back yards, so to speak and to begin with burying the stacks of abundant corpses. Later, this General who never championed so called, 'family values' or a 'religious right,' would become President. He would envision a grand plan - a colossal undertaking like Genghis Khan, regarding commerce, which up to this time now, is the last major federal project to positively affect the American nation on such a large scale. That project was termed the Federal Interstate Freeway System that eventually connected every state in the union to a huge network of separated two-way highways across the land. Commerce flowed more freely with little impeding traffic stoppage. Goods cost less to ship and arrived sooner. Automobile traffic became much safer for travel. The cost of real estate and labor was far lower in those days than what it would be now were it delayed. One can hardly imagine the huge amount of employment such an undertaking required over the several decades it took to build towards fruition.It is (disgustingly) amazing that the present day's Republican candidates or even our present President do not offer any related plan relative to President Eisenhower's successful venture and yet tout nebulous, solutionless slogans regarding Economic recovery. One political party is so engrossed in Organized Religion related issues that what little grey matter they have is possessed by church issues such as contraception, abortion, gay marriage denial, death and dying restrictions etc. Many of this party's followers actually believe that their man-God will come down from the sky and solve the economic downturn no less than their God concept will eventually correct planetary heating and over-population through some form of rapture and resurrection. These are the voting folks, who like Congresswoman Bachmann, former Governor Palin and former Senator Santorum, all believe and worse – tout, that human life and the Age of Dinosaurs began but six thousand years ago. Now the politicians are claiming to somehow revive the economy and of course fictitiously create more jobs to win votes but none of them have emerged with any significant battle plan other than go to war again with some rich oil state and emerge the country into deeper debt.

Military-Industrial Complex

Eisenhower made his last speech as president on 17th January, 1961; probably the most controversial speech of his career. He gave the American people a serious warning about the situation that faced them,

Until the latest of our world conflicts, the United States had no armaments industry. American makers of plowshares could, with time and as required, make swords as well. But now we can no longer risk emergency improvisation of national defence; we have been compelled to create a permanent armaments industry of vast proportions. Added to this, three and a half million men and women are directly engaged in the defence establishment. We annually spend on military security more than the net income of all United States corporations. This conjunction of an immense military estab-lishment and a large arms industry is new in the American experience. The total influence - economic, political, even spiritual - is felt in every city, every State house, every office of the Federal government. We recognize the imperative need for this development. Yet we must not fail to comprehend its grave implications. Our toil, resources and livelihood are all involved; so is the very structure of our society. In the councils of government, we must guard against the acquisition of unwarranted influence, whether sought or unsought, by the Military-Industrial Complex. The potential for the disastrous rise of misplaced power exists and will persist.

A Colossal Undertaking

During the Republican primary elections, the three candidates, mentioned earlier, were vociferous in their criticism of President Obama. The other candidates also criticized the President and his programs but what separated out the aforementioned candidates were the lack of solutions or their own lack of creativity as to what they would implement toward more effectively responsive government economic problem solving. All of the candidate's views were projected upon the media on a daily basis. It did not take long for the so-called and self-identified 'conservative' sided electorate to weed out the two women candidates, along with Santorum who managed to win over ten southern states whose Republican Primary voters were mostly influenced by Organized Religion. Viewing all of this political projection for several months and the antics of these three candidates primarily, I became determined to at least offer a primary project that I had thought and re-thought over the years - a 'colossal solution' so to speak, for America that seems to merit a powerful direction for the nation to move towards and at least I can separate, for my own self-esteem, a distance as far as possible from the narrow, unfruitful thinking of these three candidates in particular. My own 'colossal undertaking' could also become an abrupt detour from what I consider America's most wasteful industry - the Military Industrial Complex which General Eisenhower had warned. Such a huge but necessary undertaking that I am about to unveil, cannot be attempted by any nation and yet maintain the military expenditure that the United States burdens its citizens with. I have thought about this project for some time and the previous year before this writing, my home state was in serious flood danger from the Missouri River. You must remember that I have seen first-hand the tremendous outlay of expenditure to keep an Army in the field in Korea and later Vietnam where I served again. In both instances, I could have avoided going into the war zone but I volunteered. Maybe it was the Native American/Mongol blood within me. I am proud that I had such experiences. It is not the Army forces upon the land bases and battlefronts alone that must be maintained but the logistics and battle support provided by the Navy and Air Force that are needed as well. From the air, I often saw the vast amount of shipping entering and leaving the war theater ports to maintain such a gigantic undertaking. It is an extremely enormous outlay and seeing it all first hand from the air has left a lasting, indelible memory.

Water Westward

America is the 'bread basket' of the world when it comes to agriculture. Just about every country cannot feed its citizens alone without importing from America. With the exponential advance of over-population the demand for food will eventually outstrip present productivity. Already, starvation is being experienced in many countries. Humans multiply, but land does not. Most people in our land will hold that 'there is no more land left.' If there was available land it would soon be put into cropland due to today's high economic return for grain, primarily. But there are millions of acres just waiting to be tilled and I find it difficult to believe that to my knowledge at least, no scientists, politicians, think tanks etc. have come up with such a practical solution to increase our country's agricultural productivity a hundred fold; maybe a thousand fold and bring the balance of payments deficit to an end. Those lands above the vast Oglala Aquifer reaching from Dakota to Texas are limited now by water shortage, this limitation can be removed and more of those lands may become opened up as well, and therefore this cannot be labeled as a South

West project only. Nebraska, Kansas, Texas and Oklahoma can no longer fear the dreaded droughts. The answer is to simply transport our bountiful water westward to the millions of acres of land to the so-termed desert areas of the Southwest and the Western South as well. Israel is a prime example of making 'the desert bloom'. Why cannot this be so here in our land? Already, hydrologists have advanced a foolish, unworkable plan to take Great Lakes' waters and pipeline the lakes to the Southwestern cities primarily for drinking water especially to the large cities therein. Little mention for agriculture is part of that plan. I consider this idea or plan as rather foolish compared to the much closer water resources that I would make use of. At least, the Great Lakes' area citizens, however, will probably endorse my plan over the one proposed for taking their waters in huge quantities enough so that their lake levels will surely lower. This Great Lakes' plan has been featured in the National Geographic. (See & Find) such article.

Nature's Pipe Line

Why these hydrologists have not considered a much closer water source to supply the Southwest is beyond me. This water would be either the Mississippi or the Missouri watershed, and more exactly the spring run-off which still inundates farms, homes and even towns on their seaward course. Possibly the dangerous Red River of North Dakota could be included with a diversion into the Missouri. First let us realize that with the machinery and dam making ability of these modern times - any huge project is possible. It may cost the end of a military build-up but eventually food will be of such demand that bullets and bombs will have to be so-called 'sacrificed.' The neo-conservatives will have to accept that food is necessary for life and the other is designed to take life. So be it. Those in the lucrative Military Industrial Complex can simply exchange their plans for tanks, airplanes and artillery to trucks, pipelines, bulldozers and excavators. They have enough lobbyists to reward themselves with many convertible contracts. If a supreme dictator were empowered it would definitely become 'doable.' Let us use the Missouri basin for an example. Remember, this water is bound for the sea. My plan, I guess we could term, is 'recycling.' Now that we are 'politically correct' - let us proceed. A vast complete pipeline westward would not be needed. The sparsely settled Dakota Badlands just to the west of the Missouri is a huge area, remotely settled. It was once an ancient inland sea; albeit a very large one. This could be a monstrous holding area a hundred miles or more in length and in turn would generate more rainfall for that area from evaporation opening up those arid areas for cropland. This new 'inland sea' borders, actually would cover the northern beginning of the Oglala Aquifer. If it went no further it could raise the water level of the aquifer which is being severely drained by agriculture southward all the way to Texas. The so-called 'natural pipeline' would or could be a series of vast lakes westward and southward. The aquifer itself, could serve as a vast underground 'pipe' to bring the water to Texas and much closer to the Southwest. Fairly simple idea – is it not? Unfortunately, white academics who control politics are very short on common sense ideas, my opinion, and experience. With this methodology, lands along the route could also benefit beside cut down the need for more costly pipelines and pumping. Water allotments already in place could be increased significantly. Any of the huge dams along the Missouri could be the beginning point for such a positive endeavour. The Oahe Dam, near South Dakota's capital - Pierre, could be a prime location to begin as only a hundred miles westward is the Badlands and the Oglala Aquifer. Pumping stations would move the waters westward where necessary. If the hydrologists proposing the movement of Great Lakes' water have originated the necessary technology then I assume this same technology would suffice for Missouri River spring runoff as well and so much closer. The Dakotas have abundant wind energy.

Hundreds of electric power-providing windmills are already in operation in the next state - Minnesota. Southern Colorado, New Mexico and Arizona would become cropland. Missouri River flooding would be history. Trillions of gallons of water would never reach the sea or be vastly reduced. Mexico could become a beneficiary as well. Remember, the spring runoff waters would only be needed and below Gavins Dam (Yankton, SD) summer barge traffic would not be curtailed. And alas, if the project transferred huge amounts of water along the way, refurbishing the lowering Oglala Aquifer, such a transfer could even make some dent in the rising worldwide sea level as most of this water will never reach the oceans. In summary; the Oglala Aquifer is a natural pipe which could flow trillions of danger prone spring runoff water wastefully bound for the rising seas. Is it doable? It certainly is a better idea than this needless war machine America constantly produces and which provides absolutely no balance of payment economics. The neo-cons will be quick to critique that without the mighty military machine our borders will no longer be secure. My rebuke is that Arab dhows are fairly puny adversaries for an invasion fleet. Ah and then the war mongers will always bring up China as our major threat to 'world peace'. If we look at the history of China even going back to the days of Genghis Khan, China has never been the adversary, the invader, 'the yellow peril'. It was the Europeans who started the Boxer War by their presence in China which Japan, not China soon ended. Americans will never admit it but it is China that keeps America afloat in the banking and monetary circles. Let us not neglect or omit the Atomic, Hydrogen, Cobalt or what have you 'bomb'. The pragmatic significance of atomic weaponry should preclude all major warfare. Who wants to set off an atomic conflagration unless it is attempted control by fanatic Organized Religion? They are about the only ones nutty enough to release such weaponry upon each other because, no doubt, 'God told them to do so!' Right here in our own country we have Pat

Robertson calling for a biblically predicted blood bath on his television channel and of course, we have the Muslims with their jihad and apostasy. If atomic war does happen it will be Organized Religion and not the Chinese who will be behind it. The Chinese are the least controlled by the religious right or the jihadists. They are the only country that is restricting legislatively the deepest threat to humanity, even more so than atomic warfare and that is over population which we shall come to. At least *Stopglobalwarming.org* is an attempt at a solution to a steadily mounting disaster that is forthcoming. Starvation should certainly be a worthy subject to confront compared to the church related issues the three candidates promote and the other three have to pay lip service to in order to cower to the ultra religious so called 'conservatives'. Does anyone have a better plan for needed betterment of our society and the world as well? I hope this projection at least removes me from the category of those complaining politicians who simply do not have the integrity to attempt to offer some form of solution toward real world problems. My mind is not cluttered by controlling religion and free to think and ponder. Theirs is! In summary: 'At least I tried!' Lastly, I suggest that you go online and look up, Stopglobalwarming.org which is deeply connected to the world's water situation. From there you may branch out to other environmental concerns of your choosing.

Four Other Issues. Heat, Thin, Gone and Too Many

I have deeply explored four other issues, enough so to have written a book on them *Nature's Way – Native Wisdom for Living in Balance with the Earth*. It is published by Harper/Collins Publishers, N. Y. The last four chapters are Heating of the Planet, Thinning Ozone, Gone Resources, and what I consider the most important chapter, Over Population. I was as precise and scientifically accurate as possible and had the serious reader in mind who wants to go on from Spirituality to Environmental

Spirituality. I would seriously be amiss if I did not touch on the dangers however; our environment is presently exposed to now.

1. Heating of the Planet – This writing is a work on Spirituality and not Science per se, yet our planet is in danger. Without a liveable environment, Spirituality/ Organized Religion will be short lived. Man is foolish, actually, totally disloyal to the human race besides the animal brethren to disregard the warnings of science. Most scientists are lining up on the side that claims planetary heating is happening. The past winter in many cities in America has had record, prolonged temperatures, extremely unusual for the northern cities. Minneapolis experienced little snowfall and what did fall melted in but a few days. Minneapolis usually has snowfall that covers the entire city beginning in November and on through April. The Pine Beetle is now devastating forests in the Black Hills of South Dakota mainly because the winter cold is not low enough to keep the insect in check which it has done so for centuries. In year 2011, one island nation is experiencing inundation and arranging to move its populace to another nation. Organized Religion's bible makes no mention of planetary heating nor does it encounter the other serious subjects listed below as I have mentioned before.

2. Thinning Ozone - Precautions have been made by man and exemplifies that humanity can correct a dangerous situation by outlawing certain product causing emissions.

3. Gone Resources – Without a doubt this subject cannot be ignored or not admitted. When I was in high school at Rapid City, South Dakota, we were often told, 'America is a land of unlimited resources.' Look at the depleted resources now and on the other end the increasing population explosion demanding and consuming more

resources. Precious metals have sky rocketed price wise causing serious economic problems for major industries: Gold and silver, to name the most notable. Copper mining is now a 24 hour a day operation due to the high price the ore brings. Worse - so much of America's resources have been wasted in the many wars it constantly becomes involved in.

4. Over-Population – The Number 1 forthcoming disaster and anyone who disputes this man-created happening is a sheer idiot. This subject is well covered already in several preceding chapters. 7 billion now inhabit the earth and soon to be 8 billion. The one billion increase becomes shorter in its multiplication time span every time a new census happens. Therefore such mathematical increase can be termed – exponential. Only one country, so called 'God-less China,' is taking on the planet's number one environmental problem. The worst offenders are dominated by Organized Religion - Mexico and India and of course millions there live in extreme poverty. The idiocy of Organized Religious man!

Ending

One associates Spirituality with the hope or faith that a Spirit World does lie beyond and one may arrive there hopefully more fruitfully equipped to fit into that realm. This is what we have strived to do while learning from these pages presented. Morality, ethics, dedication, appreciation, seeking truth and striving to equip our minds with much observant knowledge are major endeavours. Shedding foolish fears, gullibility, naïveté, controlling man, superstitions, shrouding falsehoods and cowardly association with the misleading crowd are the other side of what we must avoid. Avoiding fanatic, wasteful leadership for a dilemma filled world already is primary! Yes and for the present, Spirituality should lead us in a harmonic social relationship with our fellow citizens. I am betting that it is the harmonic and earth respecting ones who will inherit the true enlightenment in the one awaiting. We will go with our own kind which means to me that a form of progressive selection seems quite probable but one has to earn such merit while here. The Native Sioux Way has a powerful statement which they consider very spiritual. It is 'Metak ou yeh Oyasin – We are all related, for all my relatives. Another closely related statement is: 'Wakaneechah Wichoni hey wichoni – Live for those yet unborn'. Another way of saying it is: Live for the future generations. Certainly do not place them in financial jeopardy as is happening now in America. The unborn of America are actually already mortgaged! What does that say for a self-proclaimed by dominant society as – a 'Christian Country'? Therefore to discuss the environment and applying corrective application to its warnings is indeed very Spiritual. What will you say when someday, in the distant future when they, your progeny, enter the Spirit World: 'What did you do for the Planet while you were there?' So Dear Reader, do not fear that your endeavours did not meet so called 'success' in mere man's theater of recognition, reward, acceptance; what have you. It is how you will look on from the Spirit World which will really matter. It will be those who have been tested and are entering that may become the worthwhile judges of your endeavours or non-endeavours. My idea about an agricultural opening of the West and a South West may meet a host of adversaries, many of whom do not want to risk their selfish gains in the Military Industrial Complex but in the end, an over-populated world clamouring for food; it may not have seemed so far-fetched after all, is my studied prediction. The very fact that you made yourself aware while you were here on your Earth journey will allow a more fruitful entrance and recognition into that realm that waits for all - Beyond.

God is all Knowledge. God is all Truth.

Afterword

There are two kinds of people in this world.
The first seeks wisdom, while the second seeks gratification.
The first trembles with anger when injustice is done to others;
the second is numb and unconcerned.
The first recognizes their duty to speak out; the second
dismisses injustice as being out of their hands or simply the way
it is.
The first is loyal and loving to their human and non-human
brothers and sisters, while the second is loyal to their nation.
The first rejects dogma and thinks independently; the second
blindly respects authority and bitterly ridicules free thinkers.
The first is humble, always knowing that they could be wrong;
the second rigidly adheres to beliefs which ossify with time.
The first removes themselves from contributing to the system of
oppression in any and all ways; the second does nothing
because they are comfortable.
Which one are you?

About the Author

Ed McGaa, Eagle Man, is an American citizen, a Teton Oglala Lakota (Sioux) who was born on the Pine Ridge Indian Reservation and successful writer. He studied under Chief Eagle Feather and Chief Fool's Crow, influential Sioux holy men, honoured as a six time Sun Dance ceremony participant and is now regarded as a world-leader in advocating indigenous wisdoms. As an author his best-selling books include *Native Wisdom: Perceptions of the Natural Way* and *Mother Earth Spirituality: Healing Ourselves and Our World*.

At one time he was a warrior, a combat warrior. As a Marine fighter pilot, he flew the F4 Phantom, during 110 combat missions in Vietnam. Of this time he admits, that facing life and death on an almost constant schedule, was certainly memorable. Being a warrior was in his blood since childhood when he was disappointed at not being old enough to serve like his hero brother who was on Tarawa and Saipan in the Marines against Japan. Ed went to Korea as a teenager, serving in the Marines. He was promoted to corporal rank which was far below on the military totem pole. He never dreamed that he would someday become a Marine pilot and hold the rank of Captain. Eventually he was promoted to Major but left the military to attend law school where he obtained his law degree. Ed was once quoted about this change in career as saying,

I probably should have remained within the Marines, content and happy to be with fellow warriors. I would never have had to write all these books I have attempted and finished.

Thankfully for his many readers and students around the world he stuck with the written word.

ww.facebook.com/ed.mcgaa

Sources

Bachelor, S. *Letting Daylight into Magic: The Life and Times of Dorje Shugden* (The Buddhist Review, 7, Spring 1998).

Catlin, G. *Episodes From Life Among the Indians* (University of Oklahoma Press, 1959).

Choegyal, T. *The Truth about Tibet,* (Hillsdale College, Michigan, April 1999).

Coleman, L. & Slick, T. *The Search for the Yeti,* (Faber and Faber, 1989).

Cooper, J M. *Allegory of the Cave - Plato's Complete Works,* (Hackett Publishing Company, 1947).

Curren, E D. *Buddha's Not Smiling: Uncovering Corruption at the Heart of Tibetan Buddhism Today* (Alaya Press 2005).

Deane, H. *The Cold War in Tibet,* (Covert Action Quarterly, Winter 1987).

Gelder, S. & Gelder, R. *The Timely Rain: Travels in New Tibet* (Monthly Review Press, 1964).

Ginsburg, G. & Mathos, M. *Communist China and Tibet,* (Springer, 1964).

Goldstein, M. *A History of Modern Tibet 1913-1951,* (Uni. of California Press, 1989).

Goldstein, M. *The Snow Lion and the Dragon: China, Tibet, and the Dalai Lama,* (Uni. of California Press, 1995)

Goldstein, M. *The Struggle for Modern Tibet: The Autobiography of Tashì-Tsering,* (Armonk, N.Y.: M.E. Sharpe, 1997),

Greene, F. *A Curtain of Ignorance,* (Garden City, N.Y. Doubleday, 1961).

Grunfeld, T. *The Making of Modern Tibet,* (Armonk, N.Y. and London, 1996).

Harrer, H. *Return to Tibet,* (New York: Schocken, 1985).

Haught, J A. *Holy Horrors. An Illustrated History of Religious Murder and Madness,* (Buffalo, NY: Prometheus Books, 1990).

Holler, C. *Black Elk's Religion,* (Syracuse Univ. Press, 1995).

International Committee of Lawyers for Tibet. *A Generation in Peril,* (Berkeley Calif. 2001).

Juergensmeyer, M. *Terror in the Mind of God,* (Uni. of California Press, 2000).

Karan, P P. *The Changing Face of Tibet,* (London Times, 4 July 1966).

Karan, P P. *The Changing Face of Tibet: The Impact of Chinese Communist Ideology on the Landscape* (Uni. Press of Kentucky, 1976).

Kenneth, C. & Morrison, J. *The CIA's Secret War in Tibet,* (University of Kansas Press, 2002).

Kurtenbach, E. *Associate Press Report,* (12 February 1998).

Leary, W. *Secret Mission to Tibet,* (Air & Space, December 1997/January 1998).

Lewis K. *Private Correspondence,* (15 July 2004).

Lopez Jr., D. *Prisoners of Shangri-La: Tibetan Buddhism and the West* (Chicago University Press, 1998).

Mann, J. *CIA Gave Aid to Tibetan Exiles in '60s, Files Show,* (L.A. Times, 15 Sept. 1998; and N.Y. Times, 1 October, 1998).

Medicine, Dr. B. *Learning to be an Anthropologist and Remaining 'Native',* (University of Chicago Press, 2001).

Parenti, M. *The Culture Struggle,* (Seven Stories, 2006).

Pomfret, J. *Tibet Caught in China's Web'* (Washington Post, 23 July 1999).

Seok, K H. *Korean Monk Gangs Battle for Temple Turf,* (San Francisco Examiner, 3 December 1998).

Strong, A L. *Tibetan Interviews,* (New World Press, 1959).

Wilson, G. *Worker's World,* (6 February 1997).

Moon Books invites you to begin or deepen your encounter with Paganism, in all its rich, creative, flourishing forms.